PRIVATE CLIENT: WILLS, TRUSTS AND ESTATE PLANNING

PRIVATE CLIENT: WILLS, TRUSTS AND ESTATE PLANNING

Helen Cousal MA (Cantab), Solicitor

Lesley King LLB, Dip Crim (Cantab), Solicitor

Published by

College of Law Publishing,
Braboeuf Manor, Portsmouth Road, St Catherines, Guildford GU3 1HA

British Library Cataloguing-in-Publication Data

A catalogue record for this book is available from the British Library.

ISBN 1 905391 09 9

Typeset by Style Photosetting Ltd, Mayfield, East Sussex

Printed in Great Britain by Ashford Colour Press Ltd, Gosport, Hampshire

Preface

The aim of this book is to provide a comprehensive introduction to the legal and taxation implications arising from estate planning work for clients within the private client department of a solicitor's practice. At the beginning of Chapter 1, there is reference to the problem of definition of private client. In view of this it has been necessary, but difficult, to define the scope of the text, although the subtitle to this book has helped to a considerable extent.

We have had the benefit of helpful, and often long, discussions with many practitioners from whose suggestions we hope to have arrived at a consensus. However, we remain aware that the private client department of a London firm is often very different from a provincial practice. We should like to express our appreciation to the many busy private client partners who have so willingly provided their advice and suggestions, and their time, in relation to the content of this book.

This book is written primarily to complement the Legal Practice Course elective, Private Client, but it is hoped it will provide a useful introduction to others interested in this type of work. Students studying for this elective will have already completed the compulsory part of the Legal Practice Course; there are, therefore, some references to that course and to other LPC Guides.

The permission to reproduce a number of precedent forms and clauses from the following publications is acknowledged with thanks: *Practical Trust Precedents* (Sweet & Maxwell); *Practical Will Precedents* (Sweet & Maxwell) (permission obtained from Withers); and White, *Post-Death Rearrangements: Practice and Precedents*, 5th edn (Sweet & Maxwell, 1995).

For brevity, we have used the masculine pronoun throughout to include the feminine. The law is stated as at 30 September 2005.

Throughout, we have endeavoured to provide the principal statutory references to enable further research to be made into a topic where this is required. In a subject as broad-based as Private Client (even as interpreted within this book), there are many relevant textbooks and precedent books to which a student or practitioner may wish to refer; these include:

Enduring Powers of Attorney

Cretney & Lush on Enduring Powers of Attorney, 5th edn (Jordans, 2001)

Trust Law

Parker and Mellows, *The Modern Law of Trusts*, 8th edn (Sweet & Maxwell, 2003)
Hanbury and Martin, *Modern Equity*, 17th edn (Sweet & Maxwell, 2005)

Precedents

Practical Will Precedents (Sweet & Maxwell)
Practical Trust Precedents (Sweet & Maxwell)
Potter and Monroe's Tax Planning With Precedents (Sweet & Maxwell)
Encyclopaedia of Forms and Precedents (LexisNexis), Trusts and Settlements
Practical Tax Planning and Precedents (Sweet & Maxwell)

Estate and Tax Planning

Estate Planning (Tolley)
Tax Planning (Tolley)
Taxation of UK Trusts (Tolley)
White, *Post-Death Rearrangements: Practice and Precedents*, 5th edn (Sweet & Maxwell, 1995)

Wills and Probate

Barlow, King and King, *Wills, Administration and Taxation: A Practical Guide*, 8th edn (Sweet & Maxwell, 2003)
Williams on Wills, 8th edn (Butterworths, 2002)

Revenue Law

Revenue Law: Principles and Practice, 22nd edn (LexisNexis, 2004)
British Tax Library Capital Taxes (Sweet & Maxwell)

HELEN COUSAL and LESLEY KING
The College of Law

Contents

Table of Cases

Table of Statutes

Table of Statutory Instruments

Table of Abbreviations

The following abbreviations are used throughout this book.

A & M	accumulation and maintenance
AEA 1925	Administration of Estates Act 1925
AEA 1971	Administration of Estates Act 1971
AIM	Alternative Investment Market
AVCs	additional voluntary contributions
CGT	capital gains tax
COB Rules	Solicitors' Financial Services (Conduct of Business) Rules 2001
CPA	Civil Partnership Act 2004
EPA	enduring power of attorney
EPAA 1985	Enduring Powers of Attorney Act 1985
FA	Finance Act
FSA	Financial Services Authority
FSAVCs	free-standing additional voluntary contributions
FSMA 2000	Financial Services and Markets Act 2000
ICTA 1988	Income and Corporation Taxes Act 1988
IHT	inheritance tax
IHTA 1984	Inheritance Tax Act 1984
ISAs	Individual Savings Accounts
ITTOIA 2005	Income Tax (Trading and Other Income) Act 2005
LCT	lifetime chargeable transfer
LPA	lasting power of attorney
LPA 1925	Law of Property Act 1925
MCA	Mental Capacity Act 2005
OEIC	open-ended investment company
PAA 1964	Perpetuities and Accumulations Act 1964
PEP	personal equity plan
PET	potentially exempt transfer
PHI	permanent health insurance
PR	personal representative
RAO	Financial Services and Markets Act 2000 (Regulated Activities) Order 2001
RPI	retail price index
SERPS	State Earnings-Related Pension Scheme
SLA 1925	Settled Land Act 1925
TA 1925	Trustee Act 1925
TA 2000	Trustee Act 2000
TCGA 1992	Taxation of Chargeable Gains Act 1992
TESSAs	Tax Exempt Special Savings Accounts
TIA	Trustee Investments Act 1961
TLATA 1996	Trusts of Land and Appointment of Trustees Act 1996
VTA 1958	Variation of Trusts Act 1958

Chapter 1

Private Client

1.1 What is private client work?

Lord Denning in *Griffiths v JP Harrison (Watford) Ltd* [1962] 1 All ER 909, HL said, 'We can recognise a "trade" when we see it. ... But we are hard pressed to define it'. In that case, he was considering whether an activity was a trading activity. He might have said much the same thing had he been considering 'private client work'.

At its broadest, private client work may be said to include all work except commercial work, although even commercial work has a private client dimension. At its narrowest, it will generally be taken to exclude such topics as conveyancing, family law, litigation and employment law, leaving a residual category of personal taxation, wills, probate and trust work.

Some firms, generally the larger firms, have separate departments with partners and assistant solicitors who concentrate exclusively on serving the needs of their private clients. Smaller firms often have a number of partners and assistant solicitors who do private client work but not necessarily within a separate department. These firms will not usually define this work as private client work as such. If asked, they would probably see it as covering most of the firm's clients except the purely commercial clients. In recent years, some large practices have developed a policy of concentrating on commercial work and referring any private client work to other firms specialising in that area.

The subtitle to this book, 'Wills, Trusts and Estate Planning', describes, and places a limit on, the scope of the book. Therefore, it covers private client work in the narrow sense. Other aspects of private client work as more broadly defined are the subject of other books in this series.

Extensive discussion with City of London firms, provincial city firms and many other firms with private client departments has confirmed that the main emphasis of their work within the private client department is 'estate planning'. This emphasis has led to an equivalent main theme for this LPC Guide.

1.2 Private client work and the compulsory subjects of the Legal Practice Course

1.2.1 Probate and estate administration

The study of private client work follows naturally from a study of probate, estate administration and related succession issues. Many of the topics introduced in the LPC Guide, *Pervasive and Core Topics*, for example lifetime gifts and the use of annual tax exemptions, are developed further. Many new topics and ideas for estate planning are also introduced. In some cases, reference is made to particular aspects of other LPC Guides. It will be necessary to re-read some of the material contained in those books.

1.2.2 Revenue law

The three principal taxes applicable to private individuals are relevant to this area of work. The principles of these taxes are set out in the LPC Guides, *Pervasive and Core Topics* and *Business Law and Practice.*

1.2.3 Financial services

Estate planning for clients will inevitably involve a consideration of financial planning, particularly in relation to investments. For example, clients may want advice in relation to their existing shares, or as to what investments they should make in the immediate future.

In some cases, a solicitor may become involved in other investment activity for a client. After giving advice, the solicitor may follow this up by making arrangements for the client to acquire (or sell) investments. In some cases, the solicitor may even be prepared to manage a client's investment portfolio. However, this is less likely since the Financial Services and Markets Act 2000 (FSMA 2000) increased the regulatory burden on firms involved in such work.

Not all solicitors' firms will wish to carry out investment business for clients, even though they undertake a substantial amount of private client work. Many practitioners prefer to 'hive off' the financial aspects of a client's business to specialist independent financial advisers leaving the solicitor to concentrate on the purely legal aspects of the work. However, some of the larger firms, as well as many medium-sized or smaller firms, take the opposite approach. They see financial services work as potentially lucrative for the practice. Thus, using their existing client database as their prime source of investment business, firms which decide to become involved in financial services work may often set up a separate financial services department. This may be 'headed up' by a solicitor with the necessary expertise or by an individual brought into the firm for the purpose. Such a person would normally have qualifications and experience gained from working in the financial services industry. Departments of this type will work closely with the private client department but will also provide a support role for other areas of the practice. Firms need to decide whether they are prepared to comply with the requirements of FSMA 2000 and be regulated by the Financial Services Authority (FSA), or whether they wish to limit themselves to activities which can be carried out under the regulation of the Law Society.

This book presupposes that the solicitor's firm has opted for regulation by the Law Society. However, we will consider the nature of the various investment products available on the market, their similarities and differences and their suitability or otherwise for any particular client. Such a client, within the context of this book, may either be an individual or a trustee.

1.3 Ownership and disposition of assets

Private client work for any client will involve the solicitor in two separate, though closely related, matters.

1.3.1 Ownership of assets

The decision to acquire assets, for example the family home or investments, is for the client to make, although the solicitor may be asked to offer advice. Even where clients do not require advice as to the selection of particular assets, they may need advice on how family assets should be owned. The solicitor will frequently need to advise on the advantages and disadvantages of sole ownership or joint ownership (as joint tenants or as tenants in common) or whether to hold assets through a trust. Hence, this book deals with (inter alia):

(a)   financial planning; and

(b)   estate planning.

1.3.2 Disposition of assets

Clients who have substantial assets will want to consider how to pass them on to family members in the most tax effective way. The options available are:

(a)   lifetime gifts: these may be outright gifts to individuals or into trusts; or

(b)   gifts by will: these may also be outright gifts to individuals or into trusts.

Chapter 2

Financial Planning

2.1 Planning the client's financial affairs

This chapter introduces some of the concepts which lie behind financial and investment planning advice for individual clients as part of their estate planning.

The object of financial planning is to maximise the wealth (capital and income) of an individual.

Financial planning is a continuing process. It requires the development of a strategy based on short- and long-term forward planning. Ideally, a plan, an investment strategy, should be developed for the client. Any immediate needs identified by the plan can be implemented at once. Longer-term planning can be given effect as the opportunities develop.

The range of financial planning and investment opportunities available to private clients is very wide. In view of this, the key to successful advice to clients lies in:

(a)   knowing all the circumstances of the particular client; and

(b)   devising a financial and investment plan which is appropriate to meet those circumstances.

2.1.1 Financial planning

Financial planning covers savings, for example, in a bank or building society, investments, life assurance and pension arrangements, mortgages, school fee schemes (see **Appendix 2**) and tax planning generally (see **Chapter 4**).

2.1.2 Investment planning

Investment planning is one aspect of financial planning. In everyday use the phrase is understood as covering a wide range of investments from unit trusts, investment trusts and other stocks and shares (see **Appendix 2**) to specialist items such as works of art, stamp collections and investment in woodlands. It is not confined to 'investments' as defined in the FSMA 2000 (see **2.2**).

2.1.3 Fees and commissions

It is, of course, usual for a solicitor to charge a client a fee for work done for the client.

Investment business often gives rise to payment of commission by the provider of the investment product. If a solicitor arranges an endowment policy for a client he will receive a commission from the life company. If, instead, the transaction is carried out through an authorised person, it may be agreed that the authorised person shares the commission he receives with the solicitor.

Receipt of fees and commissions requires consideration of the Law Society's Code of Conduct 2004 and the general principle that there must be no conflict of interest between the solicitor and the client.

Rule 1 – The core duties include the obligation not to allow the solicitor's independence to be compromised in the face of pressure from others, the obligation to act in the best interests of clients and not to act where there is a conflict between the interests of the solicitor and the client.

This does not prevent receipt of commission. However, placing a client's business with the company which pays the biggest commission may be in the solicitor's best interest, not the client's. A breach of Rule 1 would occur.

Rule 2.06 – The solicitor must account to the client for any commission received if more than £20 unless the client, in full knowledge of the amount or basis of calculation of the commission, agrees that the solicitor should retain the commission.

Commissions for investment business will frequently exceed £20. Even where the commission is less than £20, a firm which wants to stay within the Financial Services (Scope) Rules 2001 provisions will have to account for it (see **2.2**).

Rule 9.03 – Solicitors who recommend that a client use a particular firm must do so in good faith, judging what is in the client's best interests.

A solicitor is entitled to receive commission for referring clients to third parties but must comply with this obligation and the other obligations imposed by the Law Society's Code of Conduct 2004, for example Rules 1 and 2.06.

Fees or commission?

A solicitor has a choice:

(a)   to charge a fee for the work and account to the client for the entire commission received;

(b)   to charge a fee for the work but to offset this (with the client's agreement) with the commission received;

(c)   to retain the commission with the client's agreement in lieu of charging a fee.

There are advantages and disadvantages to each method. One particular point to note is that the amount charged, whether as fees or by way of commission, can always be challenged if not 'fair and reasonable' for the amount of work done (Solicitors' (Non-contentious Business) Remuneration Order 1994, SI 1994/2616).

As we will see at **2.2**, a solicitor who is not authorised to carry on regulated activities under FSMA 2000 will often use an authorised person to arrange investments for a client. This will exempt the solicitor from the need to obtain authorisation under the Act so long as he does not receive any pecuniary award or advantage for which he does not account to the client.

The Law Society's Professional Ethics department has stated that the Law Society believes that retaining commission with the consent of the client in accordance with Rule 2.06 will be treated as having accounted to the client. The Financial Services Authority has confirmed this. Note that all commission must be disclosed to the client, even commission of £20 or less.

2.2 The Financial Services and Markets Act 2000

The FSMA 2000 is discussed in the LPC Guide, *Pervasive and Core Topics*. Any solicitor who is involved in developing and implementing an investment strategy for a client must comply with the relevant provisions of FSMA 2000 and the Financial Services and Markets Act 2000 (Regulated Activities) Order 2001, SI 2001/544. Remember that carrying on a regulated activity without the necessary authorisation is a criminal offence under FSMA 2000, s 19.

Under FSMA 2000 firms carrying on regulated activities as defined by Financial Services and Markets Act 2000 (Regulated Activities) Order 2001 (RAO) have to be regulated by the Financial Services Authority (FSA).

However, Pt XX of FSMA 2000 makes special provision for professional firms which do not carry on mainstream investment business but which may carry on regulated activities in the course of other work such as probate and trusts. This enables solicitors to be treated as 'exempt professional firms' and to carry on 'exempt regulated activities' under the supervision of the Law Society which is a Designated Professional Body for this purpose.

In this book we deal with exempt professional firms but not with regulation by the FSA. Readers interested in obtaining authorisation from the FSA should consult a specialist text.

2.2.1 Regulation by The Law Society

Designated Professional Bodies are required to make rules to ensure that their members only carry on regulated activities arising out of or complementary to the provision of professional services to the client. The Law Society has made the Solicitors' Financial Services (Scope) Rules 2001 which set out the scope of activities that solicitors can undertake within the Pt XX exemption. It is most important that solicitors do not stray outside the Scope Rules as this is likely to amount to a criminal offence under FSMA 2000, s 19.

In the course of probate and trust work a firm will frequently perform services which fall within the definition of regulated activities in the RAO. They need to ask the following questions:

(a)   Does the activity involve a specified investment?
(b)   Is the activity capable of being a regulated activity under the RAO?
(c)   If so, does it fall within any of the exclusions in the RAO?
(d)   If not, does it fall within the Scope Rules?

There is a further problem. The FSMA 2000 provides that any communication which amounts to an invitation or inducement to engage in an investment activity must be made (or in some cases approved) by an FSA-authorised person.

Solicitors regulated by the Law Society must be careful not to breach this requirement. Communication can be oral or written. Almost anything a solicitor says or writes in connection with many transactions could be construed as a financial promotion. For example, a solicitor who advises executors to sell the deceased's shares could be inviting them to deal in investments.

Fortunately there is an exemption for 'one-off' communications, which will normally cover solicitors unless the communications are part of an organised marketing campaign.

2.2.1.1   Does the activity involve a specified investment?

Investments are specified in RAO, arts 74–89. They include:

(a)   shares or stock;

(b)   debentures;

(c)   government securities;

(d)   unit trusts and open-ended investment companies (OEICS);

(e)   long-term insurance policies such as endowments and whole life assurance.

The following are not investments:

(a)   National Savings products such as National Savings Certificates, Premium Bonds, SAYE contracts;

(b)   land;

(c)   bank and building society accounts;

(d)   TESSAs;

(e)   mini-cash ISAs.

2.2.1.2   Is the activity capable of being a regulated activity under the RAO?

The activities are listed in RAO and usually the activity is expressed in relation to a particular type of investment so it is the combination of activity plus particular investment which produces the regulated activity.

Some of the activities have particular exclusions associated with them which are dealt with below.

Regulated activities include:

(a)   dealing in shares as principal or agent;

(b)   advising on or arranging the acquisition or disposal of shares;

(c)   advising on or arranging the assignment of life policies;

(d)   arranging deals;

(e)   safeguarding and administering investments on behalf of clients;

(f)   managing investments.

Note: Advising means giving specific advice about a specific investment. Solicitors can give generic advice to a client without carrying on a regulated activity. For example, they can advise on the relative merits of buying shares as opposed to land.

2.2.1.3   Does the activity fall within any of the exclusions in the RAO?

If the activity falls within one of the exclusions then the activity is not regulated and the firm will not be subject to the Scope Rules at all in connection with the activity. There are a number of exclusions. The most relevant to private client work are:

Articles 22, 29 and 33 – using an authorised person or introducing a client to an authorised person

A solicitor can:

(a)   Introduce a client to an authorised person with a view to the provision of independent advice (art 33).

The solicitor must do no more than introduce the client to the adviser. If the solicitor retains any sort of ongoing role (for example, acting as a channel of communication, discussing the matter with the client or explaining the meaning of certain terms) this will amount to more than mere 'introducing'.

(b) Arrange deals for a client who enters into them with or through an authorised person:

    (i)   on the advice of an authorised person, or

    (ii)   where it is clear that the client, in his capacity as investor, is not seeking the advice of the solicitor (or if the client did seek it, the solicitor declined to give it and recommended that the client obtained advice from an authorised person) (art 29).

(c) Enter into deals as agent for a client with or through an authorised person:

    (i)   on the advice of an authorised person, or

    (ii)   where it is clear that the client, in his capacity as investor, is not seeking the advice of the solicitor (or if the client did seek it, the solicitor declined to give it and recommended that the client obtained advice from an authorised person) (art 22).

In order to come within arts 29 or 22 the solicitor must not receive any pecuniary reward from anyone other than the client which is not accounted for to the client. In each case the solicitor must be careful not to comment on the advice of the authorised person in such a way that it amounts to separate advice coming from the solicitor.

Article 66 – trustees

This exclusion relates to four functions which trustees or personal representatives (PRs) might perform in relation to investments. The exclusion does not apply if the solicitor trustee receives any additional remuneration on top of remuneration received for acting as trustee or PR. The trustee/PR is not regarded as receiving additional remuneration if he simply receives remuneration calculated on a time basis for time spent dealing with the investments.

(a) *Arranging.* Arrangements made by a solicitor acting as trustee or PR will be excluded if for or with a view to a transaction which is made by:

    (i)   him, and any fellow trustees or PRs, acting in their capacity as PRs or trustees;

    (ii)   by a beneficiary under the trust, will or intestacy.

    It is only available where the solicitor acts *as* trustee or PR and not where he acts *for* them. However, it is available where a member of the solicitor's firm carries out the activity on behalf of the solicitor trustee.

(b) *Managing.* Managing investments as a trustee or PR is excluded. Again there must be no additional remuneration. This exclusion is not available if the solicitor holds himself out as providing a discretionary management service over and above that which a lay trustee would provide.

(c) *Safeguarding.* There is an exclusion for safeguarding investments, but it is not available if the solicitor holds himself out as providing a discretionary management service over and above that which a lay trustee would provide. Again there must be no additional remuneration.

(d) *Advising.* There is an exclusion where a solicitor who is a trustee or PR advises:

    (i)   a fellow trustee or PR for the purposes of the trust or estate; or

    (ii)   a beneficiary under the trust, will or intestacy concerning his interest in the trust fund or estate.

Article 67 – necessary part of other professional services

There is an exclusion if the activity may reasonably be regarded as a necessary part of other services provided in the course of that profession or business. The exclusion does not apply if the service is remunerated separately from the other services. This simply means that the solicitor must not make a separate charge on the bill.

An example of reasonable necessity in connection with probate work would be arranging the sale of *all* assets to provide funds for payment of debts and inheritance tax. The Law Society has said that a decision as to *which* asset to sell to provide funds is unlikely to be 'necessary' as the solicitor can always go elsewhere for the advice.

2.2.1.4   Does it fall within the Scope Rules?

There are three main conditions.

Rule 4(b) – the manner of providing the service must be 'incidental to the provision' by the firm of professional services

To satisfy this condition the exempt regulated activities must not be a major part of the firm's practice. The FSA would consider whether the scale of regulated activity was in proportion to other professional services provided; whether the regulated activities were held out as separate services and the impression given through the firm's advertising of the way in which the firm provides the regulated activities.

In addition the regulated activity must be incidental to the particular client. A firm cannot carry out a regulated activity in isolation for a particular client. The professional service must be the primary service and any regulated activity should be subordinate to that professional service. Thus, in a probate matter where the client is the executor, advice given to a beneficiary will not satisfy the test.

Rule 4(c) – the firm must account to the client for any pecuniary reward or other advantage which the firm receives

If a firm receives commission or any other financial benefit from a third party because of acting for or giving advice to a client, the firm must account for the commission or benefit to the client. Accounting to the client does not mean simply telling the client that the firm will receive commission. It means that the commission or reward must be held to the order of the client. As we saw at **2.1.3**, the Law Society believes that solicitors will still account to the client if they have the client's informed consent to keeping the commission.

If the firm is charging the client on a fee basis, the firm can offset the commission against the firm's fees. The firm must send the client a bill or some other written notification of costs to comply with Solicitors Accounts Rules 1998, Rule 19.

The requirement for informed consent will not be satisfied by the firm seeking a blanket consent in its terms of business to the keeping of unspecified commission.

The firm must be able to demonstrate that the client has given informed consent to any retention of the commission, having had full disclosure of the amount. The FSA's Perimeter Guidance indicates that the firm should inform the client that, in effect, the commission belongs to the client.

The £20 de minimis provision contained in the Law Society's Code of Conduct 2004, Rule 2.06 does not apply to a firm seeking to remain within the Scope provisions. Commissions of £20 or less arising out of regulated activities must be treated in the same way as commissions in excess of £20.

Rule 4(d) – the activity must not be on the list of activities prohibited from coming within Pt XX

Under the Financial Services and Markets Act 2000 (Professions) (Non-exempt Activities) Order 2001, SI 2001/1227, the Treasury has listed activities which cannot be provided within the Pt XX Designated Professional Body regime. They include:

(a) market making and dealing in the same way as a stockbroker;

(b) operating a regulated collective investment scheme;

(c) advising a person to become a member of a particular Lloyd's syndicate;

(d) managing a stakeholder pension scheme.

2.2.2 The Conduct of Business Rules

If the firm carries out an exempt regulated activity it must comply with the Solicitors' Financial Services (Conduct of Business) Rules 2001 (COBS Rules) as well as with the Scope requirements.

The COBS Rules apply only when solicitors are carrying out an exempt regulated activity and not when the firm is doing something which does not amount to a regulated activity at all. For example, using an authorised third party. However, it is safest to make sure that the firm always follows the COBS Rules as this will avoid any risk of accidental non-compliance. In any event, the Rules merely set out good practice.

Of particular relevance to private client departments are the following:

(a) Rule 6 – The firm must keep records of all commissions received in respect of regulated activities and how that commission was dealt with.

(b) Rule 7 – Where a firm safeguards and administers another's assets it must operate 'appropriate systems'. These should include the following:

 (i) to register assets in the client's name;

 (ii) to record all title documents held, and safeguard documents adequately;

 (iii) to maintain a central record of all documents of which it has custody;

 (iv) to check records against title documents at least once a year;

 (v) to report to clients at least once a year on title documents held.

2.3 Developing the investment strategy for clients

Although you are unlikely to be developing such a strategy, it is important to appreciate what professional investment advisers should be doing.

2.3.1 'Know your client'

When taking instructions in relation to any financial planning for clients, it is essential to 'know the client'.

There are two main aspects to this:

(a) investigating, ie, ascertaining from the client all relevant personal and financial details; and

(b)   determining the suitability of investments, ie, only recommending investments suitable to the particular client.

2.3.2 The client's personal details

The information which should be obtained will include the following four major categories:

(a)   Personal details:
    (i)   name, address and occupation;
    (ii)   dates of birth and retirement;
    (iii) whether single, married, divorced, or widow(ed);
    (iv) whether employed, or self-employed.

(b)   Family details:
    (i)   spouse (name and age);
    (ii)   children, grandchildren (names and ages).

(c)   Gifts previously made (including the amounts and whether outright or in trust).

(d)   Provision by any will (including the date of will).

2.3.3 The client's financial details

The financial details obtained from the client will generally concentrate on two broad areas:

(a)   the client's current assets and liabilities; and

(b)   the client's current income and expenditure.

Generally, there will be some 'signpost' or 'indicator' in the client's existing financial affairs which leads to the opportunity to provide financial planning advice. Some of these indicators are as follows.

2.3.3.1 Savings predominantly on deposit in a bank or building society account

Savings in a bank or building society are 'safe' and convenient in that the money can be withdrawn quickly (although some accounts do require up to 90 days' notice to be given unless interest is to be lost, see further **Appendix 2**). Interest payable is subject to income tax. The main danger in holding a lot of money in such an account is the loss of purchasing power because of inflation. Inflation is the investor's number one enemy. At 5% inflation, £100 today will be worth £95 next year.

Although it is prudent to hold some money in savings accounts as a ready source of money in case of emergency, clients should consider withdrawing some of it for investment elsewhere.

2.3.3.2 Investments all yielding high income returns

High income yields will be superficially attractive to the client but there are features of such a return which indicate a review of the investment strategy, for example, because:

(a)   High yields may be earned at the expense of high risk, ie, there may be a higher risk of losing the invested capital because of the nature of the investment. If so, it may be prudent to diversify the investment portfolio to an appropriate extent; and

(b)   High income indicates the probability of income tax rates of 40%. This may be alleviated by the transfer of some investments into the name of the client's spouse if he or she pays income tax at a lower rate, or by rearranging the investment portfolio into assets where the concentration is on capital growth rather than income yield.

2.3.3.3   No life assurance

For a consideration of the available types of life policy, see **Appendix 2**. Although premiums do not generally attract income tax relief, it is always prudent to use life policies as a method of saving to produce substantial sums of money on the occurrence of anticipated future events. Traditionally, these are the repayment of a mortgage, the retirement of the client and the death of a client. They can also be used to cover school fees.

2.3.3.4   No occupational pension scheme or personal pension

Ideally, anyone who is in work should be able to look forward to retirement in the knowledge that he will then benefit from a pension which provides an acceptable level of income. Payment of national insurance contributions during working life will ensure receipt of the State retirement pension. This is payable at State pension age. In some cases, a 'top up' pension will be payable as well, ie, the State earnings related pension. However, further 'top up' through an occupational pension scheme or a private pension is also desirable.

Occupational pension schemes

The absence of contributions by an employee to an occupational pension scheme should not necessarily be taken as meaning that the employee will not benefit from an occupational pension on retirement. These schemes may be offered by employers on a 'non-contributory' basis, ie, only the employer pays contributions. If approved by the Revenue, occupational pension schemes attract considerable tax advantages for employer and employee contributions and for the pension fund itself. Sadly, the increasing cost to employers of providing such schemes means that many are closing.

Personal pension schemes

Personal pension schemes are available to the self-employed and to those employed in 'non-pensionable' employment, ie, to employees who are not offered an occupational pension scheme by their employers. They are also available to employees who prefer not to join the pension scheme provided by their employer. If approved by the Revenue, these schemes also attract considerable tax advantages for contributions to the scheme as well as for the fund itself.

Stakeholder pension schemes

These became available on 6 April 2001 and are really a type of personal pension scheme. They are low cost and available to everyone, even those who are not in paid employment. They are much more flexible than traditional personal pension schemes as contributors can contribute varying amounts and stop and restart contributions. Employed people can take the pension with them when they change jobs. They have substantial tax advantages as for every £1 contributed, the Revenue will contribute 28p even where the contributor is not a tax payer.

See **Appendix 2** for a more detailed discussion of pensions.

2.3.3.5 Assets held in the name of one spouse alone

The home, investments and other assets may, with advantage, be transferred into the joint ownership of spouses through the use of a joint tenancy or a tenancy in common. The various estate planning opportunities available to spouses are discussed in **Chapter 4**. It is frequently preferable to own as beneficial tenants in common rather than as beneficial joint tenants as this gives greater flexibility.

2.3.4 Suitability of investments for a particular client

The investment strategy for the client will reflect the information obtained from the client. Two particular factors will be the age of the client, and the client's existing investments and earnings.

2.3.4.1 The client's age

Younger clients, especially if married with children, may have little spare money beyond what is needed for everyday life, including mortgage payments. Because of the possibility of moving house and other changing circumstances, such clients should place any spare money in savings accounts whereby the income is reasonably high but the capital is free from risk and can easily be recovered if needed. For example, high interest building society and bank deposit accounts provide safe, high returns. Should further money be available, a more complex strategy will be needed.

Middle-aged clients, with growing families, should begin planning for retirement and old age by improving their income and capital position as far as possible. They may, however, be burdened by the costs of school and university fees. So far as possible, they should try to fund pensions. Spare earnings and investment income should be invested to produce maximum capital growth.

Retirement-age clients, who no longer have mortgage and school fee commitments, may need to change the emphasis of their investment strategy from capital growth to income yield. Loss of earnings will need to be balanced as far as possible by investment yields and pension income. If a tax-free capital lump sum is withdrawn from the pension fund at retirement, this should be invested to improve the income position.

Elderly clients, often with low incomes, need to ensure that maximum advantage is taken of the increased levels of personal tax allowances – the age related allowances (see **Appendix 1**) – by holding high income yielding investments where possible. By s 480A of the Income and Corporation Taxes Act 1988 (ICTA 1988), interest payable to depositors in banks and building societies is paid net of lower rate tax (20%). Non-tax payers can recover this tax if they submit an appropriate claim to the Revenue. However, if the client is not a tax payer, there is considerable advantage to be gained from holding money in a bank or building society because interest can be paid without deduction of lower rate tax at source. The elderly client will need to certify to the bank or building society that he is not a tax payer so that he can receive gross interest payments.

Planning the financial and other affairs of clients will become difficult where they are unable to take part in decision-making through loss of mental capacity. In order to overcome problems caused by loss of mental capacity, it is appropriate for the solicitor to recommend to clients that they make an enduring power of attorney (EPA) (or, when the Mental Capacity Act 2005 is in force, a lasting power of attorney (LPA). The client may choose to appoint a member of the family or perhaps the solicitor to be his attorney.

However, EPAs and LPAs should not be regarded as something reserved for elderly clients. People of any age can lose capacity as a result of accident or illness. They will then need someone to deal with their affairs for them. It is often convenient to raise the question of making an EPA or LPA at the same time as the client is making a new will or codicil. EPAs and LPAs are considered in detail in **Chapter 3**.

2.4 Portfolio planning

Every client is different, and each client will have different requirements. Excluding the buying of a house, a general plan for investments will probably be:

(a)   'ready cash' saved in a bank or building society;

(b)   protection through life assurance for the client and dependants;

(c)   pension; and

(d)   longer-term investments purchased with any spare cash.

2.4.1 High risk/low risk

Investments can be categorised as low, medium or high risk. Often the higher the return, the higher the risk. Each category might include the following.

Low risk

(a)   savings accounts in the bank or building society;

(b)   government stock ('gilts');

(c)   National Savings, for example National Savings premium bonds.

Medium risk

(a)   unit trusts;

(b)   investment trusts;

(c)   shares in public companies, ie, in blue chip 'equities';

(d)   loans to companies, financial institutions and local authorities.

High risk

(a)   shares in small public companies and in private companies;

(b)   'collectibles' such as works of art and stamp collections;

(c)   woodlands.

2.4.2 Short-term/longer-term

Short-term investments often mean 'savings', ie, short-term cash investments made for the purchase of a particular item such as a new car. Probably the bank or building society offers the best opportunity but interest rates may be low (and no capital growth).

Longer-term 'investment' depends on the client's available resources, personal likes and dislikes etc and may include many of the investments in **Appendix 2**.

2.4.3 Capital growth/income yield

If the client has adequate income, he may prefer to invest for capital growth rather than for dividends or interest. Company shares are the most likely type of investment if capital growth is required, although companies showing good capital growth usually pay good dividends as well. In the last few years, it has proved unusually difficult to obtain capital growth.

If income yield is required, savings in higher rate bank and building society accounts may be sensible. So too may be investment in certain companies where the dividend record is good or even government stocks ('gilts').

2.4.4 Income tax and capital gains tax

'Savings' producing an income and 'investments' producing both an income and capital growth will mean that both income tax and capital gains tax will affect the client. Some savings and investments are tax free and should always feature in the portfolio planning for clients who are, or who become because of the investment, tax payers. Examples include ISAs (see further **Appendix 2**).

2.5 Introduction to types of investment products

There are very many different types of investment product on the market. The term 'investment product' covers savings, ie, money deposited in a bank or building society, as well as stocks, shares, unit and investment trusts, ISAs, life policies, etc. All these products have different characteristics, uses and tax positions associated with them. They must be selected with care to suit the particular type of client.

The main categories of savings and investments producing tax-free income are detailed in **Appendix 2**. Where possible, a gross income should be obtained if the client is not a tax payer so as to avoid the need to obtain a refund of tax deducted at source from the Revenue. Some of these investments are free of capital gains tax as well as income tax.

Chapter 3

Enduring Powers of Attorney, Lasting Powers of Attorney and Living Wills

The Mental Capacity Act 2005 contains substantial changes to the law concerning mental capacity and enduring powers of attorney. However, it is not yet in force. This chapter considers both the law as it is at the time of writing and the position when the Mental Capacity Act 2005 comes into force.

3.1 What is an EPA?

An ordinary power of attorney, whether granted under the Trustee Act 1925 (TA 1925) or as a short form power under the Powers of Attorney Act 1971, ceases to have effect when the donor of the power loses his mental capacity. This means that the attorney appointed by the power is no longer able to act at just the moment when the power is most needed.

The enduring power of attorney (EPA) was introduced by the Enduring Powers of Attorney Act 1985 (EPAA 1985) as a means of allowing the authority of the attorney to continue notwithstanding the intervening lack of mental capacity of the donor. An EPA has a number of features including the following.

(a) It must be granted by an adult donor with the appropriate mental capacity to make the EPA. He will have such capacity if he understands the nature and effect of the power, ie, that the attorney may assume authority over his affairs and that the power may continue if he becomes mentally incapable.

(b) Under an EPA, one or more attorneys can be appointed. Where two or more are appointed, the donor must specify whether they are joint attorneys or joint and several attorneys. Failure to do so means that the EPA is invalid. Joint attorneys must all act together; if one should die, become bankrupt or lose mental capacity, the power ceases to be effective.

Joint powers provide protection for the donor but are inconvenient.

Joint and several attorneys can act independently of the other or others. This may be convenient but could lead to lack of protection for the donor's property. A joint and several attorney can continue to act when a co-attorney has died or lost capacity.

(c) The EPA may continue despite the loss of mental capacity of the donor but special duties then arise for the attorney (see **3.3.2**). In particular, the attorney must apply to the Court of Protection to register the EPA.

(d) The EPA may give the attorney general or specific authority to act on the donor's behalf. If general authority is given, this confers authority 'to do on behalf of the donor anything which the donor can lawfully do'. If specific authority is given, the authority is limited to the particular activity, for example, to contract to sell and execute a transfer of the donor's freehold property.

(e) Any authority given by the EPA is limited to acts relating to the donor's property and financial affairs. Thus, it can cover such transactions as buying and selling shares or a house on behalf of the donor. But even an EPA giving general authority is significantly limited. It does not cover such matters as where the donor should live, whether or not medical treatment should be given or withheld or the execution of a will for the donor. This limitation on the authority of the attorney will not necessarily matter until such time as the donor of the power loses mental capacity. Decisions relating to matters not covered by the EPA must be taken by individuals and not by the attorney acting under the power. If the donor of the EPA does not have sufficient mental capacity to make a will, the Court of Protection may be asked to make a 'statutory will' on behalf of the donor.

(f) Attorneys have authority to use the donor's property to make provision for others under s 3(4) and s 3(5) of the EPAA 1985.

Subsection (4) provides as follows:

Subject to any conditions or restrictions contained in the instrument, an attorney under an enduring power, whether general or limited, may (without obtaining any consent) act under the power so as to benefit himself or other persons than the donor to the following extent but no further, that is to say—

(a) he may so act in relation to himself or in relation to any other person if the donor might be expected to provide for his or that person's needs respectively; and

(b) he may do whatever the donor might be expected to do to meet those needs.

Thus, the attorney must ask three questions:

(i) Is the provision required to meet a need?

(ii) Might the donor be expected to provide for this person's needs?

(iii) What would this particular donor have done to meet these needs?

Subsection (5) provides as follows:

Without prejudice to subsection (4) above but subject to any conditions or restrictions contained in the instrument, an attorney under an enduring power, whether general or limited, may (without obtaining any consent) dispose of the property of the donor by way of gift to the following extent but no further—

(a) he may make gifts of a seasonal nature or at a time, or on an anniversary, of a birth or marriage, to persons (including himself) who are related to or connected with the donor, and

(b) he may make gifts to any charity to whom the donor made or might be expected to make gifts,

provided that the value of each gift is not unreasonable having regard to all the circumstances and in particular the size of the donor's estate.

The attorney can make gifts to charity at any time. Gifts to non-charities can be made only if they are seasonal (eg, at Christmas), or for a birthday or marriage. It is doubtful whether 'seasonal' extends to the end of one tax year and the beginning of another. Presents given for particular events such as christenings, engagements, graduations, barmitzvahs or confirmations are effectively excluded.

3.2   Creation of an EPA

3.2.1   The Enduring Power of Attorney (Prescribed Form) Regulations 1990

An EPA can be validly created only if the instrument complies with the following requirements:

(a)   The EPA is in the form prescribed in the 1990 Regulations (see **Appendix 3**). The Act provides that 'immaterial differences in form' can be ignored, thus making it possible for firms of solicitors to have their own forms of EPA on word processor. The Court of Protection has indicated that it considers it safer to use printed versions of the form purchased from law stationers.

(b)   The EPA form incorporates the prescribed explanatory information together with all the relevant marginal notes. Part A of the form entitled 'About using this form' must be included together with Parts B and C. The entire form must be explained to the donor of the power before it is signed.

(c)   The EPA must be executed in the prescribed manner by both the donor and the attorney, in each case in the presence of an independent witness. If the donor (or the attorney) is physically disabled then the EPA can be executed on his behalf, but in this case the signature must be made in the presence of two independent witnesses.

3.2.2   Postponing the attorney's authority to act

Once the EPA has been correctly executed, the attorney may act under its authority immediately, and without further formality. The execution of the EPA does not deprive the donor of the ability to take decisions on his own behalf should he so wish; indeed, he can revoke the power at any time. However, he must retain sufficient mental capacity if he is to act on his own behalf or to revoke the power.

Some donors prefer the attorney's authority to act only to arise at a future date and not immediately the power is executed. They do not want the attorney to act while they still retain capacity. If the attorney's authority is to be delayed, the EPA should be drafted to include an appropriate restriction on the attorney's authority. For example, the authority may be delayed until such time as the attorney believes that 'the donor either is, or is becoming, mentally incapable', ie, the authority will arise at the same time as EPAA 1985 places a duty on the attorney to register the EPA with the Court of Protection (see **3.3**). Great care must must be exercised when drafting this type of restriction.

3.3   Registration of the EPA with the Court of Protection

3.3.1   Donor's mental incapacity

Unlike an ordinary power of attorney, an EPA is not revoked by the donor's subsequent loss of mental capacity. However, once the donor has become incapacitated the attorney is unable to act under the authority of the EPA until it has been registered with the Court of Protection. The EPAA 1985 imposes special duties on the attorney which arise once the attorney 'has reason to believe that the donor is or is becoming mentally incapable'.

3.3.2 Special duties

The attorney is required to notify the donor of the EPA and certain specified relatives of his intention to apply to the Court of Protection for registration of the EPA.

The specified relatives who must receive notification of intention to apply for registration of the EPA include:

(a)   the donor's husband or wife;

(b)   the donor's children (including illegitimate children);

(c)   the donor's parents;

(d)   the donor's brothers and sisters, whether of the whole or half blood;

(e)   the widow or widower of a child of the donor;

(f)   the donor's grandchildren.

The list continues with further remoter categories of relatives.

The EPAA 1985 requires that three individuals be ascertained by working from the top of the list. All members of a particular category must be notified once any member of the category is counted to establish the minimum number of three. However, there is no requirement for the attorney to notify, inter alia:

(a)   a person who has not attained 18, or

(b)   himself, even if he is a specified relative, but he should be included when counting the number of relatives to notify.

Example

Adam is married with five adult children and a number of other surviving relatives. He has appointed his solicitor, Brian, to be his attorney. When Adam becomes incapable of managing his affairs, Brian must notify Adam's wife and all five children (plus Adam himself unless the court dispenses with this).

The Court of Protection has a general power of dispensation from the duty of notification. It can order dispensation if satisfied that it would be undesirable or impractical for the attorney to give notice, or if no useful purpose is likely to be achieved by it. However, clear medical evidence of detriment to health would be required before the court dispenses with notification to the donor.

The application to the Court of Protection for registration of the EPA should be made within 10 days of giving notice to the donor and the specified relatives.

3.3.3 Effect of registration

The registration of the EPA with the Court of Protection effectively revalidates the EPA and restores to the attorney the powers granted by the EPA. Once registered, the donor can no longer revoke, extend or restrict the extent of the EPA.

3.4 When should an EPA be granted?

As in the case of an ordinary power of attorney, there is no precise occasion when an EPA should be granted. However, it may be appropriate to do so:

(a)   When the donor is intending to be absent abroad for a given period of time. If the EPA is not restricted, the attorney would be able to act during the donor's absence.

(b)   At the same time as the donor is making a will. Most clients will raise the question of a will with their solicitor but, apart from unusual circumstances, it is not likely that a client will consider making an EPA. It is, therefore, generally necessary for the solicitor to find an appropriate occasion when the subject of an EPA can be introduced. Often this will be when instructions are taken for the will. It is good practice to consider giving advice about a will and an EPA at the same time. Although younger testators are unlikely to be keen on the idea of an EPA, they should remember that either accident or illness can result in loss of mental capacity. Without an EPA the person's affairs would be managed by a receiver appointed by the Court of Protection.

Many solicitors offer clients a 'package' of a will, an EPA and 'living will' setting out their wishes with regard to medical treatment in the event of loss of mental capacity.

3.5 Effect of the Trustee Delegation Act 1999

Prior to the Trustee Delegation Act 1999 it was possible for trustees to delegate their powers by using an EPA (EPAA 1985, s 3(3)). Section 3(3) had been drafted in haste in response to the decision in *Walia and Others v Michael Naughten Ltd* [1985] 1 WLR 1115. There was a feeling that the section had gone too far. There were three main problems with s 3(3):

(a)   The delegation remained effective indefinitely, unlike a delegation under TA 1925, s 25 which could last for only 12 months.

(b)   Various safeguards present in TA 1925, s 25 were not present in EPAA 1985. The trustee did not have to give notice to the person entitled to appoint new trustees and was not liable for the acts of the delegate.

(c)   The delegation remained effective after the trustee lost capacity.

The Trustee Delegation Act 1999, s 5 therefore provides (subject to one important exception) that any delegation of trustee functions must comply with TA 1925, s 25, as substituted by s 5. The delegation cannot exceed 12 months; the trustee must give notice to any co-trustees and to any person able to appoint new trustees; the trustee will remain liable for the acts of the attorney.

The exception is contained in s 1, which allows a person who is beneficially interested in land (or the proceeds of sale of land) to delegate trustee functions without complying with s 25. The appointment can, therefore, continue for more than 12 months.

The usefulness of the s 1 exception is to some extent eroded by s 7, which provides that where two trustees are required (for example, to give a good receipt for capital money) the requirement is not fulfilled by one person acting in two capacities, as a trustee and as an attorney of another trustee.

Example

H and W are co-owners of a house. H appoints W as his attorney under an EPA. He becomes mentally incapable and W registers the power. W wants to sell the house but she will not satisfy the requirement for two trustees. She can, however, appoint a further trustee under s 8.

3.6 What is a living will?

Living wills (also known as advance directives) are intended to allow individuals to specify the extent and nature of the medical treatment they would or would not find acceptable should they lose capacity in the future. The term 'living will' can be confusing since such documents have no connection with ordinary wills, but this term is probably too well established to change.

A mentally capable adult has no right to demand a particular treatment, but has the right to refuse any medical treatment (*Sidaway v Board of Governors of the Bethlem Royal Hospital and Maudsley Hospital and Others* [1985] AC 871).

The right to refuse treatment extends to a refusal made in advance. There are various cases which support advance directives.

After the Tony Bland case (arising from the Hillsborough stadium disaster) a *Practice Note (Persistent Vegetative State: Withdrawal of Treatment) (26 July 1996)* [1996] 4 All ER 766 was issued dealing with the procedure to be followed when an application is made to withdraw treatment from a person in a persistent vegetative state. It included the following statement:

> Previously expressed advance directions of the patient, in writing or otherwise, will be an important factor, and the High Court may determine the effect of advance directives as to future medical treatment.

In *Re T (Adult: Refusal of Treatment)* [1992] 2 FLR 458, the Court of Appeal said that an advance refusal is legally binding provided:

(a)   the person making it had capacity at the time of making it;

(b)   a situation has arisen which was envisaged when the directive was made;

(c)   the person making it was not under any undue influence at the time the directive was made.

It is not easy to draft effective advance directives. It is difficult to anticipate the circumstances that may arise and make the direction sufficiently specific. In *Re B (Consent to Treatment: Capacity)* [2002] EWHC 429 (Fam), [2002] 1 FLR 1090, Ms B had made a living will but it was not appropriate to deal with the circumstances that arose. Doctors therefore ignored it.

Even if a person has written a perfectly effective advance directive, there is the further problem that an emergency doctor may give treatment before becoming aware of the existence of the advance directive.

However, despite the problems, living wills are likely to become more, rather than less, popular.

3.7   Changes contained in the Mental Capacity Act 2005

The MCA 2005 contains a number of changes of general application in relation to mental capacity.

Section 2 introduces a single test for capacity. It provides that:

(a)   a person lacks capacity *in relation to a matter* if at the material time he is unable to make a decision for himself in relation to the matter because of an impairment of or a disturbance in the functioning of the mind or brain;

(b)   it does not matter whether the disturbance is permanent or temporary.

Section 3 provides that a person is unable to make a decision for himself if he is unable to:

(a)   understand the information relevant to the decision; or

(b)   retain the information relevant to the decision; or

(c)   use the information relevant to the decision as part of the process of making the decision; or

(d)   communicate the decision (whether by talking, using sign language or any other means).

A person is not to be treated as unable to make a decision simply because he makes an unwise one. A person is not to be treated as unable to make a decision unless all practicable steps to help him to do so have been taken without success. The fact that a person is able to retain information relevant to the decision only for a short time does not prevent him being regarded as able to make the decision. The information relevant to making a decision includes information about the reasonably foreseeable consequences of:

(a)   deciding one way or another; or

(b)   failing to make the decision.

Section 1 provides that a person is to be assumed to have capacity until the contrary is established on the balance of probabilities. It also states that anyone making a decision on behalf of a person who lacks capacity must act in the best interests of that person.

Part 2 of the MCA 2005 provides for the creation of a new Court of Protection which will deal with persons who lack capacity. The Act also contains some specific changes which include the creation of lasting powers of attorney and the creation of advance decisions to refuse treatment.

3.7.1   Lasting power of attorney (LPA)

One of the important changes contained in the MCA 2005 is that once the Act is in force it will no longer be possible to create an EPA (see **3.1**). However, existing EPAs (whether registered or not) will continue to be valid and operate as usual. Instead a person will be able to create a LPA.

3.7.1.1   What is a LPA?

According to s 9 of the MCA 2005, under an LPA a person (the donor) is able to confer on the attorney(s) authority to make decisions about the donor's personal welfare and/or the donor's property and affairs, including authority to make such decisions in circumstances where the donor no longer has capacity (as defined in ss 2 and 3).

3.7.1.2   Who can be appointed as attorney?

According to s 10 of the MCA 2005, the attorney must be an individual over the age of 18 or, if the authority is only in relation to the donor's property and affairs, the attorney could also be a trust corporation.

The donor may appoint more than one attorney, and may specify whether the appointment is joint or joint and several. It is possible to provide that for some functions the attorneys must act jointly, and for other functions they may act jointly and severally. If the donor does not specify, the appointment will be regarded as joint.

If the attorney is appointed to deal with the donor's property and affairs the attorney cannot be bankrupt. However, if there are joint and several attorneys, the bankruptcy of one of the attorneys will not affect the validity of the appointment of the other non-bankrupt attorneys.

The donor may provide for a successor or substitute attorney to replace an attorney in certain circumstances, for example the death, loss of capacity or bankruptcy of the attorney.

It is not clear whether it is possible to appoint different attorneys to deal with different decisions, for example, one person to deal with decisions on property and affairs and another to deal with decisions on personal welfare. A solicitor or other professional adviser may be happy to act as attorney in relation to property and affairs, but is unlikely to wish to act in relation to personal welfare.

3.7.1.3   How to create an LPA?

Only an adult with capacity can create an LPA. It must be made in the form prescribed from time to time in regulations, and contain prescribed information, including:

(a)   that the donor has read and understood the prescribed information and intends to confer authority to make decisions in circumstances where he has no capacity;

(b)   who the donor wishes to be notified of any application for the registration of the LPA (or that he wishes no one to be notified);

(c)   that the attorney has read and understood the prescribed information and understands his duty to act in the best interests of donor;

(d)   a certificate, signed by a person of a 'prescribed description', as to the capacity of the donor.

The person of a 'prescribed description', and the person named by the donor to be notified, cannot be the attorney. At the time of writing there are no regulations expanding on these requirements.

Unlike EPAs, which could come into operation as a power of attorney from the moment of execution, the LPA will not have any effect at all until it is registered with the Public Guardian. The Public Guardian is appointed by the Government to deal with various matters concerning people who lack mental capacity.

The donor or attorneys (or, where there are joint and several attorneys, any of them) must apply to register the LPA, in prescribed form, and pay a fee. Whoever applies for registration must have first notified anyone named by the donor as a person to be notified in such circumstances.

On receipt of an application for registration, the Public Guardian must notify:

(a)   the attorneys if the donor applied; or

(b)   the donor if the attorneys applied (and any attorneys who did not join in the application to register).

The donor, attorneys or the other persons notified can object to the registration on various grounds, but otherwise the Public Guardian will register the power and notify the donor and attorneys of this. The Public Guardian will keep a register of LPAs.

Once registered, the LPA is valid and could be used by the attorney(s), subject to any express restrictions in the LPA.

An attorney making a decision under an LPA for a person who lacks capacity must act in the best interests of the donor, which means complying with s 4 which sets out various matters to which the attorney must have regard.

3.7.1.4   Authority in relation to personal welfare

The MCA 2005 provides that the attorney cannot make certain decisions, for example, organ donation, but it does provide for the attorney to be able to give or refuse consent to health care treatment. However, this is only if the donor does not have capacity to make such a decision. Further, if the decision involves the refusal of life-sustaining treatment the attorney must have express authority in the LPA to make such a decision.

3.7.1.5   Authority in relation to property and affairs

An attorney who has authority in relation to the donor's property and affairs cannot dispose of the donor's property by making gifts unless in accordance with s 12. Section 12(2) provides that the attorney may make gifts:

(a)   on customary occasions to persons (including the attorney) who are related to or connected with the donor; or

(b)   to any charity to whom the donor made or might have been expected to make gifts.

In either case the value of the gift must not be unreasonable in all the circumstances. 'Customary occasions' is defined in s 12(3) to mean:

(a)   the occasion or anniversary of a birth, a marriage or the formation of a civil partnership; or

(b)   any other occasion when presents are customarily given within families, or among friends or associates.

Unlike EPAs, therefore (see **3.1**), gifts to non-charities can be made other than at 'seasonal' times.

Under s 23(4), the court may authorise gifts not covered by s 12(2), for example a gift made for tax planning purposes.

3.7.2   Advance decisions to refuse treatment

The MCA 2005 provides for an adult with capacity to make an advance decision to refuse specified medical treatment in future specified circumstances. Provided the provisions contained in the advance decision apply to the particular circumstances encountered by the persons supplying treatment, it will be as if the person had capacity to refuse the treatment, and those persons will not be liable for complying with the advance decision to refuse treatment. Such persons will also not be liable if they reasonably believe the advance decision to apply.

The advance decision can be revoked or modified by the person who made it at any time when he has capacity to do so. If a person who has made an advance decision later makes an LPA giving express authority to an attorney to make decisions on such matters, this LPA will supersede the advance decision.

Chapter 4

Estate Planning

4.1 Introduction

The object of estate planning is to pass on wealth to the desired objects as efficiently as possible.

Estate planning can range from advising on a will leaving everything to a spouse to complex 'off-shore' tax avoidance schemes. The majority of practitioners find that their cases fall somewhere between these extremes. The client offering the greatest scope for estate planning is wealthy, married with children (and possibly grandchildren).

4.1.1 Estate planning

Estate planning is a combination of financial planning (see **Chapter 2**); lifetime giving, outright and/or into trusts (see **Chapter 5**); and will drafting (see **Chapter 11**). For clients with relatively limited means, it may only be possible to plan through a will, for example, by leaving a legacy to the children to take advantage of the nil rate band with the residue passing to the surviving spouse. Wealthy clients, however, should consider a combination of lifetime transfers and gifts by will. Where lifetime estate planning is contemplated, it is essential that consideration should also be given to a complementary will. If a client dies intestate or leaves a will that does not take lifetime planning into account, unexpected claims can arise, such as, for example, from the Revenue for additional tax. There may be a claim in negligence against the solicitor by a surviving spouse or children who receive less than was intended.

4.1.2 Aims

The aims of a client are usually:

(a)   the provision of financial security for self and family; and

(b)   the avoidance of tax.

It is not always possible to achieve both objectives and many practitioners believe that tax savings should not be achieved at the expense of financial security.

Estate planning often involves a person giving away assets during his lifetime, perhaps to a spouse or children. Once the gift is made, it cannot be claimed back, for example, if the parties subsequently divorce or the donor parent falls on hard times. If planning through a will, the will of the deceased spouse should not prejudice the standard of living of the survivor by leaving too much property away from that surviving spouse.

Whereas with basic tax planning through wills the intention is to limit the amount of inheritance tax (IHT) payable on a death, the tax planning element of lifetime estate planning is often as much concerned with avoiding capital gains tax (CGT) or minimising an income tax bill as it is with IHT. Because of the interaction of the taxes, clients may have to accept a small CGT bill as part of the cost of avoiding a large IHT bill, or a potential IHT charge for a considerable saving of CGT.

Example

James has been told that to give away assets which are likely to increase in value is sound IHT planning. Accordingly, he plans to give his daughter his 10,000 shares in Widgets plc which have considerable growth potential. He hopes to reduce the IHT payable at death on his already large estate. Stockbrokers have advised that he will realise a gain of £20,000 if he gives the shares away now. There are no relevant reliefs which James can claim.

Compare the following:

Lifetime gift

(a)   CGT: chargeable gain of £11,500 (£20,000–£8,500 annual exemption) taxed at 40% = £4,600.

(b)   IHT, potentially exempt transfer (PET): even if death occurs within seven years, IHT will be calculated on the value of the shares at the date of the gift. The increase in value will occur in James's daughter's estate, not in his estate.

No lifetime gift: tax on death

(a)   CGT: none (tax-free uplift to value of shares at the date of death).

(b)   IHT: on value of the shares at death as part of James's estate attracting tax of up to 40%.

Where a client is contemplating estate planning, the solicitor must balance the cost of the legal work involved against the tax saving to ensure that the costs of the scheme do not outweigh the advantages. Making lifetime property transfers may give rise to an immediate tax bill which may make the proposal unattractive to the client even though it will save tax in the long run. Clients may also have to accept that the payment of some tax is inevitable (whether during their lifetime or on death) in order to ensure the best practical financial arrangements for the family.

In this chapter we consider estate planning by lifetime transfers. Estate planning through will trusts is dealt with in **Chapter 12**.

4.1.3   Some ground rules

When advising clients, solicitors should consider the following.

4.1.3.1   How much to give away?

Apart from the obvious – not too much – other factors to be taken into consideration are: ill health, separation or divorce, retirement, death of one of the parties to the marriage and the effects of inflation on the purchasing power of income and on the value of retained capital. Any of these may suggest retaining more rather than less.

4.1.3.2   What to give away?

Where possible, assets likely to appreciate in value should be considered for lifetime giving. Shares in a private company will often rise substantially in value if the company is floated on the Stock Exchange. So too may the value of a painting following the death of the artist. Making the gift *before* the value increases ensures the growth occurs in the estate of the donee. It 'freezes the value' of the property (ie, a PET) at the value at the time of the gift, which will be relevant should death occur within seven years. A 'disposal' for CGT will occur but the disposal consideration will be the market value at the date of the gift.

4.1.3.3   How to give away?

Outright gifts are straightforward but are inflexible; if circumstances change, the property given away cannot be recovered. If the proposed donee is a minor, such a gift (if substantial) would not be sensible. The donor may come to regret making an outright gift; for example, the donee may become addicted to drugs, or may become mentally or physically handicapped. In either case, the money might be better held by trustees for the benefit of the donee.

4.1.3.4   Gifts into trust provide flexibility

Because unexpected events do occur, flexibility is an important part of planning, and therefore trusts are attractive. However, trusts require proper administration. Dealing with income and investment of trust funds, preparing trust accounts and making tax returns for the trust all cost time and money. These disadvantages must be weighed against the advantages of flexibility. So too must possible adverse change in tax law affecting trusts. Over recent years, such changes have made discretionary trusts less attractive to estate planners and their clients.

4.1.3.5   Don't let the tax tail wag the dog

The objective is to plan affairs so that the client's property is enjoyed by the beneficiaries (often the family) to the best advantage. In achieving this, tax avoidance is only one aspect.

4.2   Tax and estate planning

The following paragraphs contain some reminders of the basic rules relating to the taxation of individuals; many of these rules also apply to the taxation of trustees. The basic rules are covered in the LPC Guides, *Pervasive and Core Topics* and *Business Law and Practice*. This chapter groups together all the points that are relevant when considering the various estate planning ideas put forward here. More complex tax law is explained in detail either here or in context.

Note that under s 103 of the Finance Act 2005, the Treasury is empowered to issue regulations making provision for the tax treatment of persons involved in a civil partnership. It is likely that such regulations will be used to ensure that for all tax purposes persons who have entered into a civil partnership will be treated in the same way as married persons. At the time of writing there are no regulations in place, but it is expected that there will be by December 2005.

4.3   Inheritance tax

The Inheritance Tax Act 1984 (IHTA 1984), s 7 provides that tax is charged in accordance with the table of rates in Sch 1 to the Act.

4.3.1   Rates of IHT chargeable on death

0% on the first £275,000 (nil rate band) from 6 April 2005.

40% on the balance.

4.3.2   Rates of IHT for lifetime chargeable transfers

0% on the first £275,000 (nil rate band).

20% on the balance.

The majority of lifetime transfers are PETs, which become chargeable only if the donor dies within seven years. However, the creation of a no interest in possession trust, eg, a discretionary settlement, is immediately chargeable. IHT must be reassessed at death rates if the settlor (the person creating the settlement) dies within the following seven years. Credit is given in the re-calculation for any tax already paid, ie, when the settlement was created.

Example

Helen gives property with a value of £321,000 to the trustees of her discretionary trust (ignore exemptions and reliefs). The trustees agree to pay the IHT.

		£
IHT at lifetime rates	£275,000 @ 0% =	nil
	£46,000 @ 20% =	9,200

Helen dies 14 months later – the IHT is reassessed.

		£
IHT at death rates	£275,000 @ 0% =	nil
	£46,000 @ 40% =	18,400
		18,400
Less: IHT already paid at lifetime rates		9,200
Additional IHT as result of Helen's death		9,200

If Helen, not the trustees, had agreed to pay the IHT when she created the settlement, the loss to her estate then would have included the IHT payable, ie, the legacies would be 'grossed up' when calculating the value transferred. This is considered further in **Chapter 5**.

4.3.2.1   Tapering relief (IHTA 1984, s 7(4))

If a transferor dies more than three years after the date of a transfer, the full death rate of tax is reduced and only the following percentages are charged:

(a)   transfers within 3 to 4 years before death 80% of death charge;
(b)   transfers within 4 to 5 years before death 60% of death charge;
(c)   transfers within 5 to 6 years before death 40% of death charge;
(d)   transfers within 6 to 7 years before death 20% of death charge.

Notice that tapering relief is of no benefit if the transfer is within the nil rate band. This is because it operates to reduce the rate of tax charged. If no tax is payable, there can be no reduction.

In the case of transfers which were immediately chargeable to tax, the effect of tapering relief may be that no further tax is payable. The relief never results in a refund of tax already paid.

Example

Suppose in the previous example Helen had died 6 years and 4 months after making the transfer.

The effect of tapering relief is that only 20% of the tax at the full death rates is payable. The full death rate tax was £18,400 so only £3,680 is payable. The trustees have already paid £9,200. No further tax is payable but the trustees are not entitled to a refund.

4.3.3 Potentially exempt transfers (IHTA 1984, s 3A)

Potentially exempt transfers (PETs) are transfers made by an individual on or after 18 March 1986 which, apart from the section, are chargeable transfers. The following are PETs:

(a) Gifts to other individuals provided the donee's estate is increased or the property transferred becomes comprised in his estate.

(b) Transfers to the trustees of an interest in possession settlement because the estate of the beneficiary with the life interest includes the property in which that interest subsists, ie, the settled property (IHTA 1984, ss 5 and 49).

(c) Transfers to the trustees of an accumulation and maintenance trust and trusts for the disabled (IHTA 1984, ss 71 and 89).

Transfers to trustees of interest in possession settlements and accumulation and maintenance trusts are considered further in **Chapter 5**.

No charge arises at the time the PET is made and it is treated as fully exempt unless the transferor dies within the following seven years. There is no obligation on the transferor to notify the Revenue of the PET. Should the transferor die within the seven years following the PET, it becomes chargeable and is treated as if it had always been chargeable. It must be reported to the Revenue.

A transfer which is covered by an exemption is fully, not potentially, exempt.

4.3.4 Exemptions applying to lifetime transfers (IHTA 1984, ss 18–23)

(a) Any property passing to a spouse (there is a limit of £55,000 on the exempt amount if the recipient spouse is non-UK domiciled – IHTA 1984, s 18(2) (see further **15.3**)).

(b) Gifts to charity. Various ways of giving to charity are considered in **4.8**.

(c) Small gifts. Gifts not exceeding £250 to any one person in any one year are exempt. Because of this limitation, it is not possible to combine the small gift exemption with another exemption, for example, the annual exemption. The gift must be outright, not in trust.

(d) Transfers of £3,000 per annum (any unused annual exemption can be carried forward one year).

Example

In Year 1, a donor makes his first ever gift of £1,000. The unused part of the annual exemption is carried forward to Year 2. In Year 2, he may give away £5,000 in exempt transfers. If the £2,000 carried forward from Year 1 is not used in Year 2, it is lost and may not be carried further forward.

A husband and wife who each use the annual exemption over a 25-year period they could give their children a total of £156,000. By the simple use of an exemption considerable estate planning for the parents could be achieved.

(e) Gifts in consideration of marriage: up to £5,000 per parent of the couple (lesser amounts for other donors). The gift may be outright or into trust provided the beneficiaries do not include persons other than the couple or their issue (or spouses of their issue). It must be 'in contemplation' of a particular marriage, and should be so evidenced in writing.

(f) Normal expenditure out of income: if claimed (it is not given automatically), this exemption applies to a gift of cash that:

(i)   is part of the normal expenditure of the donor;

(ii) taking one with another, is made out of income; and

(iii) after other such gifts, leaves the donor with sufficient income to maintain his usual standard of living.

It is a question of fact whether a gift qualifies for the exemption. What is 'normal expenditure' for one person is not necessarily so for another. Even though it is not one of a series of regular payments, a gift may none the less be 'normal' if there is evidence that payments of an ascertainable amount are likely to recur (see further *Bennett v Inland Revenue Commissioners* [1995] STC 54).

The exemption is most commonly used to fund the payment of premiums on policies of assurance written in trust, for example:

(i)   an endowment policy written in trust by a parent in favour of a child on which the parent pays the annual premiums;

(ii) premiums on a policy written in trust to be used to fund a potential IHT liability should the donor die within seven years of a PET.

4.3.5 Valuation

4.3.5.1 Market value

The IHT legislation contains provisions relating to the valuation of property given away by a donor. The normal rule is that property is valued at 'the price [it] might reasonably be expected to fetch if sold on the open market at the time; but that price shall not be reduced on the grounds that the whole property is to be placed on the market at one and the same time'. Thus, it is not possible to argue for a reduced valuation because 'the market is flooded' where a lot of a similar type of property is available at once (IHTA 1984, s 160).

The 'open market rule' applies on a death, although changes in value of an estate caused by the death can be taken into account (IHTA 1984, s 171). For example, life policies which mature on death are valued at the maturity value (not the surrender value) and personal goodwill in a business is valued at a figure (usually lower) after allowing for the loss of the proprietor of the business.

4.3.5.2 Joint ownership of assets

Co-owners of land can discount the value of their respective shares to take into account the fact that it may be difficult to sell a share in co-owned property on the market; the purchaser will occupy the property with the other co-owner. A discount of 10%–15% is normal.

Example

Two brothers own a house equally. If the open market value of the house is £200,000, the value of a one-half share may be agreed by the Revenue to be £90,000.

Valuation of other jointly owned assets does not attract such a discount. In these cases, the open market value is divided proportionately between the joint owners.

Where spouses are co-owners of land, a discount is not normally available. This is because of the related property rules (see **4.3.5.5**) which require each party's interest to be valued as a proportion of the whole.

4.3.5.3 Quoted shares

For IHT (as for CGT) the price is taken to be the price 'one quarter up' from the lower to the higher price for dealings on the day in question on the stock market. Thus, if a share is shown as 100p–104p for the day of dealing, the valuation would be 101p per share held by the donor.

4.3.5.4 Shares in unquoted companies

Shares in private/family companies are notoriously difficult to value; such a valuation is not an exact science. The principal reason for the difficulty is the lack of any real market. Final agreement of value may take many years of negotiation between the donor's valuers and the Revenue. Many factors will be relevant, including:

(a)   The success or otherwise of the company.

(b)   Other recent dealings in the shares (if any).

(c)   The number of shares as a percentage of the entire issued capital of the company:

- a 75% holding   can pass special resolutions;
- over 50% holding   can pass ordinary resolutions;
- 50% or less   a minority holding, with less voting influence (especially if small holding).

(d)   The existence of typical pre-emption rights in the company's articles of association requiring shares first to be offered to other shareholders. Here the lack of a market is the real problem. Nevertheless, the courts have over a long period held that shares must be valued on the assumption that the shares could be sold on the open market but that the purchaser will then himself become subject to the restrictions contained in the articles of association.

To reach agreement the Revenue will need from the company or its advisers much information including:

(a)   a full description of the business carried on by the company;

(b)   the last three years' accounts of the company published before the date of valuation;

(c)   if minority holdings are to be valued, details of any restrictions on the transfer of shares;

(d)   if there are different classes of shares, a statement of the rights of each class, in particular those concerning voting, dividends and distributions on a liquidation of the company.

4.3.5.5 Related property (IHTA 1984, s 161)

Assets which make up a pair or set are worth more than the aggregate value of each item valued separately; for example, one of a pair of valuable earrings is not worth a lot on its own. The related property rules are designed to prevent tax payers who can make exempt transfers (eg spouses) avoiding IHT by dividing ownership of valuable assets between them. Section 161(1) provides 'where the value of any property comprised in a person's estate would be less than the appropriate proportion of the value of the aggregate of that and any related property, it shall be the appropriate proportion of the value of that aggregate'.

Example

Harriet has a 60% holding in H and T Ltd. She transfers half of this to her husband, Tim, so that they now each have a 30% holding. (This transfer is exempt for IHT and at no gain or loss for CGT purposes.) Taken separately, each holding is valued at £25,000, but together the controlling holding of 60% is valued at £75,000. Harriet considers giving her shareholding to their child, Rowland. Under the related property rule, her shareholding would be valued as the appropriate proportion of the value of their total holding, ie, £75,000 ÷ 2 = £37,500.

If Harriet makes her gift, she will make a PET. If she dies within seven years the PET will have become a chargeable transfer. Business property relief at 100% will be available if Rowland owns the shares when his mother dies.

4.3.6   Reliefs

4.3.6.1   Agricultural property relief (IHTA 1984, ss 115–124)

Agricultural property relief is given automatically for transfers of value of 'agricultural property'. 'Agricultural property' is defined as including agricultural land and pasture; and cottages, farm buildings and farmhouses together with the land occupied with them as are of a character appropriate to the property.

The Revenue is quick to argue that houses are not of a 'character appropriate' in an attempt to deny the relief.

The relief is given against the 'agricultural value' of the agricultural property. Agricultural value is defined as the value which would be the value of the property if the property were subject to a perpetual covenant prohibiting its use otherwise than as agricultural property. Thus, any value attributable to possible development or to mineral deposits under the land would not be eligible.

Agricultural property relief applies to property which was either:

(a)   occupied by the transferor for agriculture throughout the two years immediately before the transfer; or

(b)   owned by the transferor throughout the seven years immediately before the transfer (provided it was occupied by someone (the transferor or another) for agriculture throughout the seven-year period).

For these purposes, periods of occupation and ownership of a deceased spouse can be included.

100% relief

Available where the transferor had the right to vacant possession immediately before the transfer or the right to obtain it within the next 12 months or, by concession (ESC F17), within 24 months from the date of the transfer. To encourage agricultural tenancies, this relief is also available where property is let on a tenancy starting on or after 1 September 1995 (Finance Act 1995, s 155).

50% relief

Available on any other qualifying agricultural property.

Examples

Giles, who farmed Greenacre for 28 months has just died. Agricultural property relief is available at 100% against the vacant possession value due to the owner occupation.

Jim ceased farming Blackacre 10 years ago. He let the farm to his son, who has continued to farm it, and he retained the freehold reversion himself. Jim has just died. His PRs will be able to claim agricultural property relief at 50% against the tenanted value of the agricultural property.

Agricultural property in settlements

Subject to the time-limits, the relief can apply to agricultural property held by trustees whether or not there is an interest in possession in the settled property. If there is an interest in possession, the life tenant (whose 'estate' under general principle is deemed to include the settled property, ie, the agricultural property) is the 'transferor' and 'owner' of the agricultural property for the purposes of the relief. The life tenant must therefore satisfy the conditions of two years' occupation of the property or seven years' ownership of it. If there are discretionary trusts, the trustees will instead be the 'transferors' and 'owners' of the agricultural property. The occasions of charge to IHT on discretionary trusts are discussed at **10.2.3**.

Agricultural property relief is given in priority to any available business property relief.

4.3.6.2   Business property relief (IHTA 1984, ss 103–114)

Business property relief operates to reduce the value transferred by a transfer of value of relevant business property by a certain percentage.

A reduction of 100% of the value transferred is allowed for transfers of certain assets. They are:

(a)   a business or interest in a business (eg, a partnership share);

(b)   shares which are not quoted on the Stock Exchange (companies on the Unlisted Securities Market and the Alternative Investment Market (AIM) count as unquoted for this purpose).

A reduction of 50% of the value transferred is allowed for transfers of any other assets which qualify for business property relief. They are:

(a)   shares which are quoted on the Stock Exchange and where the transferor had control; control exists broadly where the transferor's entire holding yields over 50% of the votes on all resolutions;

(b)   land, buildings, machinery or plant owned by the transferor personally but used by a partnership of which he is a member or by a company of which he has control.

The relevant business property must have been owned by the transferor for at least two years immediately prior to the transfer. An exception to this rule applies where a spouse inherits business property under the will or intestacy of the deceased spouse. In that circumstance only, the surviving spouse is deemed to have owned the property from the time it was originally acquired by the deceased spouse.

Example 1

In 1999, James acquired 75% of the shares in X Ltd, a private company. James died in 2004 leaving those shares to his wife Kim. In 2005, Kim dies leaving all her estate, including the shares, to her son. The 100% relief will be available on Kim's death.

The exception does not apply where the relevant business property is transferred to the spouse *inter vivos*.

Example 2

In Year 1, Judy sets up her own business, Y Ltd, and holds 100% of the shares.

In Year 5, she transfers 20% of those shares to her husband, Keith.

In Year 6, Keith dies leaving the 20% shareholding to his son.

No relief is available against the value of the 20% holding as Keith has owned the shares only for one year.

These inter-spouse transfer rules also apply to agricultural property relief.

Inter vivos transfers – availability of relief

Where the charge to IHT arises as a result of a PET or chargeable lifetime transfer (a transfer to discretionary trustees) which is followed by the death of the transferor within seven years, any IHT (or additional IHT) will be calculated with the benefit of business property relief *provided*:

(a)   the transferee still owns the assets (or replacement assets which qualify as business property) at the death of the transferor (or, if earlier, the transferee's own death); and

(b)   the asset qualified as business property immediately before the transferor's death but (for this purpose) ignoring the two-year ownership requirement.

There is, therefore, the danger that at the time of the death relief will not be available.

Business property in settlements

As with agricultural property relief, relief can be available where business property is held by trustees.

In an interest in possession settlement, the availability of this relief is gauged by reference to the position of the life tenant; as with agricultural property relief, the life tenant's 'estate' includes the settled property. If the *life tenant* satisfies the two-year ownership test, 100% relief is available where the assets in the trust are either a business or unquoted shares; 50% relief is available for controlling holdings in quoted companies and for land, buildings, machinery or plant in the trust used in the life tenant's own business or a company which he controls.

If property is held on discretionary trusts, relief will be available if the *trustees* satisfy the conditions. The occasions of charge to IHT on a discretionary trust are discussed at **10.2**.

4.4   Capital gains tax

4.4.1   Rates

Capital gains tax (CGT) is charged on gains on disposals by treating them as the top slice of the tax payer's income, ie, at 10% (to the extent gains fall within the starting rate band), 20% (to the extent gains fall within the basic rate band) and/or 40% (to the extent they exceed the basic rate limit). For trustees the rate is 40% (2005/06) (see **Chapter 14**).

4.4.2   Calculation

The gain is calculated as the difference between the disposal consideration (less the costs of selling) and:

(a)   the acquisition cost (less the cost of buying); and

(b)   any cost of improvements/enhancing expenditure.

An indexation allowance, removing inflationary gains from CGT, may also be deducted when calculating gains (but not losses) on any asset owned between 31 March 1982 and 5 April 1998. The indexation allowance is calculated by applying to the initial and subsequent expenditure the retail price index (RPI) percentage increase since the date of the expenditure to the date of disposal (or April 1998 if earlier).

From April 1998, the indexed gains of individuals, personal representatives and trustees can be further reduced by taper relief. The percentage relief depends on the number of complete years between 6 April 1998 (or later acquisition) and the date of disposal. An additional bonus year is available for non-business assets owned on 17 March 1998. Taper relief is generally more generous for business assets than for non business assets.

'Business assets' are assets used for the purposes of a trade carried on by an individual, his partnership, or his 'qualifying company'. Such a company is a trading company which is:

(a)   unlisted (eg, private companies and those traded on the AIM); or

(b)   listed on the Stock Exchange and the individual is either:

   (i)   an employee or officer of the company (there is no requirement for full-time employment); or

   (ii)   able to exercise at least 5% of the voting rights.

Shares in a qualifying company are also 'business assets'.

Capital losses are normally set against capital gains of the same year (before taper relief is applied). Losses can be set against gains which attract the least taper. To the extent that losses exceed gains for the year, they can be carried forward to the following year.

4.4.3   Exemptions

(a)   The first £8,500 (£4,250 for trustees) of chargeable gains each year.

(b)   A husband and wife is each entitled to the annual exemption.

(c)   Any gain arising on the disposal by gift or sale of the taxpayer's main or only residence. Where a taxpayer owns more than one residence, he may elect for one to be treated as his main residence. A husband and wife living together have only one principal private residence exemption.

(d)   Any gain on the disposal of a property owned by trustees where the property is the residence of a beneficiary entitled to occupation under the terms of the trust or at the discretion of the trustees.

For a further discussion of the points mentioned in paragraphs (c) and (d) above and other matters relating to the main residence, see **4.7.4**.

4.4.4   Death (Taxation of Chargeable Gains Act 1992 (TCGA 1992), s 62)

Death provides an automatic CGT-free revaluation of assets. The probate value becomes the acquisition cost for subsequent disposals by PRs, beneficiaries and trustees if a trust arises under the will or intestacy. This is because there is no disposal on death but there is an acquisition by the PRs, etc. One consequence is that inbuilt gains accruing during the lifetime of the deceased person are not charged to CGT. This point needs careful consideration as part of general estate planning. Disposal of the same asset during lifetime could well result in immediate liability to tax if the gain exceeds the annual exemption and where hold-over relief is not available.

No liability arises when assets are vested in legatees by the PRs; the PRs' acquisition (on death) is taken to be the legatees' acquisition for their future CGT purposes. A 'legatee' includes any person inheriting under a will or intestacy whether beneficially or as a trustee if a trust arises following the death.

Example

Shares worth £50,000 at death were acquired by the testator 10 years earlier for £5,000. The gain of £45,000 over the period of ownership does not attract CGT. Gains on all subsequent disposals will be based on an acquisition cost of £50,000. If instead the shares were given away by lifetime gift, the gain on the disposal would attract CGT unless relief was available.

A similar CGT-free revaluation of trust assets occurs when the life tenant of an interest in possession settlement dies. This is in line with the general approach that CGT is not payable as a result of a death.

Example

Under a testator's will the trustees are holding £100,000 of quoted shares 'for Susan for life, remainder to George'. Susan has just died and the shares are worth £250,000.

(a)   The gain of £150,000 during the trust period does not attract CGT.

(b)   The trustees are 'deemed' to dispose of the investments at market value at Susan's death.

(c)   The investments transferred to George are 'deemed' acquired by him for his future CGT purposes at their market value at Susan's death. Not all the investment will be transferred to George because some will have been sold by the trustees to pay IHT due as a result of Susan's death.

The position of the trustees where a 'deemed disposal' occurs is considered further in **10.1.4.2**.

4.4.5   Reliefs

4.4.5.1   Inter-spouse transfers

Inter-spouse transfers are deemed to occur at no gain no loss. Effectively, tax on any gain since the acquisition by the donor spouse is deferred until there is a disposal by the donee spouse (TCGA 1992, s 58).

Example

In 1994, Archie bought a painting for £10,000. He gave his painting to his wife Belinda in 2005 when its value had increased to £18,000. Indexation for the relevant period was £500.

	£
Archie's deemed disposal consideration	10,500
less: Acquisition cost	10,000
	500
Indexation allowance	500
	nil

Belinda's acquisition cost is Archie's disposal consideration, ie, £10,500. Taper relief is not applied on the disposal to Belinda, but can be claimed by her on her later disposal for their combined ownership period.

4.4.5.2   Hold-over relief

Hold-over relief is now provided in relatively limited circumstances by TCGA 1992, ss 165 and 260. These two provisions operate in the same way, by permitting gains which accrue to the donor to be held over. Tax is effectively deferred by permitting the donee to acquire the gifted property at the donor's acquisition cost after allowing for indexation. Tax remains deferred until the donee disposes of the property when he either cannot or chooses not to make a further hold-over election. Taper relief is not applied until the donee disposes of the property at a future date. Only the donee's period of ownership is relevant when calculating taper relief.

To obtain hold-over relief, an election is required by both the transferor and the transferee, although where the transferee is a trustee only the election of the transferor is required.

Once made, the result of the election is that:

(a) the amount of any chargeable gain which the transferor would otherwise have made on the disposal, and

(b) the value at which the transferee would otherwise be regarded as having acquired the asset,

shall be reduced by an amount equal to the held-over gain on the disposal.

Example

John gives his shares in his personal company to his daughter Julia. Their market value is £100,000.

A joint election for hold-over relief under s 165 is made.

		£
(a)	Disposal consideration (market value)	100,000
	less: Cost price (say)	10,000
		90,000
	less: Indexation allowance (to April 1998, say)	20,000
	held-over gain	70,000

1. John's gain on disposal is reduced to nil.
2. Julia's acquisition cost is reduced to £30,000 (£100,000 – £70,000).

(b) Julia sells her shares for £150,000. Her gain is calculated as follows:

	£
Disposal consideration (sale proceeds)	150,000
less: Cost price (see above)	30,000
gain	120,000

Julia's chargeable gain is made up of the gain during her period of ownership of £50,000 (£150,000 – £100,000) and £70,000 (the gain held over). Her tapered gain is calculated by applying taper relief based on Julia's period of ownership.

Disposal of business assets within s 165

Section 165 applies to gifts by individuals and deemed disposals by trustees on the ending of a trust of:

(a) An asset, or an interest in an asset, used for the purposes of a trade, profession or vocation carried on by:

(i)   the donor; or

(ii) his personal company; or

(iii) a company which is a member of a trading group of companies of which the holding company is the donor's personal company.

(b)   Shares or securities of a trading company or of the holding company of a trading group where:

    (i)   the shares or securities are not quoted on a recognised stock exchange; or

    (ii)   the trading company or holding company is the transferor's personal company.

(c)   Agricultural property, or an interest in agricultural property, which is not used for the purposes of a trade carried on as mentioned in (a) above.

A 'personal' company is one in which the individual owns not less than 5% of the voting rights.

Disposal of business assets held in settlements

Section 165 relief in a modified form is extended to business assets owned by trustees by TCGA 1992, Sch 7. The asset must be used in a business carried on by the trustees, ie, the trustees of a discretionary settlement, or by a beneficiary of a settlement with an interest in possession in the settled property, ie, the life tenant. In the case of disposals of shares in a trading company by trustees, the company must be unquoted, or at least 25% of the voting rights must be exercisable by the trustees.

Disposals within s 260

Private client practitioners are likely to meet three types of disposal, which attract hold-over relief under s 260:

(a)   *Chargeable transfers within the meaning of IHTA 1984 (and transfers which would be chargeable transfers but for IHTA 1984, s 19 (the annual exemption)) and which are not potentially exempt transfers.*

The effect of this relief is that a gift which is immediately chargeable to IHT (even at 0%) is not also charged to CGT. A double charge to tax is thus avoided. PETs do not attract IHT (at least immediately) and so CGT will normally arise on the disposal (unless s 165 relief applies).

If the donor dies within seven years of making a PET and as a result the PET becomes chargeable, relief is still not available since it was not immediately chargeable when made. The most common type of chargeable transfer occurs on the creation and termination of discretionary settlements. Such transfers are included even if the value transferred falls within the nil rate band (IHT is charged, but at 0%).

(b)   *Exempt transfers within IHTA 1984, s 24 (transfers to political parties), s 26 (transfers for public benefit), s 27 (transfers to maintenance funds for historic buildings) and s 30 (transfers of designated property).*

(c)   *Termination of an accumulation and maintenance settlement where a beneficiary becomes absolutely entitled to the settled property.*

The termination of an accumulation and maintenance settlement is specifically within the provisions even though IHT is not chargeable (see **Chapter 10**). Note that the *creation* of an accumulation and maintenance settlement is a PET and so relief under s 260 is not available.

Example

Kathy transfers assets valued at £275,000 to the trustees of her newly created discretionary settlement. She has made no other transfers. Even though no IHT is actually payable there is an occasion of immediate charge (at 0%). Hold-over relief is available at Kathy's election. The trustees do not need to join in the election.

Hold-over relief and settlor interested trusts

Prior to 10 December 2003, if a person created any trust by settling business assets, CGT hold-over relief was available under TCGA, s 165. Also, if a person created a discretionary trust, CGT hold-over relief was available under TCGA, s 260, as this was a disposal that was a chargeable transfer for IHT. However, tax payers began to use hold-over relief creatively to avoid CGT, so in 2003 the Government passed anti-avoidance measures.

As from 10 December 2003 hold-over relief is not available under s 165 or s 260 for any disposal to a trust which is a 'settlor interested' trust immediately after the disposal. If the settlement later becomes a settlor interested trust the relief will be clawed back.

A settlor interested trust is one where any property may be payable to the settlor or the settlor's spouse in any circumstances (see **6.2.11**).

Hold-over relief and the foreign element

Neither s 165 nor s 260 applies where the transferee is neither resident nor ordinarily resident in the UK. Thus, disposals of chargeable assets to non-resident individuals or settlements are, for this reason, not particularly attractive.

A clawback of CGT can arise where the donee emigrates within six years following a hold-over election. If the donee ceases to be resident and ordinarily resident in the UK, CGT liability on the held-over gains is immediately triggered. The CGT is primarily payable by the donee (now overseas). If he fails to pay the tax within 12 months it can be recovered from the donor who has a (probably worthless) right of recovery from the donee.

Because of the risk of a clawback charge, the donor should be advised to consider insurance cover, retention of part of the gifted property for six years and indemnities from the donee.

Gifts attracting IHT and CGT

If chargeable gains on a disposal are held over, the transferee may add any IHT paid on the transfer to him to his CGT acquisition cost. In this way, some relief against the overlap between IHT and CGT is available.

Example

Jason transferred assets worth £200,000 to the trustees of his recently established discretionary settlement. They elected to hold over the gain of £80,000. Assume £20,000 IHT was paid. The trustees now sell the assets for £250,000 and re-invest the proceeds. The calculation of the trustees' CGT liability is:

	£	£
Disposal consideration		250,000
less: acquisition cost		
(200,000 – 80,000)	120,000	
IHT paid	20,000	140,000
		110,000
indexation allowance (to April 1998, say)		30,000
indexed gain		80,000

The trustees' gain may be further reduced by taper relief based on their period of ownership.

Note: the principle illustrated in the example also applies if the lifetime gift was a PET which later becomes chargeable. Provided a CGT hold-over election was made by the donor and donee, the IHT payable on the donor's death can be added to the transferee's acquisition cost, as in the example.

Some planning considerations in relation to hold-over relief

The fact that hold-over relief is not generally available on lifetime gifts may make them less attractive for tax planning purposes.

A gift which attracts CGT at 40% made purely to save IHT at 40% may not be particularly attractive in cash-flow terms. The same gift made by will would avoid CGT and give the donee the benefit of an uplift in his acquisition price (to market value at the date of death) for future CGT purposes.

However, CGT is charged on gains (after allowing for indexation and taper relief) whereas IHT is charged on full values (subject to reliefs).

Gifts of assets expected to appreciate in value may attract an immediate CGT charge on the gain to date but IHT will be limited to the value of the asset at the time of the gift, ie, 'asset freezing' applies should the PET become chargeable.

Section 165 of IHTA 1984 provides that CGT paid by the donee reduces the value transferred by the chargeable transfer for IHT. Normally CGT is payable by the donor but, in circumstances where hold-over relief is not available, consideration should be given to the donee paying the tax to take advantage of s 165. For this to happen, agreement must be reached between the donor and donee.

A disposal (PET) giving rise to a chargeable gain which cannot be held over, followed by the death of the donor within seven years, could cause IHT to become payable by the donee. In such a case any CGT paid by the donor will not be treated as part of the loss to the estate (IHTA 1984, s 5(4)). As discussed in the previous paragraph, if the donee pays the CGT, the value transferred is treated as reduced by the CGT paid (IHTA 1984, s 165(1)) and therefore the IHT bill for the donee will be reduced.

> Example
>
> A gift (PET) of quoted shares worth £500,000 results in a CGT liability of £50,000.
>
> (a) If the donor pays the CGT, the value transferred for IHT is £500,000. It is not £550,000, ie, the loss to the estate of the donor is not increased by the CGT paid.
>
> (b) If the donee pays the CGT, the value transferred for IHT is £450,000, ie, it is reduced by the CGT paid.
>
> Obviously the donee will need to be in a position to fund both tax liabilities. Insurance against the potential IHT may be possible but not the CGT because this is an immediately quantifiable amount.

4.5 Transfers between husband and wife

4.5.1 Financial and estate planning

It is advisable for the wealth of a married couple to be split between them. Whilst the division need not be equal, it is inadvisable for one spouse to own the majority of the assets. 'Equalisation' will provide greater financial security for the 'poorer' spouse, and the greatest scope for tax planning.

4.5.1.1   Life insurance

Insurance on the taxpayer's own life

Most clients who are married or with young children should consider personal life insurance (see **Appendix 2**). If nothing further is done when the life cover is purchased, the insured sum will be paid to the PRs on the death of the insured and will form part of his estate.

A grant of representation will be required before the proceeds are available, and the amount will be taxable if left to a beneficiary other than the deceased's spouse (or charity). Both problems can be avoided if the life insurance policy is written in trust.

Where a new policy is being purchased as part of financial advice, it can be written in trust from the outset. Life insurance companies have standard trust documents which the insured can complete with the names of the trustees and the chosen beneficiary or beneficiaries.

Existing policies can also be written in trust but whenever possible it is better to create the trust at the time of purchase. This is because existing policies may have a surrender value, meaning that if the insured cancels the policy before his death he will receive a lump sum based on the amount of premiums he has paid. When an existing policy is written in trust, the insured gives up this surrender value to his beneficiary and this is a transfer of value for IHT purposes. Usually the policy will be valued at the higher of the market value or cost of providing the policy, ie, the premiums already paid (IHTA 1984, s 167). In practice this is rarely a problem as the surrender value is relatively small compared with the maturity value and is likely to be covered by the insured's £3,000 annual IHT exemption. To the extent this is exceeded the transfer of the surrender value will be a potentially exempt transfer (PET). It does mean, however, that in the year the policy is put into trust, the annual IHT exemption may not be available to set against other non-exempt gifts.

Once a policy has been written in trust the annual premiums paid by the insured to the insurance company are paid by the insured for the benefit of the beneficiary. These premiums are transfers of value for IHT but, unless disproportionately large when compared with the annual income of the insured, they should be exempt as normal expenditure out of income, or if not then covered by the £3,000 annual exemption. They are not PETs (IHTA 1984, s 3A).

Insurance on the life of another

Where a couple have young children it is quite possible that one parent, usually the mother, does not have paid employment. The couple should calculate how much it would cost to employ a housekeeper and nanny or purchase child care if the mother were to die. Where the father's income is unlikely to be sufficient to cover the cost, he might consider insuring the mother's life, ie, he pays premiums and receives a lump sum if the mother dies. As the insurance cover is likely to be required only whilst the children are of school age, term assurance (see **Appendix 2**) could be considered.

> #### Example
>
> Adam and Betty have two children aged 6 and 4 respectively. Betty does not work and Adam's income is £32,000 per annum. He calculates the family's expenditure to be £22,000 per annum, and believes home help and child care would cost an extra £12,000 per annum if Betty died. This could not be supported by his income. If he

insured Betty's life he would receive a lump sum on her death from which to pay the £12,000 per annum.

4.5.1.2   The matrimonial home

This is often the major asset owned by an individual or married couple. Whilst care should be taken in using it purely as an object of tax planning, certain steps might be considered by most married couples.

Sole ownership versus co-ownership

Unless there are personal reasons for not doing so, spouses should consider property being owned as co-owners rather than in the sole names of either.

Co-ownership can reflect the contributions each has made to the purchase price or may provide a non-contributing spouse with the security of legal ownership. The couple may make the initial purchase as co-owners or a sole purchaser may subsequently transfer an interest in the property to the other. Most lenders insist that a property which is to be used as a matrimonial home is held as co-ownership.

Joint tenancy

Holding a property as joint tenants means that on the death of one spouse his or her interest in the property immediately and automatically passes to the surviving spouse, ie, accrues by survivorship. This cannot be prevented by anything said about the property in the will. All that the surviving joint owner needs to prove absolute ownership of the property is the death certificate of his or her spouse. Joint tenancy therefore avoids the costs and delays involved in obtaining a grant of representation on the death of the first joint tenant to die and, because the survivor is the spouse, the interest in the property is IHT exempt on that first death.

Example

Carla and David own a house worth £295,000 as joint tenants. David dies and the house vests in Carla absolutely. There is no IHT payable. Carla dies six weeks later leaving her estate (the house) to Emma. IHT of £8,000 is payable.

Where the combined value of a husband and wife's assets (including the house) exceed the IHT nil rate band, they should consider owning the matrimonial home as tenants in common. Coupled with appropriate wills this can provide a limited opportunity for tax avoidance whilst ensuring security for a surviving spouse.

Tenancy in common

Property held under a tenancy in common passes by will or intestacy, not automatically to the surviving co-owner. A tenancy in common allows the first spouse to die to leave his share to someone other than the survivor. The effect would be shared ownership between the surviving spouse and children or other relative(s) or friend(s) of the deceased. The danger is that the child etc may want the house sold to realise his inheritance. This risk should be contemplated only where the value of the property is such that the surviving spouse's share is sufficient to purchase suitable alternative accommodation and the survivor is happy at the possibility of having to move.

Because of the problems involved in giving an interest in the matrimonial home to others, it is normally preferable to adopt a more cautious approach. A husband and wife can make wills leaving their respective interests in the property to each other subject to a survivorship period. In the normal course of events, one spouse will survive the other by a considerable period of time, in which case the property passes to the survivor, whose right to the home is thus guaranteed. Where, however, both die within a short period of time their respective interests in the property pass to, for example their children, and both nil rate bands are utilised.

Example

Carla and David own a house worth £295,000 as tenants in common. They make wills leaving their respective shares of the house to each other conditional on surviving at least three months and if not, to Emma. David and Carla die within six weeks of each other.

David's ½ share (£147,500) is held by his PRs for Carla if she survives by three months. As she dies within this period it passes to Emma. There will be no IHT because it falls within his nil rate band.

Carla's ½ share (£147,500) passes to Emma. There is no IHT because it falls within her nil rate band.

Where a house is held by beneficial joint tenants, either co-owner may sever the joint tenancy converting it into a tenancy in common. The consent of the other co-owner is not required to the severance which can be effected by giving notice to the co-owner signed in writing that the joint tenancy is terminated and that the parties now hold as tenants in common.

Mortgage

Where the matrimonial home, however owned, is subject to a mortgage, that mortgage debt should be covered by suitable insurance (see **Appendix 2**). This will enable the mortgage to be paid off in full on the death of the borrower without the need for the house or other assets to be sold to meet the debt. Where two people are jointly responsible for the mortgage they can choose whether the insurance should pay out on the first or second death.

4.5.2 Transferring assets (other than the matrimonial home) into joint ownership

4.5.2.1 Practical reasons

The reasons for making such a transfer are likely to be practical. The transfer allows each spouse access to particular assets and means that on the death of the first spouse to die the survivor automatically becomes sole owner of those assets. There is no need to obtain a grant of representation (so the administration is quicker and cheaper) and the survivor has immediate access to finances.

4.5.2.2 Effect for IHT

Joint ownership offers no IHT saving. Although on the first death the transfer is spouse exempt, the combined estates are taxed on the second death.

4.5.2.3 Effect for income tax

The basic rule is that any income arising from a jointly held asset will be treated as belonging equally to the husband and wife (ICTA 1988, s 282A). This is so irrespective of how they contributed to the account or purchase of the asset or account (eg, with a bank or building society).

Example

Harry has a building society account into which he periodically pays additional savings. He transfers this account into the joint names of himself and his wife Isobel. Isobel makes no contributions to the account. For income tax purposes she is nevertheless treated as owning one half of the annual income.

Spouses can override this general 50:50 rule by making a declaration to the Inland Revenue of how they in fact beneficially enjoy the income. The declaration relates to the income and to the underlying property. The income cannot be shared in proportions different from the property which produces it. The declaration has effect from its date; notice must be given to the Inspector of Taxes within 60 days of a declaration which must be made on Form 17.

Where one spouse has insufficient income from his or her own resources to be paying income tax, or is paying income tax at the starting (10%) or basic (22%) rate whilst the other spouse is a higher (40%) rate income tax payer, it may be sensible to transfer some part of the beneficial ownership in the jointly owned property to the spouse with the lower tax rate, followed by a declaration that that spouse is entitled to an equivalent proportion of the income. The transfer of the beneficial ownership will generally be by declaration of trust made by the spouses.

Example

John and Kate are the joint holders of a building society account. The annual interest is £100 gross. John pays income tax at 40%. Kate pays income tax at 20%.

(a)   Without a declaration

John will pay 40% tax on his one half	£50 × 40%	= £20
Kate will pay 20% tax on her one half	£50 × 20%	= £10
Total income tax		£30

(b)   Transfer of beneficial ownership and declaration that Kate is entitled to 90% of the interest

John will pay 40% tax on his 10% share	£10 × 40%	= £ 4
Kate will pay 20% tax on her 90% share	£90 × 20%	= £18
Total income tax		£22

4.5.2.4   Effect for CGT

The transfer of an asset from a sole name into the joint names of the husband and wife is at 'no gain no loss' (see **4.4.5.1**).

On a subsequent disposal, whether a sale or by gift, each spouse will be regarded as owning a half share of the asset and charged to CGT accordingly. Where a husband and wife, who pay income tax at different rates, contemplate the disposal of an asset with an inbuilt capital gain, the effect is that up to one half of the gain will be taxed, if at all, at the lower of their rates.

Example

Len transfers a shareholding which he bought for £2,000 into the joint names of himself and his wife Mary.

Len pays CGT at 40% and Mary at 20%. The shares are sold for £21,000 (assume indexation nil).

	Len will pay	Mary will pay
	£	£
Disposal consideration	10,500	10,500
less: Acquisition cost	1,000	1,000
	9,500	9,500
less: Annual exemption	8,500	8,500
	1,000	1,000
Chargeable gain (taper ignored):	£1,000 @ 40%	£1,000 @ 20%
	= £400	= £200

Where a declaration as to the beneficial enjoyment of the income from a jointly owned asset has been made, it will have a corresponding effect for CGT purposes.

Example

Neville and Olive declare that the income from a shareholding is enjoyed 25:75. They will have a corresponding beneficial ownership of the shareholding. The shares were bought for £400 and have just been sold for £16,000. Assume indexation nil.

	Neville's chargeable gain		Olive's chargeable gain	
	£	£	£	£
Disposal		4,000		12,000
less: Acquisition cost	100		300	
less: Annual exemption	8,500		8,500	
		8,600		8,800
Chargeable gain		nil		3,200

4.5.2.5 Conclusion

Transferring assets into joint names may provide beneficial effects. It allows both spouses access to the assets. It is a means of making provision for the recipient spouse without the donor spouse losing control of the property. However, holding property jointly may cause IHT to be payable when the couple die. If all assets are in joint names, the IHT nil rate band of the first spouse to die will not be utilised and their estates will be aggregated on the second death. Clients whose combined assets do not exceed the nil rate band will find that the practical and income tax advantages of owning property jointly exceed the theoretical IHT disadvantages. For wealthier clients, particularly those with combined estates of £550,000 (twice the nil rate band) or more, there may be practical reasons for holding some assets in joint names but the IHT disadvantage of losing one IHT nil rate band means that the majority of assets should be held in individual names.

Some clients value the independence and control of having assets in their sole name over and above any tax saving which may result from holding assets jointly.

4.5.3 Transferring assets from one spouse to another

It is not efficient for inheritance tax purposes for all of a couple's assets to be in the name of one spouse. It is preferable for ownership to be divided so that each spouse can make use of his/her nil rate band. It is common, therefore, for spouses to transfer assets between themselves with a view to 'equalising' their estates.

Take care, when selecting the assets to be transferred, that available tax reliefs are not lost or reduced by the gift, for example business property relief or agricultural relief.

Example

Peter and Rose wish to minimise the amount of IHT that their daughter Susan will pay on their deaths. Peter transfers his 40% shareholding in their private company Z Ltd worth £200,000 to Rose as part of the 'equalisation' process. He has owned the shares for four years. Rose dies six months later leaving everything to Susan.

The shareholding is taxable on its full value as Rose has not owned the shares for two years (see **4.3.6**).

Had Peter retained the shares and given them by lifetime gift or by will to Susan, 100% business property relief would have been available.

Note: Parents may consider giving property eligible for 100% business or agricultural relief to their children. It is sensible to do this by will (provided there are sufficient other assets to provide adequately for the surviving spouse) as these assets can be passed to the children without attracting inheritance tax. However, it is not necessarily a good idea to make lifetime gifts of assets attracting 100% relief. If the donor dies within seven years the transfer will become chargeable and relief may not be available at that point, for example where the child no longer owns the asset or it no longer qualifies for relief. It may be preferable for the parent to retain the asset until death. This is something of a gamble, though, as there is the possibility that the present generous tax regime for business and agricultural property may not continue until death.

4.5.3.1 Income tax reasons

Wherever possible, a husband and wife should ensure that they each utilise their own personal allowance as well as their own starting and basic rate bands before either of them starts paying income tax at the higher rate. Where only one spouse is a higher rate tax payer, as much investment income as possible should be attributed to the other spouse.

As seen in **4.5.2**, this can be achieved by a transfer of assets into joint names with a declaration as to the beneficial ownership of the income. The couple must remember to make the declaration if the income is to be apportioned other than 50:50. The maximum split is 1:99 and the division will have to be declared by the couple on their income tax returns. Many couples may prefer assets to be transferred outright as all the income then belongs to the transferee spouse from the date of the transfer.

4.5.3.2 CGT reasons

Where a large capital gain is anticipated on the disposal of an asset held by one spouse who will pay CGT at 40%, consider transferring (without liability to CGT) that asset to the 'poorer' spouse who will then pay tax on the whole or a substantial part of the subsequently realised gain at only 20% or less.

A husband and wife are both entitled to an annual exemption of £8,500, but any unused annual exemption cannot be transferred to the other spouse nor can it be carried forward for use in future years. All clients (whether married or not) should be advised to use the exemption each year if possible.

4.5.3.3 IHT reasons

IHT savings are often the main purpose in making inter-spouse transfers. Whilst no tax saving is achieved from the transfer itself, because such transfers are IHT exempt, having assets in the individual ownership of each spouse does allow maximum use of exemptions, reliefs and the nil rate band for passing on family wealth. The purpose of an inter-spouse transfer is to permit both spouses to make gifts by will and lifetime gifts to children and other relatives.

Using the nil rate band

Example 1

Ursula and Victor are married with two children. Ursula has assets worth £575,000 and Victor assets of £100,000. They have undertaken no estate planning and have made no previous transfers. Neither owns property attracting any relief for IHT. Their estates pass by will to each other, and their children inherit the entire estate on the second death.

IHT on the first death will be nil (spouse exemption).

IHT on the second death calculated on the combined estates of £675,000 will be £160,000.

Note: the tax bill would be identical if the estates were equalised but the wills remained unaltered.

Example 2

Facts as before, but Ursula and Victor do some limited planning through their wills. As a result the children will inherit some property on the death of the first parent.

Ursula's will leaves £275,000 to the children and the residue to Victor or to the children if he has predeceased her.

Victor's will leaves all his estate to the children.

(a)   Assume Victor dies first

IHT on Victor's death:	£100,000 @ 0% = nil
IHT on Ursula's death:	£275,000 @ 0% = nil
	£300,000 @ 40% = £120,000

(b)   Assume Ursula dies first

IHT on Ursula's death:	£275,000 @ 0% = nil
	£300,000 exempt = nil
IHT on Victor's death:	£275,000 @ 0% = nil
	£125,000 @ 40% = £50,000

Example 3

Ursula and Victor have undertaken estate planning by lifetime equalisation of the value of their estates, and made wills utilising their respective nil rate bands.

(a)   Ursula transfers £237,500 to Victor so that each spouse has £337,500 IHT exempt

(b)

Ursula's will:	£275,000 to children
	residue to Victor
Victor's will:	£275,000 to children
	residue to Ursula
IHT on first death:	£275,000 @ 0% = nil
	£62,500 exempt = nil
IHT on second death:	£275,000 @ 0% = nil
	£125,000 @ 40% = £50,000

Note: although the tax bill in Example 3 is the same as in Example 2(b), that depended upon Ursula dying before Victor. In Example 3, it does not matter which parent dies first as the tax bill will be the same.

Using lifetime exemptions

There is scope for the tax bill to be reduced further by each parent making lifetime gifts to or for the benefit of their children. For example, each parent can give £5,000 to a child on the occasion of the child's marriage; each parent can make annual gifts of £3,000; each parent can make gifts using the normal expenditure out of income exemption. Before these exemptions can be claimed, each parent must have sufficient assets to make the gifts. Unused exemptions cannot be transferred from one spouse to the other.

Anti-avoidance rules

The anti-avoidance legislation and cases (see **4.10**) should not be a problem in the context of straightforward family estate planning provided that at the time of the inter-spouse transfer the recipient spouse is not under a binding obligation to use the property as directed by the donor spouse.

4.6   Transfers from parents to children and remoter issue

Most parents wish to provide for their children, and those who can actually afford to do so wish to ensure that such provision is made in the most tax-effective way.

It is not always possible to achieve the client's intentions and avoid a tax bill. The skill is to put forward ideas that will satisfy the practical objectives at the minimum tax cost.

Again, the solicitor must be aware of the interaction of the capital taxes; for example, is the CGT cost of a course of action less than the IHT bill which will arise if the action is not taken?

The choice for parents is a lifetime gift either outright or through the creation of a trust (see **4.6.4**), or by will which is either an outright gift or gift into trust. The use of will trusts is discussed in **Chapter 11** and will not be discussed in detail here.

4.6.1   Outright gifts

A gift is an immediate outright transfer of property from one person to another. There can be no conditions attached.

When making gifts of small sums of money or family possessions, or wishing to benefit an adult child, an outright gift may be the most sensible and appropriate course of action. However, where the intended recipient is a minor or is irresponsible with money, the donor may feel that it is inappropriate to hand over valuable assets or large amounts of cash. In such circumstances, consideration might be given to the provision of the intended benefit via a trust (but see **4.6.4.1**). A minor is unable to hold the legal estate in land so it is impossible to make an outright gift of land to a person under 18 years of age. Where such a gift is attempted, statute imposes a trust.

4.6.2   The taxation of outright gifts

4.6.2.1   Inheritance tax

The current IHT legislation encourages lifetime giving, whether by a parent, grandparent or others and, wherever possible, clients should take full advantage of the exceptions and reliefs offered.

The annual exemption (IHTA 1984, s 19)

Every taxpayer can make gifts of £3,000 per annum, and as the unused exemption can be carried forward for one tax year only, it should be used every year if the client can afford to do so. A husband and wife each has their own annual exemption.

PETs (IHTA 1984, s 3A) – 'asset freezing'

All gifts between individuals are PETs when they are made, as indeed are gifts into accumulation and maintenance trusts and into trusts for the disabled. Gifts into discretionary trusts are immediately chargeable transfers (charged at half the death rate). The effect of the PET is that no IHT is payable at the time of the transfer. The transfer becomes exempt from IHT if the transferor lives for seven years. Should the transferor die within the seven-year period, the PET becomes chargeable. The value which is taxed is the value of the property at the date of the transfer, unless the value has fallen when it is the lower value which is taxed – see below. It is therefore sensible for clients to consider giving away assets which are likely to increase in value. Rates at the date of the death are used unless they have increased since the gift. If so, the rates at the date of the gift are used instead.

Example

Keith owns a painting by an elderly living artist. He paid £20,000 for it and believes that its value will quadruple after the artist's death. Keith utilises his annual exemptions on other transfers.

Year 1: Keith gives the painting (value £20,000) to Laura (PET).

Year 4: Keith dies and the painting is valued at £115,000. IHT rates have not increased subsequently. The gift of the painting becomes a chargeable transfer and tax is charged on £20,000, which, assuming Keith had made no previous transfers, will be covered by his nil rate band.

Where a PET is of an amount which exceeds the transferor's nil rate band, IHT will be payable by the donee if the transferor dies within seven years. Whilst this tax cannot be avoided, the transferee or transferor can mitigate its effect by insuring the transferor's life for seven years (for an explanation of such term assurance, see **Appendix 2(16)**) for a sum equal to the potential tax bill. If the transferor insures his own life the insurance policy should be written in trust for the transferee.

Example

Mike, who has made no gifts other than of £3,000 per annum, gives his daughter Nina £295,000 to buy a house.

If Mike dies within seven years, Nina could face a tax bill of up to £8,000.

Unless she insures her father's life (which she may not be able to afford to do) Nina therefore has the choice of only spending £287,000 and putting the rest aside to meet the anticipated tax bill, or having to sell or mortgage the house on Mike's death to raise the tax.

Alternatively, Mike could insure his life for £8,000 for seven years and give the benefit of the insurance policy to Nina. The annual premiums should be covered by his normal expenditure out of income exemption. If Mike dies within seven years, Nina receives cash of £8,000 with which to pay the tax and so can safely spend the full £295,000 on buying her house.

PETs – loss in value

If property other than cash is given away and the value of that property falls between the date of the PET and the death, relief is provided by IHTA 1984, s 131. IHT is calculated on the reduced value instead of the original value (the relief applies similarly following a lifetime chargeable transfer). This relief reduces the value which is taxed; it does not affect the value of the original PET. This means that the original value remains in the transferor's cumulative total when calculating any IHT on later lifetime transfers and on the estate on the death. Any taper relief is based on the IHT actually payable, ie, the IHT payable on the reduced value.

IHT is charged at the rate(s) in force at death unless the rates have increased, in which case the rates in force at the date of the PET are used.

Example

In January 2002 Harold gave his grandson his shares in Z plc, which were then worth £315,000. Harold died in March 2006 when the shares were worth £291,000. Apart from using his annual exemptions, Harold has made no other transfers.

(a) On Harold's death within seven years, the PET becomes chargeable on the reduced value of £291,000.

(b) IHT, at rates in force when Harold died:

		£
nil rate band	£275,000	nil
balance	£16,000 @ 40%	6,400
		6,400

(c)   Taper relief – Harold died more than four but less than five years later.

£6,400 @ 60% = £3,840 (payable by Harold's grandson).

(d)   The original value of £315,000 remains in Harold's cumulative total when calculating the IHT due on his estate at death.

Note: if Harold's grandson had sold the shares for £291,000, IHT on Harold's death would be calculated in the same way as above. If he had given them away, no relief is given and IHT would, instead, be calculated on the full value in 2002, ie, £315,000 (IHTA 1984, s 131(1)).

Order of gifts – some considerations

Clients planning a number of gifts, some PETs and some lifetime chargeable transfers such as gifts to the trustees of a discretionary settlement, should be advised that the possible IHT consequences may differ depending upon the order of the gifts.

Transfers made on the same day (IHTA 1984, s 266)

If a number of PETs are intended (but the client does not wish to make a discretionary settlement) and all are made on the same day there is, of course, no IHT payable at the date of the gifts. If the donor should die within seven years so that IHT becomes payable, it is charged on each PET on a pro rata basis. Each gift benefits from a proportion of the nil rate band. Had the gifts been made on separate days, the earlier gifts would benefit from the donor's nil rate band whereas the donees of later gifts would suffer IHT once the nil rate band was exceeded.

PETs and discretionary settlements (lifetime chargeable transfers – LCTs)

Here the order of gifts is important. There is an advantage to the later taxation of a discretionary settlement if the discretionary settlement is made before (or at the latest on the same day as) the PETs. If the PETs come first and later become chargeable, they will be taken into account when calculating IHT payable by the trustees during the life of the discretionary settlement. This liability of the trustees is considered in **Chapter 10**. If the client intends creating more than one settlement, the gifts to the discretionary trustees should be made on different days so as to avoid the settlements being treated as 'related settlements' (IHTA 1984, s 62). The effect of related settlements on the calculation of the trustees' IHT liability is considered at **10.2.4**.

Effect on PETs and discretionary settlements (lifetime chargeable transfers – LCTs) of death between three to seven years

Although it is beneficial to the subsequent taxation of a discretionary settlement to make the LCT before the PET, there are circumstances where this can result in the payment of more tax on the transfers themselves. This occurs where the donor dies more than three years but less than seven years after his gifts as illustrated in the examples which follow. No annual exemptions are available.

Example 1: PET precedes LCT by one day

			IHT
			£
(a)	PET	£280,000	nil
(b)	LCT	£416,000	
	first	£275,000 – nil	
	balance	£141,000 @ 20%	28,200
(c)	Donor dies after six years.		
	PET	£280,000 – £275,000 = £5,000	
		£5,000 @ 40% × 20% (taper relief)	400
	LCT	£416,000 @ 40% × 20% (taper relief)	33,280
		credit (tax already paid)	(28,200)
	IHT due on LCT		£5,080

Total IHT – £33,680

Example 2: LCT precedes PET by one day

			IHT
			£
(a)	LCT	£416,000	
	first	£275,000 – nil	
	balance	£141,000 @ 20%	28,200
(b)	PET	£280,000	nil
(c)	Donor dies after six years.		
	LCT	£416,000	
	first	£275,000 – nil	
	balance	£141,000 @ 40% × 20% (taper relief)	11,280
		credit (tax already paid – no refund)	(28,200)
			no IHT due
(d)	PET	£280,000 @ 40% × 20% (taper relief)	£22,400

Total IHT – £50,600

Lifetime transfers – transfers on death

Clients who are estate planning through a combination of lifetime giving and gifts by will should be aware of the effect of PETs on their death estates. Lifetime gifts which become chargeable on death have first call on the deceased's nil rate band and this may result in unexpected IHT being payable on property passing under the will.

Example

Oswald has always used his annual exemption but otherwise has made no previous lifetime transfers.

Year 1: Oswald makes a will leaving a legacy of £275,000 to his children and the residue to his wife.

Year 2: He makes a PET of £100,000 to his eldest son.

Year 3: Oswald dies.

Step 1: The PET becomes chargeable, but as Oswald had made no previous lifetime transfers the £100,000 is covered by his nil rate band.

Step 2: The £100,000 is cumulated with his death estate and means that only the remaining £175,000 of the nil rate band is available to set against the legacy to his children. The balance of the legacy (£100,000) is taxable at 40% (subject to grossing up); the residue is exempt.

Use of a 'formula clause' limiting the legacy to the amount available of the nil rate band at death (here £100,000) when drafting the will can anticipate and avoid this situation (see **12.5.1**).

Using the reliefs

Property which attracts business property relief or agricultural property relief (especially at 100%) should, where possible, be given to non-exempt beneficiaries rather than exempt ones as otherwise the benefit may be wasted. There is also the danger of losing the relief completely where the conditions for business property relief are not fulfilled at the date of death (see **4.3.6.2** for an example).

In view of the danger of losing relief where lifetime gifts of eligible property are made, it may be preferable to make the gift of such property by will (see **4.5.3**).

Excluded property – inheritance tax

Section 5 of IHTA 1984 defines a person's estate as including everything 'to which he is beneficially entitled … but does not include excluded property'. By IHTA 1984, s 48 a reversionary interest (with three anti-avoidance exceptions – see below) is excluded property. Section 47 defines any future interest under a settlement as a reversionary interest, whether the interest is vested or contingent, and includes the interest expectant on the termination of an interest in possession, ie, the interest which falls into possession on the death of a life tenant. The interest of a beneficiary under a discretionary settlement is not, therefore, within the definition.

Because a reversionary interest is not included in an individual's estate, it can be given away as part of estate planning without liability to IHT (and without CGT liability, see below).

Perhaps the most common example of excluded property is 'an interest in remainder'.

Example

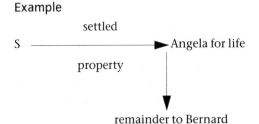

While Angela is alive Bernard has an 'interest in remainder'. Assume Bernard is wealthy and has a house, shares and cash totalling £400,000. He is a widower and intends to leave everything to his daughter Davina.

(a)   If Bernard does nothing:

On Angela's death the trust fund, then valued at £305,000, is taxable as part of Angela's estate. (Assume that her residuary estate is exempt and that her cumulative total is zero.)

IHT of £12,000 is payable on the trust fund.

Bernard receives £293,000.

When Bernard dies his estate is £293,000 + £400,000 and Davina will pay IHT of £167,200.

(b)   If Bernard gives his interest in remainder to Davina while Angela is still alive.

There will be no IHT (IHTA 1984, s 5) and no CGT on the gift (see below; TCGA 1992, s 76).

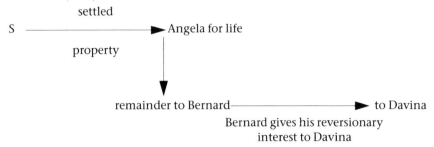

On Angela's, death, Davina will receive £293,000 (as Bernard did in (a)).

When Bernard dies his estate is £400,000 as the trust fund no longer forms part of his taxable estate. Davina will now pay IHT of £50,000 on her father's estate. This represents a tax saving of £117,200, ie, IHT at 40% on the £293,000 trust fund.

The three anti-avoidance exceptions within s 48 where the reversionary interest is not excluded property are:

(a)   where the interest was purchased for money or money's worth;

(b)   where the interest is one to which the settlor or his spouse is beneficially entitled;

(c)   where it is the lessor's interest expectant on the ending of a lease granted for life; where such a lease for life is granted a settlement exists for IHT.

Excluded property – capital gains tax

No gain arises for CGT where a beneficiary disposes of his beneficial interest under a settlement provided that it had never previously been acquired for a consideration in money or money's worth (other than consideration consisting of another interest under the settlement, for example, on a 'swap' of interests by beneficiaries). Once any consideration in money or money's worth has been given, all future disposals of the interest will attract CGT (TCGA 1992, s 76).

If, in the previous example, Bernard had sold his interest to Davina, no CGT would be payable by him (assuming no prior consideration had been given for the interest) because s 76 would apply. On Davina's later disposal (by sale or by gift) she would be liable to CGT on any gain she realises.

If instead Bernard had given his interest to Davina, neither he nor Davina would pay CGT. Whether she sold or gave away the interest subsequently, she would not pay CGT.

4.6.2.2 Capital gains tax

Although a gift may not result in an IHT charge, it may attract an immediate charge to CGT. A gift is a disposal by the donor and, if it is of a chargeable asset, CGT will be calculated in the usual way (subject to appropriate reliefs and exemptions).

Example

Susan gives quoted shares worth £60,000 to her daughter Tina and cash of £50,000 to her son Vernon.

Both gifts are PETs for IHT purposes and the cash is not a chargeable asset for CGT.

Susan will pay CGT on the difference between the purchase price of the quoted shares and their open market value at the date of the gift to Tina, after taking into account the indexation allowance and annual exemption. She may also be able to claim taper relief.

Where the gift is of a business asset hold-over relief will be available (for the definitions and conditions, see **4.4.5.2**), but if the donor's annual exemption is available or he has unused losses, it may be better not to claim the relief.

Example

William gives his 10% shareholding in O Ltd to his daughter Yasmin. William acquired the shares for £100 and they are currently worth £8,700. Yasmin expects to sell the shares within the next two years. Last year, William made capital losses of £2,000.

(a)   If hold-over relief claimed:

William pays no CGT and retains losses of £2,000.

Yasmin acquires the shares at £100 (ignore indexation).

In 2 years' time she sells the shares for £9,600.

CGT is payable on any chargeable gain (ignore indexation and taper relief).

	£
Disposal consideration	9,600
less: Acquisition cost	100
	9,500
less: Annual exemption	8,500
Chargeable gain	1,000

(b)   If hold-over relief not claimed (ignore indexation):

William's gift is a disposal of a chargeable asset.

	£	£
Disposal consideration	8,700	
less: Acquisition cost	100	
		8,600
Part of unused losses	100	
Annual exemption	8,500	
		8,600
William's chargeable gain		nil

When Yasmin sells:

	£	£
Disposal consideration		9,600
less: Acquisition cost	8,700	
less: Annual exemption (part)	900	9,600
Yasmin's chargeable gain		nil

Note: Brought forward losses need only be used to reduce gains to the level of the annual exemption unlike current year losses which must be used to reduce gains to zero before any portion of the loss can be carried forward.

Payment of CGT by instalments (TCGA 1992, ss 280, 281)

31 January following the end of the tax year of the disposal is the normal date for payment of a CGT liability. In limited circumstances, the tax may be paid by equal yearly instalments starting on 31 January. Interest is payable on the outstanding tax.

CGT may be paid by instalments if the following apply.

(a)   Sales (s 280) – if the consideration is payable over a period exceeding 18 months and the Revenue is satisfied payment of the tax in a lump sum would cause hardship. The instalment period is eight years (or the payment period if the consideration is payable over a shorter period).

(b)   Gifts or deemed disposals by trustees (s 281 – see **10.2.7**) – where the property is land, a controlling shareholding in either a quoted or an unquoted company or a minority holding in a company whose shares are unquoted, provided that hold-over relief was not available under either TCGA 1992, s 165 or s 260, ie, neither the asset (s 165) nor the occasion (s 260) was appropriate to enable hold-over relief to be claimed. Failure to make the appropriate election for hold-over relief, in cases where it is available, does not mean that the tax can then be paid by instalments. When available, the CGT may be paid by 10 equal annual instalments.

4.6.2.3   Income tax

A gift of an income-producing asset to an adult child by his parent will give the child an increase in his taxable income (taxable at his own rates) and a corresponding decrease in the level of the parent's taxable income (and a saving of tax at his own rates). The potential saving of tax, possibly at 40%, by the parent makes such gifts attractive, particularly when the child's rate of tax may be at basic rate or less.

Parental gifts for minor children (ITTOIA 2005, s 629)

Despite the obvious practical advantage of an outright gift, there is a potential income tax problem if the child is unmarried and under 18 years when the gift is made. Income tax rules state that any income (of more than £100) paid to or for the benefit of the unmarried minor child from a 'settlement' created by his parent will be taxed as though it is still the income of the parent (s 629). This is deliberate policy to prevent a parent who pays income tax at 40% from benefiting the child who pays income tax at lower rates or possibly is not a tax payer at all. If income is accumulated and not paid to or for the benefit of the minor child, it will not be taxed as income of the settlor.

'Settlement' is defined in very wide terms by ITTOIA 2005, s 620, as including 'any disposition, trust, covenant, agreement, arrangement or transfer of assets'. An outright gift by a parent to a minor child is clearly within the provision, so that any income of the property given away is taxed as if it still belongs to the parent. The actual 'ownership' of the income does not belong to the parent even though it is deemed his for income tax purposes. The parent has a right of reimbursement from the child for the extra tax suffered where the income is deemed to be his for income tax purposes (s 646). Once the child attains 18 or marries, s 629 ceases to apply. The income is then taxed as the child's, not his parent's.

4.6.3   Post-death disclaimers and variations

Where a parent leaves assets by will to a wealthy adult child, that child may in turn decide to give that property to his own children. A post-death alteration of the will may be the most tax-effective way of passing inherited property to the next generation (see **Chapter 13**).

4.6.4   Gifts into trust

The practical advantage of a gift into trust over an outright gift is flexibility. By using a settlement the settlor (the person making the gift into the trust) can determine who will benefit, when and how. Conditions can be imposed, for example, 'To Ben if he attains 21 years of age', so that Ben will receive the trust fund (gift) only if he reaches his 21st birthday; or to limit the amount of the gift received, for example 'the income to Carol during her life and on her death the income and capital to Doreen'. This is not possible with an outright gift.

In estate planning the most common types of trust are:

(a)   an accumulation and maintenance trust for children and/or grandchildren;

(b)   a discretionary trust;

(c)   an interest in possession trust.

Each trust has its own particular uses and conditions, and all three types are considered in more detail in **Chapter 5**. Trusts with trustees resident outside the UK also play a considerable role in tax and estate planning. These are considered in **Chapter 15**.

4.6.4.1   Parental settlements (ITTOIA 2005, s 629)

The income deeming provisions discussed at **4.6.2** apply to 'settlements' as defined by s 620. If, therefore, a parent creates a trust of any of the types just mentioned of which his infant unmarried child is a beneficiary, s 629 will apply to income paid out to the child for so long as the child remains under 18 years and unmarried. The provision does not apply if income is accumulated. The income produced by the property in the settlement will be taxed as though it is still the income of the parent/settlor. The income remains the income of the trustees who will use it under the terms of the trust for the benefit of the beneficiaries. The parent/settlor has a right to recover from the trustees the extra income tax he pays because of these provisions.

4.6.5   Gifts with a reserved benefit (Finance Act 1986, s 102 and Sch 20)

No estate planning involving gifts can take place without at least a brief consideration of the rules governing 'reservation of benefit'. Anybody, whether parent, grandparent, uncle, etc, making a gift must ensure that the donor does not continue to have any interest (with minor exceptions) in the subject matter of the gift or the gift will be ineffective for IHT purposes. This principle applies to outright gifts and gifts into trust, and is illustrated by the following examples.

Example 1

Gina says to Henry 'I give you the Matisse which hangs in my drawing room'. Henry lets Gina keep it on her wall.

Example 2

For many years, Ian has owned a country cottage in which he spends his holidays. Ian transfers the ownership of the cottage to his son John but spends his holidays there as before.

In both examples there has been a valid gift for succession and CGT purposes and a PET for IHT purposes. However, the Revenue will not fully recognise the gift for IHT purposes because there has been a reservation of benefit – the continued enjoyment of the Matisse and the occupation of the cottage.

The death of the donor within seven years will attract IHT in the usual way on the PET. However, because the gift is caught by the 'reservation of benefit' provisions, the property will also be taxable as part of the donor's IHT estate at death. This prima facie double liability is, to an extent, alleviated by the Inheritance Tax Double Charges (Relief) Regulations 1987 (SI 1987/1130).

If the reservation ends before the donor's death, he is treated as making a PET at that time. Again, the 1987 Regulations provide relief should each PET (the original gift and the ending of the reservation) be within seven years of the donor's death.

The reservation of benefit provisions apply where an individual disposes of any property by way of gift and either:

(a)   full possession and enjoyment of the property is not bona fide assumed by the donee at or before the beginning of the relevant period (s 102(1)(a)); or

(b)   at any time in the relevant period the property is not enjoyed to the entire exclusion, or virtually to the entire exclusion, of the donor by contract or otherwise (s 102(1)(b)).

The relevant period means the period ending on the date of the donor's death and beginning seven years before that date, or if it is later, on the date of the gift.

Example 1

David gives away (ie, transfers the legal title to) his house to his only child Ella.

(a)   If Ella moves in and David dies two years later – full possession and enjoyment at the beginning of the relevant period (of two years) – no reservation.

(b)   If Ella moves in and David dies eight years later – as before, no reservation.

(c)   If after one year David resumes occupation for six months to write his autobiography, the property is no longer enjoyed to the entire exclusion of David – gift with reservation.

Example 2

Fiona settles a property on discretionary trusts naming herself as one of the discretionary beneficiaries. Even though she has no more than an expectation of benefiting as a beneficiary of a discretionary settlement, all the trust property will remain taxable as part of her estate on death.

Section 102(1)(b) (above) requires that 'the property' is 'enjoyed to the exclusion ...' etc. Identifying the property given is not normally difficult but is obviously essential before the rules can be applied appropriately. It also requires 'virtually entire exclusion' from the gifted property. Some continued enjoyment of the property is therefore possible. There is no statutory definition but the Revenue interprets the phrase as meaning (and therefore including) 'cases in which benefit to the donor is insignificant in relation to the gifted property' (Inland Revenue Tax Bulletin Issue 9, November 1993). Flexibility is applied by the Revenue when applying the interpretation so that a donor can have limited access to the property given away.

The following are some of the situations which in the Revenue view will not bring the rules into play:

(a)   A house which becomes the donee's residence but where the donor subsequently:

(i)   stays, in the absence of the donee, for not more than two weeks each year, or

(ii)   stays with the donee for less than one month each year.

(b)   Social visits, excluding overnight stays, made by a donor as a guest of the donee, to a house which he had given away. The extent of the social visits should be no greater than the visits which the donor might be expected to make to the donee's house in the absence of any gift by the donor.

(c)   A temporary stay for some short-term purpose in a house the donor had previously given away, for example:

(i)   while the donor convalesces after medical treatment;

(ii)   while the donor looks after a donee convalescing after medical treatment.

(d)   A house together with a library of books which the donor visits less than five times in any year to consult or borrow a book.

(e)   A motor car which the donee uses to give occasional (ie, less than three times a month) lifts to the donor.

(f)   Land which the donor uses to walk his dogs or for horse riding, provided this does not restrict the donee's use of the land.

Conversely, the following are instances (in the Revenue view) where the rules may apply:

(a)   A house in which the donor then stays most weekends, or for a month or more each year.

(b)   A second home or holiday home which the donor and the donee both then use on an occasional basis.

(c)   A house with a library in which the donor continues to keep his own books, or which the donor uses on a regular basis, for example because it is necessary for his work.

(d)   A motor car which the donee uses every day to take the donor to work.

Inland Revenue Tax Bulletin Issue 9 also provides some guidance on the meaning of the exclusion provided by Finance Act 1986, Sch 20, para 6(1)(a). By this provision, if land or chattels are given away and the donor provides full consideration for his future enjoyment of the property, the reservation provisions do not apply. What constitutes full consideration for the use has caused estate planners problems. Would anything less than full consideration be fatal? In the context of rent payable for the future use of property the Revenue view is:

> While we take the view that such full consideration is required throughout the relevant period – and therefore consider that the rent paid should be reviewed at appropriate intervals to reflect market changes – we do recognise that there is no single value at which consideration can be fixed as 'full'. Rather, we accept that what constitutes full consideration in any case lies within a range of values reflecting normal valuation tolerances, and that any amount within that range can be accepted as satisfying the para 6(1)(a) test.

Further aspects of the reservation rules and the family home are discussed at **4.7.4**.

The reservation of benefit provisions do not apply (inter alia) to transfers qualifying for the four following IHT exemptions:

(a)   the spouse exemption;

(b)   the small gift exemption;

(c)   the gift in consideration of marriage exemption; and

(d)   the gifts to charity exemption.

In *Inland Revenue Commissioners v Eversden and Another (executors of Greenstock, deceased)* [2003] EWCA Civ 668, [2003] STC 822, a wife transferred an interest in 95% of the matrimonial home to her husband for life and then to a discretionary trust which included herself and her daughter as beneficiaries. She retained 5% of the house absolutely. On the husband's death, IHT was paid on his interest in possession in the trust. When the wife died, the Inland Revenue argued that the value of the house was to be included in her estate because there was a reservation of benefit. The Court of Appeal agreed that inclusion in the class of beneficiaries of a discretionary trust would normally amount to a reservation of benefit. However, this was not the case where the interest followed a transfer which was spouse exempt. The length of the spouse's interest was irrelevant, so it would be possible to give a spouse a very short interest to be followed by a discretionary trust and to avoid the reservation of benefit rules.

The decision resulted in many taxpayers giving terminable life interests to their spouses, to be followed by discretionary trusts which included the taxpayer as a beneficiary. The terminable life interest would be terminated after a very short period leaving the taxpayer a beneficiary of a discretionary trust and not subject to the reservation of benefit rules.

However, in the Finance Act 2003, the Revenue introduced anti-avoidance provisions to apply to gifts made after 20 June 2003. The legislation provides that in such cases the original gift of the life interest to the spouse is ignored when deciding whether or not the reservation of benefit rules apply. The taxpayer is treated as making the gift direct to the discretionary trust.

Income tax charge on pre-owned assets

The Finance Act 2004 introduced further provisions (s 84 and Sch 15) with the aim of catching situations not covered by the reservation of benefit regime. The effect is that where a person owns certain assets (land, chattels or intangible property) and disposes of them, other than by sale at arm's length, but still derives some benefit from them, that person will suffer an income tax charge on the annual value of this benefit. The charge also applies if a person has contributed towards the purchase of such property by another, but the contributing person derives some benefit from the property. These provisions came into effect on 6 April 2005, but the charge affects anyone who has owned and disposed of assets since 17 March 1986, or contributed to the purchase of an asset since that date.

This charge will not apply in various situations, including:

(a)   where under the reservation of benefit rules the asset is treated as part of the IHT estate of the donor;

(b)   where the annual value of the benefit is below £5,000; or

(c)   where the asset is owned by the donor's spouse.

4.7   The family home

The principal tax-saving opportunity available to the home owner is the CGT private residence exemption. Income tax saving is no longer possible since the withdrawal of mortgage interest tax relief from 2000/2001 onwards. As a substantial asset in its own right, home owners will frequently raise questions about gifts of the home, or at least an interest in it, as part of estate planning with a view to saving, principally, IHT on its value at death. There are many problems associated with gifts of this type, some of which are discussed later.

4.7.1   Insurance cover

It is sensible to provide insurance cover designed to repay the mortgage secured on the family home. In the case of property owned jointly by a husband and wife the policy will normally mature on the death of the first spouse to die leaving a mortgage-free property for the survivor. Various types of policy are available and are discussed in **Appendix 2(16)**. Of these, the endowment policy, linked to the redemption date of the mortgage, has traditionally been the most popular. Recent under-performance by life companies has led to 'endowment mortgages' becoming far less common, leaving borrowers to make other arrangements for the repayment of their mortgages. Often the choice of policy is limited by the financial resources available to the borrower; in addition to the mortgage interest payments the policy premiums can be too expensive. Because of this, the mortgage and the policy should be viewed as two separate but closely linked transactions. A mortgage protection policy alone may be sufficient; an endowment policy (with profits) can be a good investment as well as providing cover to repay the mortgage, but the premiums may be expensive.

4.7.2   Joint tenancy and tenancy in common

Joint tenancy and tenancy in common have already been discussed (see **4.5.1.2**) as the two common ways property is held by spouses. For IHT purposes, there is no distinction made between joint tenancy and tenancy in common; it is the beneficial interest behind the trust of the legal estate that is important when considering the 'estate' of each spouse. The differences between joint tenancy and tenancy in common from a succession point of view have also been considered earlier.

4.7.3   Capital gains tax private residence exemption (TCGA 1992, ss 222–226)

Gains made on the disposal by sale or by gift of an individual's dwelling house used as his only or main residence, including grounds of up to 0.5 hectares (or such larger area as is reasonably required for its enjoyment), are exempt. It is a question of fact in each case as to what constitutes a dwelling house. A caravan was held to be a dwelling house in *Makins v Elson (Inspector of Taxes)* [1977] 1 All ER 572 but not in *Moore v Thompson* [1986] STC 170 (the caravan not having its own water or electricity supply).

Problems can also arise in deciding whether separate buildings can constitute the tax payer's residence. For example, a separate bungalow occupied by a caretaker and situated in the grounds of the tax payer's house was within the exemption when sold, ie, physical separation of the buildings did not deny the tax payer the exemption (*Batey (Inspector of Taxes) v Wakefield* [1982] 1 All ER 61). Later cases (where CGT was payable) show that the separate building must be physically close to the main building so as to enhance the tax payer's enjoyment of it (*Markey (Inspector of Taxes) v Sanders* [1987] 1 WLR 864 – bungalow 130 metres away), or within the 'curtilage' of the main building (*Lewis (Inspector of Taxes) v Lady Rook* [1992] 1 WLR 662 – cottage 200 yards away).

4.7.3.1   Land and residence sold separately

The order of sales can be important where the tax payer plans to sell land used with the main residence and the main residence itself. Land of up to 0.5 hectares (or a permitted larger area) is within the exemption if used in connection with the residence. Thus sale of the residence with its grounds will be exempt, but gains on the later sale of the retained land will be chargeable (*Varty (Inspector of Taxes) v Lynes* [1976] 3 All ER 447).

4.7.3.2   Part business user

Use of part of the house exclusively for business purposes will mean that part of the gain on the disposal is chargeable. Exclusive use can easily be avoided, for example, by having a television set in a room otherwise used as an office for a business run from home.

4.7.3.3   More than one residence

A taxpayer with more than one residence can elect for one to be treated as his main residence (TCGA 1992, s 222(5)). This avoids difficult questions as to which of two or more residences is the only or main residence for the purposes of the relief. The election should be made within two years of acquiring the second residence. Failure by the taxpayer to elect will mean that the Inspector of Taxes will do so. The relative CGT liability on each property will generally influence the election of a particular property, for treatment as the taxpayer's main residence.

A husband and wife can have only one main residence between them. When a couple marry, each owning a residence, the election for treatment as their main residence must be made within two years of the marriage.

4.7.3.4 Periods of absence

Exemption is available if a taxpayer occupies a property as his only or main residence throughout the period of ownership. Periods of absence will therefore cut back the exemption so that a proportion of the gain on disposal is chargeable.

Certain periods of absence can be ignored (so not prejudicing the exemption):

(a) the first 12 months' ownership due to delay in building or alteration (Statement of Practice D4);

(b) periods not exceeding three years in total;

(c) periods of employment overseas;

(d) periods of up to four years when the owner was employed elsewhere and so could not occupy the property;

(e) the last three years of ownership, for example, where the owner moves into new property and has delay in selling the former.

Note: for (b) to (d) above, absences are ignored only if there was no other available residence and the property was occupied before and after the periods of absence.

4.7.3.5 Private residences occupied under the terms of a trust (s 225)

If the trustees sell a dwelling house occupied by a beneficiary as his main residence under the terms of the trust, their capital gain is exempt. The exemption will apply where the beneficiary has an interest in possession, ie, he is entitled to occupy under the terms of the settlement.

It will also apply if he occupies as a result of the exercise of a discretion, for example, where he is a beneficiary of a discretionary trust and the trustees exercise a power in the settlement to permit him to occupy (*Sansom and Another v Peay (Inspector of Taxes)* [1976] 3 All ER 375). In this latter situation, the Inland Revenue will often argue that, following the exercise of their discretion, the beneficiary has acquired an interest in possession, ie, the right to occupy the property (Statement of Practice 10/79 and see *Woodhall v IRC*, Simons Weekly Tax Intelligence 1653). The IHT consequence which flows from acquiring a right to occupy is that the 'estate' of the beneficiary will include the value of the underlying property, the value of the private residence, so that on his death IHT is calculated as if it was held in an interest in possession settlement.

Chapter 5 discusses the essential differences between interest in possession and discretionary trusts.

The Finance Act 2004 has introduced a new TCGA 1992, s 226A, with effect from 10 December 2003. This provides that where hold-over relief is claimed under TCGA 1992, s 260 on a transfer of a house to a discretionary settlement, the principal private residence exemption will not be available if the trustees allow a beneficiary to occupy that house and the trustees then dispose of it. If hold-over relief is not claimed when the house is transferred to the settlement, the principal private residence exemption will be available on a later disposal by the trustees (assuming that they have first allowed a beneficiary to occupy the house).

4.7.4 Estate planning and the family home

The dilemma here is, on the one hand, the wish to give away part or all of the value of the home to save IHT; and on the other hand, the necessity to maintain a roof over the donor's head. Saving tax in relation to the home (bearing in mind its value in the client's estate) is an obvious consideration but the best advice is often 'don't let the tax tail wag the dog', ie, it is frequently better not to enter into arrangements just to save IHT. Joint tenancy between a husband and wife may often be the most practical approach for spouses.

Normally, IHT planning considerations will revolve around a gift of the house, or of an interest in it, to another individual who will usually be the donor's child. It is possible to give the house to trustees – and retain a right of residence – but this course is unlikely to be followed in most cases.

There is a danger in giving the family home to a child. The child may become bankrupt or be divorced. The donor's house would then be taken by the child's trustee in bankruptcy or be at risk in the divorce settlement.

The gift with reservation of benefit provisions (Finance Act 1986, s 102) and the pre-owned assets regime discussed at **4.6.5** present the main obstacle to estate planning where the family home is involved. There are some exceptions to the reservation rules, some of which are discussed below.

4.7.4.1 'Occupation virtually to the entire exclusion of the donor' (Finance Act 1986, s 102(1)(b))

A gift of the home to a child followed by occasional visits (as interpreted by the Revenue in Tax Bulletin Issue 9, November 1993) should have no adverse IHT consequences.

4.7.4.2 'Occupation resulting from change of circumstances of the donor' (Finance Act 1986, Sch 20, para 6(1)(b))

A gift of land which is subsequently reoccupied by the donor following unforeseen and unintentional change in his circumstances is excluded by para 6 provided:

(a)   the donor is through age or infirmity unable to maintain himself;

(b)   the reoccupation is reasonable provision by the donee for the care of the donor; and

(c)   the donee is a relative of the donor or his or her spouse.

The scope of this exemption is clearly limited as shown in the following example.

> Example
>
> A father on his retirement gives to his daughter the family bungalow. He later returns to live there following serious ill health. No IHT consequences should follow from the reoccupation.

4.7.4.3 'Occupation of land and possession of a chattel for full consideration in money or money's worth' (Finance Act 1986, Sch 6, para (1)(a))

A gift of the home and the arrangement of a right of continued occupation through a lease or licence should have no adverse IHT consequence. Full consideration is required throughout the period of occupation so that a full rent, reviewed regularly, will be essential (see the Revenue's view as to this published in Tax Bulletin Issue 9, referred to at **4.6.5**). A scheme using this paragraph will reduce the donor's estate for IHT but requires the donor to have sufficient income to pay the rent in full and regularly.

4.7.4.4 'Co-ownership' between the parents (donors) and the children (donees)

The parents could give the child(ren) an interest in the house as tenant(s) in common. A gift of the beneficial interest as tenant in common is a PET and carries with it the right to occupy the entire property with the other co-owner(s). The occupation by the donor(s) is by virtue of the co-ownership, rather than by virtue of reservation of benefit. Even if schemes of this sort work, the practical result is ownership and occupation shared with other (younger) members of the family. Often this will make such schemes unattractive. In view of the legal and practical uncertainty, the best advice is probably not to 'tax plan' in this way with the matrimonial home.

4.8 Gifts to charity

In addition to, or perhaps instead of, gifts to family and friends, a tax payer may wish to make gifts to his favourite charity or charities.

Although not always considered part of estate planning, such gifts can be achieved in a number of tax-efficient ways and the method chosen will normally be determined by the timing and anticipated amount of the gift.

4.8.1 Inheritance tax

All gifts to a charity, whether made inter vivos or by will, and regardless of the amount, are exempt from IHT (IHTA 1984, s 23). A wealthy client may well make sizeable lifetime gifts to charity. These will be exempt and never enter his cumulative total.

Many clients will not be able to afford or wish to make such lifetime donations but will make provision for a charity in their will. This may take the form of a legacy or a gift of residue. The amount given must be deducted as an exemption in the calculation to find the deceased's total chargeable estate.

The will or intestacy of a deceased person may also be varied (see **Chapter 12**) to provide an exempt gift to charity.

4.8.2 Capital gains tax (TCGA 1992, s 256)

The most common form of charitable gift is of cash and therefore CGT is not relevant.

Where, however, a taxpayer is transferring chargeable assets to a charity, the gift will be at no gain no loss (the rule works in a similar way to inter-spouse transfers, see **4.4.5.1**).

For property left to charity by will, the organisation will receive the property at probate value at the testator's death. As with inter vivos gifts, when the charity disposes of the property any gains should be exempt from CGT.

4.8.3 Income tax

There are various schemes for inter vivos payments to charity which are income tax effective for the donor and which should, therefore, be especially attractive to higher rate tax payers.

4.8.3.1 Deeds of covenant (ITTOIA 2005, s 627(2)(b))

Traditionally, deeds of covenant have been a popular method of making regular annual payments to a charity, for example, where the payment is an annual membership fee to charities such as the National Trust.

Following the relaxation of the gift aid provisions by the Finance Act 2000 (FA 2000) (see below), covenanted donations to charity are far less common, although the possibility of their continued use remains.

To be effective, the covenant should be made in writing and signed and dated by the taxpayer. It must be capable of lasting for a period of more than three years, hence many charities have offered a standard form of covenant to last for four years (or the life of the donor if shorter) which the tax payer can complete.

The effect of the covenant is that the tax payer has a charge on his income, so reducing the amount of his taxable income (see LPC Guide, *Pervasive and Core Topics*).

A 'deposit covenant' couples an ordinary covenant with an immediate loan of the full amount payable under the covenant to the charity. The advantage is the early receipt of the total sum by the charity while giving annual tax relief for the individual. Each year, as the annual amount falls due under the covenant, a corresponding sum is deducted from the total sum payable under the covenant.

Example

£1,000 (net) pa is payable to a charity for five years. The charity receives £5,000. In the first year, £1,000 attracts income tax relief for the payer and the total due under the covenant is reduced to £4,000. A similar process occurs in each of the following four years after which the covenant ceases and the payer is no longer entitled to tax relief.

4.8.3.2 Payroll giving (ICTA 1988, s 202)

The payroll giving scheme was introduced by the Government with the sole purpose of encouraging charitable giving. Employers are encouraged to operate a scheme whereby part of an employee's wages or salary is deducted by the employer who pays that sum to an approved charitable agent. The agent then distributes the sum to the charity or charities of the employee's choice. Employees do not have to be involved and must expressly join the scheme if they want to make payments. There was a 10% supplement on donations until 5 April 2004. Contributions are deducted from the employee's gross pay, so reducing the amount of his taxable income.

4.8.3.3 Gift aid (Finance Act 1990, ss 25–26)

Gift aid is another Government-initiated scheme to encourage charitable gifts. Whereas payroll giving is aimed at encouraging small regular annual payments, gift aid is aimed at larger 'one-off' gifts to charity paid out of the tax payer's income.

There is no limit as such to the amount that may be given but, effectively, the maximum is the total income of the individual in the tax year of the gift.

The tax payer will make the donation net of basic rate tax and thereby obtains relief at that rate. The tax payer obtains his higher rate tax relief on the gross amount received by the charity by making a claim in his tax returns. The charity reclaims the tax deducted from the Revenue.

Example

Roger makes a payment of £1,560 net of basic rate income tax to his favourite charity. The Revenue will receive £440. The charity obtains a refund of this £440 and so receives £2,000 in total.

Roger's actual outlay is £2,000, ie, £1,560 paid to the charity and £440 (basic rate tax on £2,000) paid to the Revenue. The cost to Roger (after tax relief) is considerably less than £2,000. If he is a higher rate taxpayer the cost is £2,000 – (£2,000 × 40%) = £1,200. He obtains £440 relief by deduction from his gross payment of £2,000 and £360 (higher rate relief) through his tax return. His total relief is, therefore, £800.

4.8.3.4 Charitable gift relief (ICTA 1988, s 587B)

Gifts by individuals to charity on or after 6 April 2000 of the following non-cash assets attract income tax relief:

(a)   quoted shares;

(b)   unquoted shares dealt on a recognised stock exchange (eg, AIM);

(c)   units in a unit trust;

(d)   shares in open-ended investment companies;

(e)   interest in an offshore fund.

Relief is given by deducting the full value of the gift when computing the donor's income for income tax purposes. In addition, the gift will be treated as a disposal for CGT on a no gain no loss basis (see **4.4.5**).

Example

Johan owns shares in XYZ plc worth £100,000, which have a negligible acquisition cost and so a very large in-built capital gain. He decides to give the shares to charity.

Income tax: if he is a 40% tax payer, his tax saving is £40,000

CGT: the in-built capital gain will be free of CGT on his 'no gain no loss' disposal

Note: If Johan had no taxable income (and so could make no income tax saving), he is not able to reduce any other capital gains he may make to save CGT.

4.9 Stamp duty and stamp duty land tax

Stamp duty is a tax on documents, not transactions. It applies in relation to transactions involving shares, interests in partnerships, loan capital and bearer instruments. Therefore where a document effects the transfer of these types of property, that document is subject to stamp duty. Where the transfer is a voluntary disposition there is no *ad valorem* stamp duty, but there is fixed duty (currently £5) and a requirement that the document be sent to the stamp office for a formal 'adjudication' stamp. However, for documents executed on or after 1 May 1987 which fall within any of the categories in the Schedule to the Stamp Duty (Exempt Instruments) Regulations 1987 (SI 1987/516) these requirements are removed.

Category

A   The vesting of property subject to a trust in the trustees of the trust on the appointment of a new trustee, or in the continuing trustees on the retirement of a trustee.

B   The conveyance or transfer of property the subject of a specific devise or legacy to the beneficiary named in the will.

C   The conveyance or transfer of property which forms part of an intestate's estate to the person entitled on intestacy.

D   The appropriation of property in satisfaction of a general legacy of money or of any interest of surviving spouse in an intestate's estate.

E   The conveyance or transfer of property which forms part of the residuary estate of a testator to a beneficiary entitled under the will.

F   The conveyance or transfer of property out of a settlement in or towards satisfaction of a beneficiary's interest, not being an interest acquired for money or money's worth, in accordance with the provisions of the settlement.

G   The conveyance or transfer of property on and in consideration only of marriage to a party to the marriage or to trustees to be held on a marriage settlement.

H   The conveyance or transfer of property in connection with divorce, etc.

I to K   (not relevant to estate planning)

L   The conveyance or transfer of property as a voluntary disposition inter vivos.

M   The conveyance or transfer of property by a post-death variation. (Note: as a post-death variation is a voluntary disposition, it could be certified as falling within Category L.)

N   The declaration of any use or trust of or concerning a life policy, or property representing, or benefits arising under, a life policy.

To be exempt the document making the transfer must be certified as coming within one or more of the categories. The certificate can be included in or endorsed on the document. Most commonly for private client work this will arise on a voluntary transfer of shares where the stock transfer form will be the document effecting the transfer. Usually the certificate is found printed on the reverse of the form. A solicitor can sign the certificate in the name of his firm on behalf of the transferor (if, as is usual, it is not signed by the transferor personally).

Form of certificate

> I/we hereby certify that this instrument falls within Category ... in the Schedule to the Stamp Duty (Exempt Instruments) Regulations 1987.

Since 1 December 2003 stamp duty was abolished in relation to land transactions. Instead, transactions in land are subject to stamp duty land tax.

A transaction in land is subject to the charge if, according to FA 2003, it is:

(a)   a land transaction;

(b)   effected for consideration;

(c)   which is not exempt.

Voluntary transactions are, thus, not liable to the tax. It is necessary for the transferee to complete a Revenue certificate to the effect that a stamp duty land tax return is not required, and this is then sent to Land Registry when the application is made to register the transfer of the land. The transferee must sign the certificate and his solicitor cannot do so on his behalf.

4.10 Conclusion

Financial planning is concerned with maximising the wealth (capital and income) of the individual. Estate planning is concerned with the passing on of that wealth within the family. This can be achieved by lifetime transfers or by will or a combination of the two. Each client is unique and requires a personal plan. The task of the solicitor is to identify the possibilities for estate planning. However much the solicitor believes in a course of action, the decision whether or not to take it is the client's alone.

Tax avoidance through the use of available reliefs and exemptions as in the previous paragraphs is a legitimate activity. However, some schemes designed for tax payers by their advisers have been so contrived, and the potential savings so great, that legislation has been enacted to combat their effectiveness. The Revenue has successfully challenged some schemes in the courts (see, for example, *Ingram and Another (Executors of the estate of Lady Ingram, deceased) v Inland Revenue Commissioners* [2000] 1 AC 293). Where the tax saving is achieved through a series of artificial steps carried out as a tax-saving measure only, the Revenue may be able to ignore the intervening steps and therefore negate the effect of the scheme. All practitioners need to be aware of the anti-avoidance legislation and cases (eg, ICTA 1988, s 674A, ss 703–728, and s 776; IHTA 1984, s 268; and a series of cases beginning with *WT Ramsay Ltd v Inland Revenue Commissioners; Eilbeck (Inspector of Taxes) v Rawling* [1982] AC 300 and *Furniss (Inspector of Taxes) v Dawson* [1984] 1 AC 474) in putting forward tax-saving schemes.

In the Finance Act 2004 a new regime has been created requiring promoters of certain tax-avoidance schemes and, in some cases, tax payers using such schemes to disclose details of the scheme to the Revenue.

The Revenue registers each scheme reported to it by promoters and provides a reference number for it. This reference number is provided by the promoter to each tax payer using the scheme, and the tax payer has to disclose this in his tax return.

Chapter 5

Introduction to Settlements

5.1 Settlements

The term 'settlement' has a variety of meanings depending upon the context in which it is used. In the private client department, the term is commonly used to include any arrangement whereby an individual 'settles' property of any kind upon trust for a beneficiary or group of beneficiaries. The term 'settlement' refers to the whole arrangement; the 'trusts' are the terms upon which the property is held.

Contrast the following statutory uses of the term:

(a) Under the SLA 1925, a 'settlement' or 'strict settlement' is a trust of land where no trust for sale is imposed. Under the SLA 1925 a beneficiary who has the right to enjoy the land (the tenant for life) has many of the powers over the property which would normally be vested in the trustees (eg, the power to sell the land). The TLATA 1996 prevents the creation of any new strict settlements (but does not prevent the use of a trust for sale). (The Trustee Act 2000 (TA 2000), Sch 2 provides that SLA 1925 investments will be made at the discretion of the trustees and no longer at the direction of the tenant for life.)

(b) In tax statutes, the term 'settlement' is frequently used and is defined in a variety of different ways. For example, a parental 'settlement' for income tax purposes includes not only a settlement upon trust, but also an outright gift (see **4.6.4.1**).

5.1.1 Trusts background – some reminders

5.1.1.1 Fixed interest trusts

When an individual ('the settlor') settles property upon trust, he may wish to determine precisely the extent to which his chosen beneficiaries are to enjoy the settled property in the future. He may, for example, divide their enjoyment of the property by creating successive interests, or he may prevent beneficiaries from obtaining access to the capital before a certain age by giving them contingent interests.

Where capital or income is to be divided between a group of individuals, the settlor may determine the extent of each beneficiary's share. Allowance may be made for future generations by describing the beneficiaries rather than naming them (eg, my grandchildren) provided that the description is sufficiently clear to enable the beneficiaries to be identified with certainty.

The settlor who creates such a trust gives fixed equitable interests to the beneficiaries. Each beneficiary has a bundle of rights resembling an interest in property which he may sell or give away (provided that any such assignment complies with s 53(1)(c) of the Law of Property Act 1925 (LPA 1925)).

If the beneficiaries are between them entitled to the whole equitable interest and are all *sui juris*, they may by agreement put an end to the trust, calling for the trustees to distribute the capital between them in such shares as they may agree (the rule in *Saunders v Vautier* (1841) 4 Beav 115 – see **10.1.3**).

Under TLATA 1996, s 19, such beneficiaries can require the existing trustees to retire and appoint specified new trustees to replace them. This procedure is often preferable to bringing the trust to an end as it avoids the potential capital gains tax liability which arises when a trust ends.

Neither option is available if any beneficiary is a minor or if there are potential beneficiaries who may be born in the future, although the court has power to consent on behalf of such beneficiaries under the Variation of Trusts Act 1958 (VTA 1958) (see **13.2.3.1**).

The period during which the settlor may dictate how the property is to be held is limited by the rule against remoteness of vesting; interests which do not vest within the perpetuity period will fail (see **6.2.7**). If the trusts in the settlement should fail for this or any other reason, the property will revert to the settlor (or his estate if he is dead).

5.1.1.2 Discretionary trusts

A settlor may not wish to determine in advance the precise extent of each beneficiary's entitlement. In such a case, he may nominate a category of beneficiaries and give his trustees the power to determine how much (if anything) each potential beneficiary should receive.

The trustees' discretion may simply concern the distribution of income. If the trustees are obliged to distribute the income, the trusts are said to be 'exhaustive'. Alternatively, the settlor may widen the trustees' discretion to allow them to retain (or accumulate) the income if they think fit ('non-exhaustive' trusts). The period during which a power to accumulate income may continue is limited by the rule against accumulations (broadly, to 21 years – see **6.2.8.2**).

A discretion over the distribution of income may be combined with fixed interests in capital.

Alternatively, the trustees' discretion may extend to capital as well as income, giving the trustees the power to distribute capital to one or more of the designated class of beneficiaries at any time (and thus if they think fit bring an end to the trust).

A beneficiary under a discretionary trust cannot claim any property as of right. He has only a hope that the trustees will exercise their discretion in his favour. Although in principle the rule in *Saunders v Vautier* would allow all the potential beneficiaries to end the trust by agreement, this is unlikely to be possible in practice as the class will be too widely drawn.

Any discretion over income or capital must be limited to the perpetuity period in order to comply with the rule against remoteness of vesting. A fixed period of 80 years is usually specified in the trust instrument and the trustees will normally distribute the whole fund within that period. If, however, all members of the class of beneficiaries should die before the trustees have distributed the capital, the trusts will fail and the property will revert to the settlor (or his estate if he is dead) on resulting trust unless a default beneficiary has been included in the trust instrument. For tax reasons, it is important to avoid any possibility of 'reverter to settlor' (see **6.2.11**) and so an 'ultimate default' provision is usually included (see **7.4**).

There is a difficult distinction between a power of appointment and a discretionary trust or 'trust power'. A trust power arises where the settlor's overriding intention is to benefit a particular class of beneficiaries, giving a power of selection to his trustees. A power of appointment involves no such overriding intention: if it is not exercised, the property will pass in default of appointment. The distinction was once important because there was a different test for certainty of objects. However, the tests are now the same (*McPhail and Others v Doulton and Others* [1971] AC 424) and the distinction is largely academic. In practice, the trustees' power of selection is commonly expressed as a widely drawn power of appointment enabling them not only to give capital outright to a beneficiary, but also to resettle it on new trusts for the benefit of particular members of the class (see **Chapter 9** and **Appendix 4**, clause 5).

5.1.2 Settlements in practice

There are many rules of equity and statutory provisions which have a practical effect on the creation and use of settlements. The most important of these are the tax provisions which govern the treatment of the settlement for tax purposes on its creation, during its life and when it comes to an end. Settlements fall into three main categories for tax purposes: interest in possession settlements; discretionary settlements; and accumulation and maintenance settlements.

The purpose of this chapter is to introduce each of the three types of settlement and to explore:

(a)   what can be achieved by using a settlement; and

(b)   the taxation cost to the settlor;

with the aim of enabling the selection of the appropriate type of settlement for a particular client.

This and the following three chapters are concerned with inter vivos creation of settlements. **Chapter 12** considers how to create settlements in wills and their tax effects.

5.2 Settlements creating interest in possession trusts

5.2.1 Introduction

An interest in possession has been defined as 'a present right to the present enjoyment' of income or assets: *Pearson and Others v Inland Revenue Commissioners* [1980] 2 All ER 479. Put more simply, it means the trustees have to pay the annual trust income to a beneficiary or allow the beneficiary to have the use of assets.

The simplest example of an interest in possession is a life interest.

Example

Adam gives £100 to trustees to hold on trust for Brenda for life with the remainder to Colin. Brenda has an interest in possession. She is entitled to all the income generated by the trust fund of £100. The trustees must pay that income to her.

The purpose of this type of settlement is to provide successive interests. There are various ways to achieve this.

(a)   The settlor may want to benefit several people, one after the other.

Example

Diana wants to benefit her son and daughter-in-law by giving them extra income. She also wants to benefit her grandson. She might set up a trust giving:

(i)   the income to her son for life; and on his death;

(ii)   the income to her daughter-in-law (if still living) for life; and on the death of the survivor of her son and daughter-in-law;

(iii)   the capital to the grandson absolutely.

(b)   The settlor may wish to give one person the right to income for a given time and then the capital to somebody else.

Example

Ernest wants to provide finance for his granddaughter while she studies to be an architect. He thinks she will need his support for about eight years but ultimately he wants all his money to go to his favourite charity.

He might set up a trust giving:

(i)   the income to his granddaughter for eight years or until she qualifies as an architect, whichever is the shorter period; and then

(ii)   the capital to the charity absolutely.

(c)   The settlor may want to stagger a beneficiary's entitlement to property.

Example

Fred wants to give a substantial sum of money to his grandson George who is 19. George is in urgent need of some money but Fred does not want him to receive everything immediately. Fred might set up a trust giving:

(i)   the income to George until he is 25 years of age; and then

(ii)   the capital to George absolutely.

Note 1: If the trustees have the power to decide whether or not to pay income to a beneficiary, it is not an interest in possession trust.

Note 2: Be aware of the fact that it is possible to create an interest in possession inadvertently by giving someone a present right to present enjoyment of the property.

Example

A gives a house to B but includes a condition that C is to be allowed to live in the house for the next five years. C has an interest in possession which will terminate at the end of the five-year period.

5.2.2   Taxation on creation of settlements with an interest in possession

5.2.2.1   Inheritance tax

The creation of such a settlement is a transfer of value by the settlor, which will be a PET in so far as not exempt (IHTA 1984, s 3A). Where a settlor dies within seven years of creating the settlement, the PET becomes chargeable. The tax is paid by the trustees from the settlement funds.

Example

Harriet sets up a trust for her brother for life with the remainder to her nephew. She transfers cash and shares valued at £341,000 to the settlement (PET). Harriet dies two years' later with assets of £130,000 which she leaves to charity (IHT exempt).

The death estate is exempt. However, the PET becomes chargeable (no taper relief as Harriet died within three years of the PET).

	£
Value transferred	341,000
Less: two annual exemptions	6,000
	335,000
IHT on the first £275,000 @ 0% =	nil
On the balance of £60,000 @ 40% =	24,000

The tax is due six months from the end of the month in which Harriet died and must be paid by the trustees from the trust fund, so reducing the present value of the trust fund by £24,000.

A settlor can avoid the fund being depleted by the tax if the transfer becomes chargeable by insuring his life for seven years and writing the policy in trust for the trustees of the settlement to receive as additional trust property on his death (see **Appendix 2 (16)** for term assurance).

Example

After creating the settlement in the previous example Harriet insures her life for £24,000 and writes the policy in trust for the settlement. The trustees will use the proceeds of the policy to pay the IHT due on the PET and so the value of the trust fund will not be reduced.

	£
On Harriet's death trustees receive £24,000 from the insurance policy	
Value of trust fund £341,000 + £24,000 =	365,000
Less: IHT as result of Harriet's death	24,000
Value of fund remains	341,000

There may be subsequent charges to IHT within the settlement if the interest in possession ends; for example, the person with the interest in possession dies or gives up the right to the income for any other reason (see **10.1**).

5.2.2.2 Capital gains tax

The transfer of property by a settlor to trustees is a disposal (TCGA 1992, s 70). If chargeable assets are settled, a chargeable gain (or allowable loss) may result. The gain (if any) will be the settlor's and he will bear the tax unless there is an agreement to the contrary.

Example

Ilyana (a 40% income taxpayer) settles her quoted shares worth £36,700 (acquired for £8,000) and cash of £30,000. She has made no other disposals in that tax year. The beneficiaries are her daughter for life with remainder to her grandchildren.

Calculate the CGT on the disposal.

Cash is exempt.

		£
Shares:	Market value at disposal	36,700
less:	acquisition cost	8,000
		28,700
less:	indexation allowance to April 1998 (say)	200
		28,500
less:	annual exemption	8,500
	Chargeable gain (or less, if taper relief is available)	20,000

CGT @ 40% on £20,000 = £8,000

Calculate the cost of the settlement to Ilyana.

	£
Value of shares	36,700
Cash	30,000
CGT	8,000
	74,700

The acquisition cost of the shares to the trustees for the purpose of any future capital gains on a disposal by them is £36,700.

If the settlor settles business property, the gain may be held over at the election of the settlor, unless it is a settlor-interested settlement (TCGA 1992, s 165 – see **4.4.5.2**). The effect is that the trustees take the business property at the settlor's acquisition cost (plus indexation, but not taper relief), and this becomes the trustee's acquisition cost for any subsequent disposal, ie, using the figures of the previous example, £8,000 + £200 = £8,200.

Once the settlement has been created, any sale of trust assets by the trustees (see **Chapter 14**) or a transfer of the trust fund, or part of it, to a beneficiary (see **10.1.4.2**) will be a disposal by the trustees giving rise to a CGT charge.

The creation of the settlement is also a PET for IHT purposes of £60,700 (ie, £30,000 plus £36,700 minus 2 × £3,000 annual exemptions). As a result of IHTA 1984, ss 5(4) and 164, the reduction in Illyana's estate caused by the payment of CGT (and any disposal costs involved in the transfer) are ignored for IHT purposes, ie, this reduction in value of the estate is not included when calculating the amount of IHT payable.

5.2.2.3 Income tax

The creation of a settlement should have no income tax consequences for the settlor (other than saving of income tax on any actual loss of income).

Trustees of an interest in possession settlement pay income tax at basic rate (22%). In many cases, they will receive only dividends which carry a tax credit of 10% and interest where lower rate tax (20%) is deducted at source. The credit and the lower rate deduction are each taken to satisfy the trustees' basic rate liability. As a result, no further income tax is payable by the trustees (see further **14.5.2**).

5.3 Settlements creating discretionary trusts

5.3.1 Introduction

Settlements creating discretionary trusts are settlements in which there is no interest in possession, ie, trusts where no beneficiary has a present right to the present enjoyment of income.

The settlor identifies the beneficiaries whom he wishes to benefit but leaves it to the trustees to select which of these beneficiaries is to benefit and how and when. Discretionary trusts are the most flexible type of settlement because the decision as to beneficial entitlement can be deferred and does not have to be determined at the time the trusts are created. The discretion is normally given over both the capital and income of the trust fund.

Example

Barry wishes to benefit his grandchildren, Cora, Doris and Edward. All three are under 5 years of age, and he does not know how they will develop and whether their needs will be the same. He settles £50,000 on discretionary trusts.

Twenty years later Cora has just qualified as a lawyer; Doris is a hairdresser and single parent; Edward is a bank clerk and physically disabled as a result of an accident several years ago. The trustees decide to distribute the money unevenly between the three beneficiaries.

5.3.2 Taxation on the creation of discretionary settlements

5.3.2.1 Inheritance tax

The lifetime charge (IHTA 1984, ss 1–3)

A transfer of property to a discretionary settlement is a lifetime chargeable transfer in so far as not exempt. It is, therefore, taxable at the time it is made. The rate of tax is one half of the death rate.

Example 1

John (who has no annual exemptions available) settles £75,000 on discretionary trusts.

IHT is charged @ 0% on £75,000 = nil

Example 2

Karen settles £331,000 on discretionary trusts on the basis that any IHT is paid out of the trust fund. She has made no previous transfers.

	£
Value transferred	331,000
Less: two annual exemptions	6,000
	325,000

IHT on the first £275,000 @ 0% = nil
On the balance of £50,000 @ 20% = £10,000.

The charge on the death of the settlor

If the settlor dies within seven years of making the transfer, IHT is recalculated at the death rates with credit being given for tax already paid.

Example 3

The facts are the same as Example 2 above but Karen dies 18 months later leaving her free estate to her husband.

IHT is payable on £325,000	£	
IHT on first £275,000 @ 0%	nil	
on balance £50,000 @ 40% =	20,000	
	20,000	
Less	10,000	(as per Example 2)
Additional IHT payable as a result of Karen's death (taper relief not available)	10,000	

Grossing up

In the above examples, it has been assumed that the tax will be paid by the trustees, ie, that the tax will be deducted from the amount going into the settlement. In Example 2, Karen's discretionary settlement will have an initial trust fund of £321,000 (£331,000 – £10,000) and in Example 3, Karen's death will reduce the fund by a further £10,000.

Where the settlor intends the settlement to retain the full amount of the transfer he must pay the IHT. Since IHT is calculated on the fall in value in the transferor's estate, tax will be charged on the value of the gift and on the IHT on the gift. This requires the transfer to be grossed up.

Example

Karen wants the full £331,000 to go into the discretionary trust. This is a net gift. IHT on the gross gift will be calculated as follows:

Step 1: Deduct available exemptions to find the value transferred,
ie; £331,000 – £6,000 = £325,000

Step 2: Gross up the value transferred at the appropriate tax rates:

Net	Gross equivalent
£275,000	£275,000
£50,000 × $\frac{100}{80}$	£62,500
	£337,500

The settlement receives £331,000 (ie, including the £6,000 covered by Karen's annual exemption).

The Revenue will receive IHT of £12,500 from Karen (£337,500 – £275,000 = £62,500 at 20%).

Any charge which arises as a result of Karen's death within seven years will be based on a value transferred of £337,500.

Subsequent events (IHTA 1984, ss 58–69)

Once the discretionary settlement has been created, there is a potential IHT charge on the trust fund every 10 years. There is also an 'exit' charge when any part of the capital of the trust fund is given to a beneficiary or an interest in possession arises (see **10.2.4**).

5.3.2.2 Capital gains tax (TCGA 1992, s 260)

The disposal of property by a settlor into a discretionary settlement is a chargeable event (unless cash is being settled). Hold-over relief is available on chargeable transfers:

(a)   irrespective of the nature of the asset being settled, therefore including land and quoted shares; and

(b)   even if the transfer is chargeable at 0%.

Example 1

Lesley settles on discretionary trusts her country cottage which she bought for £50,000 and is now worth £80,000. She has made no previous transfers.
IHT will be payable but at 0% because the £80,000 falls within Lesley's nil rate band.
CGT hold-over relief is available.

Example 2

Morris settles quoted shares purchased for £1,000 and now worth £6,000 on discretionary trusts. He has made no other transfers but has made chargeable gains this year of £8,500 on disposal of other assets.

The transfer to the discretionary settlement is a transfer of value but for IHT purposes the value transferred is nil because of Morris's unused annual exemptions.
CGT hold-over relief is available.

Only the settlor need make the hold-over election. Since 10 December 2003 hold-over relief is not available if the settlor or his spouse has an interest in the settlement (see **4.4.5.2**).

Sales by the trustees after the settlement has been created will be subject to CGT depending on the availability of the trustees' exemptions and reliefs. Transfers of capital from the trust fund to a beneficiary may also attract CGT, although hold-over relief may then be available, see **Chapter 10**.

5.3.2.3 Income tax

The usual rate of income tax on all trust income over £500 is a single flat rate of 40% (or 32.5% on dividends) (see **Chapter 14**).

5.4 Settlements creating accumulation and maintenance trusts

Settlements creating accumulation and maintenance (A & M) trusts can be set up only to benefit young people under the age of 25 years when the settlement is created. They are settlements without an interest in possession but, provided they comply with the rules in IHTA 1984, s 71, are afforded special IHT treatment (see **5.4.2.1**). If a settlement does not comply with s 71, it cannot be an A & M settlement.

5.4.1 The requirements

Section 71 lays down three requirements, all of which must be satisfied:

(a) One or more beneficiaries will, on or before attaining a specified age not exceeding 25, become beneficially entitled to, or to an interest in possession in, the settled property.

(b) No interest in possession subsists in the settled property and the income from it is to be accumulated so far as it is not applied for the maintenance, education, or benefit of such a beneficiary.

(c) Either:

    (i) not more than 25 years have elapsed since the day on which the settlement was made; or

    (ii) all the beneficiaries are grandchildren of a common grandparent, or are children, widows or widowers of such grandchildren who were themselves beneficiaries but died before becoming entitled as in (a) above.

Each of these requirements will be considered in turn.

5.4.1.1 At least one beneficiary will become entitled to the trust property, or an interest in possession in it, on or before his 25th birthday

This requirement gives the settlor a choice. He may give an entitlement to the capital of the trust fund on or before 25 years, or he may give an entitlement to income on or before that age.

Capital entitlement

A & M trusts create contingent benefits. In a simple settlement, a beneficiary will be entitled to the capital of the trust fund, or a portion of it, only if he reaches the specified age.

> **Example 1**
>
> £10,000 is settled on trust for Adam if he attains 18 years of age.
>
> If Adam reaches 18 years (ie, satisfies the contingency) the trustees must give him the £10,000.

If Adam dies, say aged 15 years, the trust will fail. The £10,000 will not form part of Adam's estate.

Example 2

Year 1: Property is settled for Brian (now aged 17) and Clare (now aged 15) if they attain 21 years of age, and if both reach 21, in equal shares.

Year 4: Brian attains 21 and he will receive half the trust fund.

Year 6: Clare is now 21 and receives the other half of the trust fund.

If Clare had died in Year 5, she would not have satisfied the contingency and neither she nor her estate would have any right to the trust fund. In those circumstances, Brian would receive the other half.

The requirement that a beneficiary 'will' become entitled does not require absolute certainty. It should be read as meaning 'will become entitled, if at all, at or before the age of 25'. Death can always prevent entitlement.

Section 71(4)(b) provides that tax will not be charged on the death of a beneficiary below the specified age. Therefore, the death of all the intended beneficiaries before the specified age does not prevent the settlement being an A & M settlement (see further *Inglewood (Lord) and Another v Inland Revenue Commissioners* [1983] STC 133).

The existence of powers which, if exercised, could result in property vesting beyond the age of 25 or being appointed to a non-beneficiary will, however, prevent a settlement having A & M status.

Income entitlement

On occasion, the settlor will not want the beneficiary to receive the capital of the trust fund on or before his 25th birthday but will want the contingency delayed to a later age, say 30. This need not be fatal to the settlement being an A & M settlement. Section 71 requires a beneficiary to become entitled to the settled property or 'an interest in possession in it' on or before 25 years.

A beneficiary has an interest in possession in a trust fund if he has a right to income from the fund.

Section 31 of TA 1925 provides that a minor beneficiary who is contingently entitled to capital of a fund nevertheless has the right to the income from that fund from his 18th birthday.

Example

Property is settled on trust for Dora if she attains the age of 30 years.

At first sight, this is not an A & M settlement because Dora will not acquire the capital of the fund until after she is 25. But, assuming s 31 of TA 1925 applies to the settlement, she will acquire the right to the income in the fund at the age of 18. As her interest in possession arises on or before 25, ie, at 18 years, this satisfies this part of s 71.

Trust draftsmen will often modify s 31 of TA 1925 or replace it with an express clause. In such circumstances, care must be taken to ensure that, if the right to capital is delayed beyond the age of 25, the right to income is given on or before the beneficiary's 25th birthday (see **Chapter 8**).

5.4.1.2 No beneficiary may have an interest in possession when the trust is created and any income not applied must be accumulated

As with the first requirement, there are two aspects, namely no interest in possession and the accumulation of income. Both are normally satisfied while the beneficiary is a minor by the effect of s 31 of TA 1925.

No interest in possession

Because of this requirement, if any beneficiary has an immediate right to the income from any portion of the trust fund, that portion of the fund will not be an A & M settlement.

Section 31 of TA 1925 applies to all settlements unless it is expressly excluded or overridden. Where s 31 applies, a beneficiary has no right to any of the income of the trust fund (ie, to an interest in possession) until he attains his 18th birthday.

Example 1

Property is settled on Ella and Francis contingent on their attaining the age of 25 years and, where both attain 25, in equal shares. Section 31 of the TA 1925 applies.

At the time the property is settled, Ella is 9 and Francis 4. As a result, neither is entitled to the income until 18 years of age. Therefore, this part of s 71 of the IHTA 1984 is satisfied.

Example 2

Property is settled on Gina (aged 22) contingent on her attaining the age of 30. Section 31 of TA 1925 applies to the settlement.

Section 31 gives Gina an immediate right to the income from the trust fund and so prevents this being an A & M settlement. (It is an interest in possession settlement whereby Gina is to receive the income until she is 30 and then the capital absolutely (see **5.2**).)

Example 3

Property is settled on Harry (aged 19) to receive both the capital and income contingent on his reaching 25 years of age (ie, s 31 of TA 1925 has been suitably modified). This requirement of s 71 of IHTA 1984 is satisfied.

Example 4

Property is settled on Ian (aged 21) and Susan (aged 17) contingently on their attaining 25 years of age. Section 31 of TA 1925 applies. Section 71 of IHTA 1984 is satisfied so far as Susan is concerned but not Ian. There is an A & M settlement for Susan (if all the other conditions are also satisfied). Ian has an interest in possession in one half of the settled property.

Accumulation

Section 71 of IHTA 1984 provides that the income of the trust fund is to be accumulated so far as not applied for the maintenance, education or benefit of a beneficiary.

Section 31 of TA 1925 gives trustees the power to apply income for the maintenance education or benefit of a minor beneficiary and requires them to accumulate the balance of the income.

Example

Property is settled on Keelash (aged 9) contingent on her attaining the age of 18 years. Section 31 of TA 1925 applies. Every year the trustees apply some of the trust income towards Keelash's education and her annual holiday and accumulate the balance. Section 71 is not breached.

5.4.1.3   **The trust must not last for more than 25 years or all the beneficiaries must have a common grandparent (or be the children, widows or widowers of such beneficiaries)**

Where the beneficiaries do not share a common grandparent, the settlement can only have A & M status for 25 years. If it continues as a settlement after the expiry of 25 years, a charge to IHT may then arise (see **10.3.2.1**).

The grandparent must be common to all the beneficiaries but need not have any blood tie to the settlor.

This requirement is designed to prevent more than one generation from benefiting from A & M status. Even so, a second generation can benefit in some cases as the provisions permit substitution where an original beneficiary has died.

5.4.2   Taxation on the creation of an A & M settlement

5.4.2.1   Inheritance tax (IHTA 1984, s 3A)

The creation of an A & M settlement is a PET (insofar as not covered by an exemption) by the settlor. If the settlor dies within seven years, any tax will be paid from the trust fund.

Therefore, if the amount being settled exceeds the settlor's nil rate band (after deducting all available reliefs and exemptions) consideration should be given to insurance. The insurance can be effected either by the settlor insuring his own life and writing the insurance policy in trust for the settlement or by the trustees of the settlement insuring the settlor's life (see **5.2.2.1**).

Subsequent events (IHTA 1984, s 71(4))

The main advantage of an A & M settlement over other settlements without an interest in possession (eg, discretionary settlements) is its IHT treatment.

Apart from the potential charge on creation, there should be no IHT charges levied on an A & M settlement either during its life or on its termination (see further **Chapter 10** and **12.6.2**, where an A & M settlement is created by will).

5.4.2.2   Capital gains tax

The transfer of property by a settlor to an A & M settlement is a chargeable event for CGT purposes. CGT is calculated in the normal way and paid by the settlor. Consideration could be given to settling cash thereby avoiding CGT or, where appropriate, assets such as business property which attract hold-over relief (TCGA 1992, s 165). Hold-over relief under TCGA 1992, s 260 is not available since a PET (not a chargeable transfer) occurs when the settlement is created (see **4.4.5.2**).

Subsequent dealings with the trust property, such as sales or distributions to beneficiaries, may attract a charge to CGT (see **Chapter 10**).

5.5   Further tax implications of creating settlements

Any settlor who is thinking of creating a settlement should consider the overall tax position, before and after its creation, both for himself and for the settlement. Tax should not be the only reason for creating a settlement but it will always be one of the most important factors. The type of settlement which is chosen may be governed by its particular tax treatment.

5.5.1 Inheritance tax

A settlor who is proposing to make more than one lifetime settlement must be aware of the cumulative effect of IHT on his second (and subsequent) settlements as well.

5.5.1.1 Cumulation

Because of the way cumulation works, a tax payer who makes a lifetime chargeable transfer (eg, settles property on discretionary trusts) has to survive for 14 years before it ceases to have any impact.

Example

Year 1:   Jake settles £200,000 on discretionary trusts.

Year 5:   Jake makes a gift of £75,000 to his sister Susan.

Year 6:   Jake settles £200,000 on A & M trusts for his grandchildren.

Year 9:   Jake dies.

Ignore annual exemptions.

Step 1:

The discretionary settlement was an immediately lifetime chargeable transfer (LCT) made more than seven years before death and so no further tax is due on it. However, as we shall we, it remains relevant to the calculation of IHT on the transfers in Years 5 and 6.

Step 2:

The gift in Year 5 was made less than seven years before death and so the PET becomes chargeable. Look back seven years from that transfer to see if there are any chargeable transfers. If so they must be cumulated. The existence of the Year 1 LCT reduces the nil rate band available when calculating IHT on the Year 5 transfer.

	£	£
Transfer – PET now chargeable		75,000
Cumulative total – LCT	200,000	
Nil rate band (part)	200,000	
Nil rate band (balance)		75,000
		nil

IHT on failed PET – nil

Step 3:

The A & M settlement in Year 6 was a PET when made but has also become chargeable. It must be cumulated with all chargeable transfers made in the preceding seven years. In this case, the cumulative total of chargeable transfers is £275,000 (the Year 1 LCT and the Year 5 PET which is now treated as chargeable) and so exhausts the nil rate band.

	£	£
A & M – PET now chargeable		200,000
Cumulative total – the failed PET and the LCT	275,000	
Nil rate band	275,000	
Nil rate band (balance)		nil
		200,000

IHT on £200,000 @ 40% payable by the trustees. Taper relief is available only if three years have elapsed since the creation of the A & M settlement.

Step 4:

Jake's estate on death is cumulated with chargeable transfers made in the previous seven years, ie, the gift in Year 5 and the A & M settlement in Year 6 which are now treated as chargeable. As these together give a cumulative total of chargeable transfers of £275,000, Jake's estate is prima facie taxable at 40%. The LCT to the discretionary settlement was made more than seven years ago and drops out of cumulation of the death estate.

5.5.1.2   Order of gifts and same day transfers (IHTA 1984, ss 62, 66 and 68)

As we saw at **4.6.2**, where a client is proposing to create a discretionary settlement and to make a PET, there is an advantage to the later taxation of the settlement in making the discretionary settlement before the PET. If the PET comes first and later becomes chargeable, it will be taken into account when calculating IHT payable by the trustees during the lifetime of the discretionary settlement.

5.5.2   Capital gains tax

5.5.2.1   Anti-avoidance

If either the settlor or his spouse has an 'interest in the settlement', CGT is payable by the settlor on any gain by treating it as the top slice of his income, ie, it is taxed at his income tax rates – see **6.2.11.2**. (Note that it is likely that a civil partner will be treated in the same way as a spouse for these purposes.)

5.5.2.2   Other settlements

From 6 April 2004, CGT on any gains made on disposals by trustees is paid at 40% (subject to taper relief). (Between 6 April 1998 and 5 April 2004 the rate was 34%, and for earlier years the rate depended on the type of settlement.)

Trustees have an annual exemption of half that available to an individual, ie, £4,250 per annum. Where a settlor has created more than one settlement, the annual exemption is divided between them.

Example

Albert creates two separate settlements. Each settlement will have an annual exemption of £2,125 (£4,250 ÷ 2).

There is, however, a minimum exemption per settlement of £850.

5.5.3   Summary

Tax on creation of settlements

	IHT	CGT
Interest in possession	PET	Disposal – only TCGA 1992, s 165 hold-over relief
Discretionary	20% rate (subject to nil rate band)	Disposal – hold-over relief available (TCGA 1992, s 260 and s 165)
Accumulation and maintenance	PET	Disposal – only TCGA 1992, s 165 hold-over relief

Chapter 6

Drafting Settlements: Some Common Points

6.1 Introduction

This chapter and the following two chapters concentrate on the drafting of settlements containing discretionary and A & M trusts.

As each client is unique, the available 'standard' precedents may not be appropriate for that client's requirements. In modifying an existing deed or drafting from scratch, settlement drafters must be aware of the effect of every clause included and the effect of excluding a particular clause. In addition, they should aim for a consistency of style and not use both 'modern' and 'traditional' styles in the same trust instrument.

The basic structure of each settlement differs very little, as the following comparative example shows. The clauses shown do not provide a definitive list of what can or should be included in a settlement but are the most important types of basic clauses. The main differences between the two settlements are the trusts of the beneficial interests, as the purposes of discretionary and A & M settlements are different. The drafting of the trusts of the beneficial interests is considered in **Chapters 7** and **8**. Additional powers required by trustees and their use are examined in **Chapters 9** and **10**. The administrative provisions are discussed in **Chapter 14** but are broadly similar to those in will drafting. These and other provisions are often placed in Schedules.

Discretionary settlement	*Accumulation and maintenance settlement*
Date	Date
Parties	Parties
Recitals	Recitals
Definitions	Definitions
Perpetuity period	Perpetuity period
Accumulation period	Accumulation period
Trust (for sale)	Trust (for sale)
Trusts of the beneficial interests	Trusts of the beneficial interests
Trustee powers over the beneficial interests	Trustee powers over the beneficial interests
Administrative provisions	Administrative provisions Restrictions on trustee's powers, so as not to take the settlement outside IHTA 1984, s 71
Appointment of new trustees	Appointment of new trustees
Exclusion of TLATA 1996, ss 11, 12 and 19	Exclusion of TLATA 1996, ss 11, 12 and 19
Exclusion of settlor and spouse	Exclusion of settlor and spouse
Schedules	Schedules
Signatures	Signatures

6.2   Drafting common clauses

6.2.1   The date and opening words

It is usual for the date on which the settlement was made to be set out at the beginning of the trust instrument. In modern style settlements, this may be preceded by a table of contents (see **6.2.4.1**). The date may be important for subsequent time-limits and the chronology of events where a settlor has made more than one settlement. Some settlements are known by titles which include their dates, for example, 'Mrs Brown's Grandchildren Settlement of 4 April 1990'.

Sample clause

> This Settlement is made the   day of   Two thousand and

6.2.2   Parties

The settlor and the initial trustees must be clearly identified. How this and the opening words are set out will also determine the style for the rest of the document, ie, is it to be modern (Clauses 1 and 2) or traditional (Clause 3)?

Sample clause 1

> BETWEEN
> (1)   DAVID SMITH of [address] ('the Settlor')
> (2)   TONY TUBBS of [address] and TOM THOMAS of [address] ('the Trustees') which expression shall where the context admits include the trustee or trustees for the time being of this Settlement

Sample clause 2

> PARTIES:
> (1) [   ] (the 'Settlor'); and
> (2) [   ] (the 'Trustees').

Sample clause 3

> Between DAVID SMITH of [address] (hereinafter called 'the Settlor') of the one part and TONY TUBBS of [address] and TOM THOMAS of [address] (hereinafter called 'the Trustees' which expression shall where the context so admits include the trustee or trustees for the time being of the Settlement) of the other part

The definition of the trustees may instead come later in a clause which collects together all definitions used in the settlement.

6.2.3   Recitals

Recitals appear immediately after the parties and in traditional style settlements are introduced by the word 'Whereas'. The numbers or letters to the recital clauses are normally placed in brackets which distinguishes them from 'operative' clauses, ie, the clauses declaring the beneficial interests.

Recitals explain the background to the settlement: why it has been created and the settlor's intentions.

A declaration that the settlement is to be irrevocable means that the settlor cannot subsequently change his mind about having created the settlement and demand his money or property back from the trustees. Whilst revocable settlements are possible, they are uncommon because of their unfavourable tax treatment. Where there is a power to revoke the trusts, the result is that the fund may revert to the settlor or his spouse (see **6.2.10**).

Sample clause

Whereas

(1)   The Settlor wishes to make this Settlement and has transferred or delivered to the Trustees the property specified in the Schedule

(2)   It is intended that this Settlement shall be irrevocable.

6.2.4   Table of contents, clause headings, definitions and Schedules

6.2.4.1   Table of contents

Because settlements are often long and complex, modern precedents generally start by setting out in a table of contents the constituent parts of the settlement, showing the operative parts separately from the administrative provisions. Whilst this simplifies the use of the settlement, it is important that a further clause ensures that the use of the table does not affect its meaning (see **6.2.4.2**).

6.2.4.2   Clause headings

Some draftsmen like to give each clause a heading as this enables a person who is reading the trust instrument to see quickly and clearly what each clause concerns. This can be particularly useful once the settlement is in use. For example, a trustee may want to know what powers of investment the trustees have. Rather than having to read every clause until he finds the investment clause he need only look at the clause headings to identify the one he needs to study. It is a matter of personal preference as to whether or not clause headings are used but they should either be used for every clause, or not at all. Where headings are used, it should be made clear by an additional clause that they are only for administrative convenience, ie, they do not affect the construction of the trust instrument.

Sample clause

Clause headings

The clause headings are included for reference only and do not affect the interpretation of this Settlement

6.2.4.3   Definitions

Many descriptions and phrases will need to be repeated, often several times, in drafting a settlement. It is, therefore, convenient to give these descriptions and phrases a 'name' by which they can be identified throughout the trust deed.

Example

Adam is settling a house, some cash and several holdings of quoted shares on discretionary trusts.

Reference needs to be made to these assets being held on trust, being available for distribution, being invested and so forth.

Unless a 'name' is used, each time reference is made to them the trust deed will have to read: 'The Trustees shall hold the freehold house known as [address], £x cash, 500 shares in A plc etc upon trust …'.

It is much neater and simpler to call the combined assets 'the Trust Fund' so that the clause would read: 'The Trustees shall hold the Trust Fund upon trust …'.

It is good practice to give the first letter of the 'names' a capital letter to indicate to the reader that they are definitions.

There is a choice of where to record the definitions of the 'names'.

(a)   Definitions can be dealt with as and when they arise in the body of the deed, for example:

> The Trustees shall hold the Trust Fund upon trust for such of them, David, Sue and Charles (hereinafter together called 'the Beneficiaries') as shall attain 18 years of age and if more than one in equal shares

> The problem with this approach is finding the definition when subsequently using the trust instrument. For example, Brenda is a trustee of an A & M settlement. She wants to know if the trustees have a power to apply income for the maintenance of a particular beneficiary. A glance through the clause headings shows her that she needs to study clause 18. In reading this clause, she comes across the expression 'the Accumulation Period'. She has no idea what it means and will have to read all the preceding clauses until she finds where the expression was used for the first time.

(b)   Definitions can be contained in a Schedule to the deed. A person reading the trust instrument who comes across a 'name' such as 'the Beneficiary' will know to turn to the Schedule whenever he meets a 'name'.

(c)   All the definitions can be set out in clause 1 of the trust instrument. This is common practice in modern style settlements.

Sample clause

(1)   Definitions

In this deed where the context so admits

(a)   'the Trust Fund' shall mean ...

(b)   'the Beneficiaries' shall mean ...

6.2.4.4   Schedules

Schedules can serve a useful purpose in keeping the various parts of the settlement deed separate. Most settlements will contain at least one Schedule and some draftsmen like to consign everything but the clauses directly related to the trusts of the beneficial interests to Schedules.

Example

The 1st Schedule:	definitions
The 2nd Schedule:	details of the trust property
The 3rd Schedule:	the necessary administrative provisions
The 4th Schedule:	miscellaneous clauses, etc

6.2.5   The trust fund

The settlement needs some property to be the subject-matter of the trusts from the outset. The settlor may add to the original trust property from time to time and other people may also transfer property to the settlement. All the trust property will be defined as the 'trust fund' and will be set out in detail in a Schedule.

When property is transferred from the settlor to the trustees, the correct mode of transfer must be used or the transfer will be ineffective. For example, shares must be transferred by signed stock transfer form and land by deed.

6.2.6   Trust or trust for sale?

Before TLATA 1996, it was usual practice for the trustees of lifetime settlements to hold property on an express trust for sale. This ensured that a strict settlement under SLA 1925 could not arise where land was settled property. TLATA 1996 prevents any new strict settlements being created after 31 December 1996 but does not prevent the continued use of a trust for sale. Such use is likely to continue only where the settlor wishes the trustees to be under a duty to sell. If, instead, a power of sale is considered sufficient, the trustees will be directed to hold the settled property 'on trust' and will be given power of sale in the administrative provisions of the settlement. This approach is already adopted in some modern style settlements drafted before TLATA 1996 was enacted.

If a trust for sale is used, it has five constituent parts as shown in the sample clause.

Extracts from sample clause – trust for sale

(1)   The Trustees shall hold the Trust Fund upon trust as to investments or property other than money in their absolute discretion to sell, call in or convert into money all or any of such investments or property

(2)   But with power to postpone such sale, calling in or conversion

(3)   To permit the same to remain as invested

(4)   Upon trust as to money with the like discretion to invest the same in their names or under their control in any of the investments authorised by this Settlement or by law

(5)   With power at the like discretion from time to time to vary or transpose any such investments for others so authorised

6.2.7   Perpetuity – the trust period

6.2.7.1   No perpetual trusts

English law does not allow a private trust (as opposed to a charitable trust) to be perpetual. It must come to an end and the capital vest in a beneficiary within a limited period of time. The time from the creation of the settlement to the moment when the capital must vest is called 'the perpetuity period'.

6.2.7.2   Selection of a perpetuity period

The settlor chooses the perpetuity period which is to apply to his settlement. It will be defined in the trust instrument as 'the trust period'. There is a common law period which is a life in being plus 21 years, but today most settlors and their professional advisers use the Perpetuities and Accumulations Act 1964 (PAA 1964) and adopt a fixed period of anything up to 80 years. The trust investment must state expressly that it selects a particular number of years as the perpetuity period. If no mention of a perpetuity period is made in the trust instrument, the common law rules apply.

Sample clause – the trust period

> The trust period shall mean the period ending on the last day of the period of 80 years from the date of this Settlement which period shall be the applicable perpetuity period.

6.2.7.3   Property must vest 'in interest'

Property does not have to vest *in possession* provided it has vested *in interest* by the end of the perpetuity period.

Example 1

Property is settled on Agnes for life with the remainder to Bert. Agnes has an immediate interest in possession (ie, the right to the income) and Bert is guaranteed the capital although the actual receipt of the capital will be delayed until Agnes dies.

Agnes's interest is vested in possession. Bert's interest is vested in interest.

You will not need to consider the perpetuity rules as the interests are already vested.

Example 2

Property is settled on Connie for life with the remainder to the first child of David to attain 25 years of age.

At the time the settlement is created, David has no children, but shortly afterwards he has one child, Edward. Edward will become entitled to the settled property only if he reaches 25. Until then his interest is contingent. Connie's interest is vested in possession. Here it is necessary to consider the perpetuity rules.

At common law, in order for a trust to be valid there must be no possibility of the interest vesting outside the perpetuity period. Depending on the perpetuity period selected, there is a possibility on these facts that the interest will vest outside the period.

In this example, if no statutory perpetuity period is selected, the perpetuity period is a life in being plus 21 years. Connie and David are both lives in being. Suppose both die one year after the creation of the settlement. Edward would reach 25 more than 21 years after the end of the perpetuity period. Prima facie the trust would be void (although the age reduction provisions in the PAA 1964 would save it).

The perpetuity period is, therefore, relevant when looking at A & M settlements where the gifts to children are contingent upon them reaching a specified age as in the previous example.

The perpetuity period also applies to discretionary settlements. Trustees select the beneficiary from within a class of beneficiaries and decide how much of the trust property to give that beneficiary. They must exhaust the trust fund, ie, give a vested interest in the trust property, within the perpetuity period. A failure to do so will render void the trusts over any remaining property.

Example

£10,000 is settled on discretionary trusts for the children of X.

There are three children: Rose, Arthur and Kate. The stated perpetuity period is 10 years.

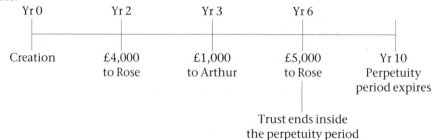

6.2.8 Accumulations

6.2.8.1 Meaning of accumulations

Discretionary and A & M settlements are settlements without an interest in possession. However, the fact that no beneficiary has a right to the trust income does not mean that the trust property is not earning income. Where income is not being paid out to a beneficiary, it is retained by the trustees within the trust. Such retained income is said to be 'an accumulation'.

6.2.8.2   Accumulation periods

There is a limit to the number of years during which income can be accumulated. PAA 1964 sets out a choice of maximum periods for which income can be accumulated. Most trust draftsmen specify that income can be accumulated for a fixed period of 21 years from the date of the settlement. Although this period is possibly shorter than PAA 1964 would allow, a fixed period provides for certainty. The specified accumulation period must not exceed the perpetuity period applicable to the settlement. At the end of the accumulation period, all income arising in each future year must be paid out to the beneficiaries unless the beneficiary is a minor (see **6.2.8.3**).

Example

Property is settled on discretionary trusts for the benefit of Susan, John and Harry. The accumulation period is 21 years. The trust income is £300 per annum.

		Susan	John	Harry	Accumulated
Accumulation period	Yr 1	100	–	–	200
	Yr 7	–	300	–	–
	Yr 8	100	100	100	–
	Yr 15	–	–	–	300
After accumulation period ends	Yr 22	100	200	–	–
	Yr 23	100	100	100	–
	Yr 24	150	–	150	–

There is a government proposal to introduce a statutory accumulation period of 125 years. At the time of writing, there is no date fixed for the introduction.

6.2.8.3   Extension of accumulation period under Trustee Act 1925, s 31

Where a beneficiary is a minor at the end of the accumulation period and s 31 of TA 1925 applies to the trust, the trustees can continue to accumulate the income of the minor's share of the trust fund until he is 18 years of age.

Example

Three brothers were the beneficiaries of a discretionary settlement. The two older boys both died leaving Adam (aged 16) the only beneficiary. The settlement's accumulation period has just ended. The trustees may accumulate income for a further two years.

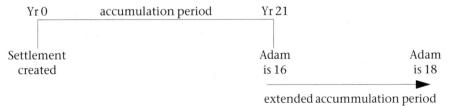

Sample clause

The Accumulation Period shall mean the period of twenty-one years from the date of this Settlement or the Trust Period if shorter

As in **6.2.7**, the trust period means the perpetuity period applicable to the settlement.

6.2.9   Appointment of new trustees

If a new trustee needs to be appointed because, for example, one of the original trustees has died or wishes to retire, in the absence of anything to the contrary in the trust instrument, the choice and appointment rests with the continuing trustee(s) under TA 1925, s 36.

A settlor who wishes to continue to exercise sole control over the selection of trustees during his lifetime can do so only if the trust instrument gives him the appropriate power (see **14.4.2**).

Sample clause

> During the lifetime of the Settlor the power of appointing new trustees shall be vested in the Settlor

6.2.10   Excluding the effect of TLATA 1996, ss 11, 12 and 19

6.2.10.1   Consultation

Under TLATA 1996, s 11(1) the trustees of a trust of land who are exercising any function relating to the land subject to the trust must consult any beneficiary who is of full age and beneficially entitled to an interest in possession (eg, a co-owner) and, so far as consistent with 'the general interest of the trust', give effect to the wishes of the beneficiary or (in the case of dispute) the majority (according to the value of their combined assets).

Section 11 will not apply if there is a provision to that effect in the trust instrument (s 11(2)). If appropriate, a declaration excluding the s 11 requirement for consultation can be included in the settlement. It is common to include such a declaration.

Sample clause

> The provisions of section 11 of the Trusts of Land and Appointment of Trustees Act 1996 shall not apply so that it shall not be necessary for my Trustees to consult any Beneficiaries before carrying out any function relating to land or for the avoidance of doubt any other property.

6.2.10.2   Occupation of land by beneficiaries

Section 12 gives a beneficiary who is entitled to an interest in possession (eg, a co-owner) in land, even if not of full age, a right to occupy the land in certain circumstances.

In order to have this right of occupation, a beneficiary must establish either that the purposes of the trust include making the land available for his occupation or that the land is held by trustees so as to be so available.

The trustees have the right to impose conditions on an occupying beneficiary (eg, the payment of outgoings or expenses in respect of the land (s 13)). These conditions may include making payments by way of compensation to a beneficiary whose entitlement has been restricted.

A settlor cannot exclude ss 12 and 13. However, where a settlor does not wish beneficiaries to have a right to occupy, he can include a declaration that the purposes of the trust do not include making land available for occupation.

Sample clause

> The purposes of the trust in clause [   ] do not include making land available for occupation of any Beneficiary.

6.2.10.3 Right to direct retirement and appointment of replacement trustees

TLATA 1996, s 19 (unless expressly excluded by the trust instrument) gives beneficiaries who are *sui juris* and entitled to the whole beneficial interest the right to direct trustees to retire and appoint specified replacement trustees (see **14.4.2**).

Settlors can exclude the s 19 right but beneficiaries who are *sui juris* are entitled to the whole beneficial interest would still be able to remove the trustees by bringing the trust to an end and then resettling the trust property with different trustees. Ending the trust would be likely to involve a charge to CGT as it will be a disposal. It is likely to be preferable in most cases, therefore, to allow beneficiaries to retain the s 19 right. However there may be settlors who wish to exclude it.

Sample clause

> Section 19(2)(a) of the Trusts of Land and Appointment of Trustees Act 1996 shall not apply to this trust.

6.2.11 Exclusion of settlor (and spouse)

To prevent settlors using settlements to obtain an unfair tax advantage for themselves, there are a number of anti-avoidance provisions in the tax legislation. Broadly, for each of the three main taxes, these provisions require that neither the settlor nor his spouse has 'an interest in the settlement'. The phrase is directly relevant to income tax and CGT; for IHT the 'reservation of benefit' provisions discussed at **4.6.5** are relevant. (Note that it is likely that a civil partner will be treated as a spouse for these tax purposes.)

6.2.11.1 The general income tax avoidance rules (ITTOIA 2005)

These complex, wide-ranging provisions are intended to prevent a higher rate tax payer from avoiding income tax on income by transferring the property which produces it to another person, who either pays no income tax or pays at a rate lower than the transferor.

The rules apply to 'settlements'. These are defined very widely (ITTOIA 2005, s 620) to include 'any disposition, trust, covenant, agreement, arrangement or transfer of assets'. Thus, although they can in theory apply to any type of settlement, they are effectively restricted to two main areas. They apply to settlements where the settlor retains an interest in the settled property (s 624) and they apply specifically to settlements by parents for the benefit of their minor unmarried children (s 629 is discussed at **4.6.2.3** and **4.6.4.1**).

Under s 624 the income of settled property 'is treated . . . as the income of the settlor and of the settlor alone if it arises . . . from property in which the settlor has an interest'. Section 625 states that a settlor is treated as having an interest in settled property if there are any circumstances in which the settled property is or may become payable to or applicable for the benefit of the settlor or the settlor's spouse.

Typically (but not exclusively), s 624 will apply where:

(a)   the settled property will revert to the settlor, for example, where the property is settled on A for life the remainder to the settlor. Such a settlement might be considered if a settlor wished to provide an elderly relative with an income but at the same time wanted to ensure return of the settled property when the relative died;

(b)   the settlement contains a power of revocation whereupon the settled property would revert to the settlor or his spouse;

(c)   the settlement contains a discretionary power to benefit the settlor or his spouse, ie, they are among the objects of the trustees' discretion.

Example

Thomas creates a discretionary settlement during his lifetime under which he and his wife Agatha may benefit because they are included in the class of beneficiaries, ie, they are among the objects of the trust. Even if neither Thomas nor Agatha actually benefits, for example because the trustees of the settlement accumulate the income or apply all of it for other beneficiaries, all of the income of the settled property will be taxed as though it belonged to Thomas.

Where the rules apply, the income of the property in the settlement is 'treated' as belonging to the settlor for all income tax purposes, although generally he can recover from the trustees any tax he has to pay on the income. If the settlor is a higher rate tax payer, the plan to save tax through using the settlement will not be achieved. Although the rules treat the income in a particular way for income tax purposes, they do not affect the entitlement of the settlement trustees to receive the income and to use it for the beneficiaries.

6.2.11.2   CGT where the settlor has an interest in the settlement

Where the settlor and the trustees are UK resident or ordinarily resident, anti-avoidance provisions (TCGA 1992, ss 77 and 78) similar to the income tax provisions (see above) prevent a settlor who would otherwise pay CGT at 40% from using the settlement to realise his gains and pay tax at a relatively lower rate. These provisions apply where the settlor or his spouse has an 'interest in the settlement' and are widely defined. They apply, inter alia, 'if the settled property or its income will or may become applicable for the benefit of the settlor or his spouse'. In such cases, all gains are deemed made by the settlor and not by the trustees. The settlor, and not the trustees, must therefore pay tax on the settlement gains at the rate appropriate to the settlor, ie, 20% or 40% depending on his income tax position. As in the case of income tax, there is a right of reimbursement from the trustees for any CGT paid by the settlor.

Since 10 December 2003 the settlor cannot claim hold-over relief under TCGA 1992, ss 165 or 260 on a transfer into a settlement in which he or his spouse is interested (see **4.4.5.2**).

6.2.11.3   Reservation of benefit and IHT

Although the phrase 'an interest in the settlement' is not found in Finance Act 1986, s 102, none the less the concept lies behind the reservation of benefit provisions. These have been discussed at **4.6.5**. If settled property is subject to reservation of benefit for the settlor, s 102 will apply with the result that the property is still within the settlor's estate for IHT. Note that the rules apply only where the settlor derives a benefit. They do not apply if the settlor's spouse benefits.

6.2.11.4   Drafting the settlement

Where a settlor could or might benefit from income or capital the settlement is ineffective for tax purposes, ie, the trust property is still taxed for income tax, CGT and IHT, as if it still belongs to the settlor. It is therefore essential that a settlor has no interest in the trust property. Because of the wording of the anti-avoidance provisions, the settlor's spouse must also be excluded from benefiting although it is permissible for a widow or widower of the settlor to be included as a beneficiary.

So as not to fall foul of these provisions, a discretionary settlement will normally contain two references to the exclusion of the settlor and spouse; the first, in relation to the power to add new beneficiaries and the second in relation to the exercise of the administrative powers (see **Appendix 4**, clauses 3(3) and 15). Only the general exclusion in exercise of the administrative powers appears in an accumulation and maintenance settlement (see **Appendix 5**, clause 14) since a power to add beneficiaries is inappropriate to such settlements.

A settlor or his spouse does not have to be named as a beneficiary to be deemed to have an interest in the settlement. If the trust property will, or might, revert to the settlor at the end of the trust period he has an interest in the settlement.

The trust instrument may give the trustees very wide powers and discretions over the trust fund (see **Chapter 9**). For example, if the trustees can use their powers to benefit the settlor or his spouse, even though the power is never used, the settlor is deemed to have an interest in the trust property.

In drafting a settlement, therefore, it is essential to ensure that the beneficial interests are fully disposed of and that in no circumstances can the settlor or his spouse be said to have an interest in the settlement – see **7.4** and **8.4**. In addition, a clause should be included in the settlement deed to the effect that the settlor and his spouse cannot and must not benefit from the trust. This clause serves as a prohibition against trustees ever exercising a trust power in favour of the settlor or his spouse.

Sample clause

> No discretion or power conferred on the Trustees by this Settlement or by law shall be exercised and no provision in the Settlement shall operate, directly or indirectly so as to cause or permit any part of the capital or income of the Trust Fund to become in any way payable to or applicable for the benefit of the Settlor or the spouse of the Settlor

Assuming that a civil partner of a settlor will be treated as a spouse for tax purposes, it will be necessary to exclude a civil partner of the settlor from benefiting. This could be done by indicating in the definitions provisions of the settlement document that the word 'spouse' will be taken to include a civil partner.

6.2.12 Stamp duty

It is not uncommon for a settlor to transfer shares into a settlement. Where shares are transferred for no consideration, the document transferring them is exempt from stamp duty if the transaction falls within the Schedule to the Stamp Duty (Exempt Instruments) Regulations 1987 (SI 1987/516) (see **4.9**). If, very unusually, the settlement deed is the document making the transfer of shares to the trustees, it should contain a certificate that the transaction does come within these regulations.

Sample clause

> It is hereby certified that this instrument falls within Category L in the Schedule to the Stamp Duty (Exempt Instrument) Regulations 1987

However, it is much more likely that the transfer to the trustees will be by separate stock transfer form, and it is this document that should contain this certificate.

If land is transferred to the trustees the transferor must provide a separate certificate to the effect that a stamp duty land tax return is not required.

6.2.13   Signatures

A trust instrument is a deed and must be signed as such by the settlor, and by the trustees as well to show their acceptance of the trusts. One witness is required to each signature.

Sample clause

> Signed as a deed and delivered
> by [name of Settlor]
> in the presence of

Chapter 7

Drafting Discretionary Trusts

7.1 Introduction

The aim of this chapter is to introduce drafting of the clauses which ensure that the settlement creates discretionary trusts. It should be read in conjunction with **Chapters 5** and **6**.

The settlement deed will begin with the identification of trustees, recitals and, if used, a definitions clause. The perpetuity period will normally be stated as being 80 years and the accumulation period 21 years from the date of the settlement. The settlement will also require trustee powers.

7.2 Beneficiaries

The major requirement of the definition of 'beneficiaries' is that it provides certainty, ie, that the trustees can clearly identify who is within the class of beneficiaries. This may be achieved by naming the beneficiaries. However, this is not possible if the identity of potential beneficiaries is not yet known, for example, unborn children or the spouses of people who have not yet married. In such circumstances, the beneficiary must be identified by description.

Sample clause

'The Beneficiaries' shall mean the following persons (whether now in existence or who come into existence during the Trust Period)

(a) the Settlor's children and remoter issue and the spouses' widows and widowers (but not such widows or widowers as have remarried) of such children and remoter issue

Example

Aisha created a settlement with a trust period of 80 years and the above clause 20 years ago. When she set up the trusts, she had three adult children, Ben, Cora and Deirdre, and one grandson, Edwin. The trustees wish to know who are the current beneficiaries.

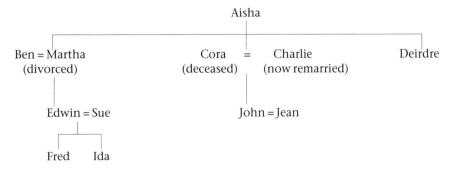

The beneficiaries are:

(a)   Ben, Deirdre, Edwin, John, Fred and Ida because they are the issue of the settlor; and

(b)   Sue and Jean because they are the spouses of the settlor's issue.

Martha and Charlie have been within the class of beneficiaries, but are now excluded. Martha's divorce from Ben means she is no longer his spouse; although Charlie was the spouse and then widower of the settlor's child, he has remarried.

If a person who was within the class of beneficiaries is subsequently excluded, because of a change in status, he does not have to pay back to the settlement any previous benefit he may have received from it.

Example

The facts are the same as in the previous example. After Cora's death the trustees gave Charlie £5,000. Charlie remarried two years later. He does not have to repay the £5,000 but cannot receive anything more from the settlement.

7.3   The discretionary trusts

The discretionary trusts apply to both income and capital of the trust fund. There are separate clauses for each. The component parts of these clauses are discussed at **7.3.1** and **7.3.2**. A full precedent of the clauses is found in **Appendix 4**.

7.3.1   Discretionary trusts of income

7.3.1.1   The primary trust

The primary trust enables the trustees to decide how to distribute the income of the trust fund amongst the beneficiaries.

Sample clause

> The Trustees shall pay or apply the income of the Trust Fund to or for the benefit of such of the Beneficiaries as shall for the time being be in existence, in such shares and in such manner generally as the Trustees shall in their discretion from time to time think fit

The clause gives trustees the choice not only of which beneficiaries to benefit but also how to provide that benefit.

Example

Property is settled on discretionary trusts for the settlor's two grandchildren, Adam and Debbie. The annual income is £100 net. Adam is at university, reading medicine; Debbie is 16, at school and wants to be an actress.

For the last two years the trustees have made an outright payment of £100 per annum to Adam as he is not managing on his grant.

This year the trustees decide to buy one year's membership to the local theatre club for Debbie at a cost of £80 and pay the insurance premium (£20) on the bicycle she has bought herself to save bus fares.

7.3.1.2   Power to accumulate income

Trustees may not wish to distribute all the income every year. The PAA 1964 limits the length of time income can be accumulated. The accumulation period applicable to the settlement must be stated (see **6.2.8.2**) and without the need for a further clause the effect of stating the accumulation period is that during the period the trustees may exercise their discretion by retaining rather than distributing some or all of the annual income.

Example

Property is settled on discretionary trusts for Roger, Sally and Thomas. The stated accumulation period is 21 years and the annual income £120 net.

	Roger	Sally	Thomas	Accumulate
Year 1	40	70	10	–
Year 5	–	–	–	120
Year 6	40	40	–	40
Year 7	–	10	20	90
etc				

At the end of the accumulation period, all future income must be fully distributed each year.

	Roger	Sally	Thomas	Accumulate
Year 20	30	40	20	30
Year 21	–	–	–	120
Year 22	40	60	20	
Year 23	40	40	40	
Year 24	–	120	–	
etc				

7.3.1.3 Power to use accumulated income

As a general rule, income received during the accumulation period and accumulated becomes part of the capital of the trust fund and so unavailable as income of future years.

The settlor may wish to give the trustees more flexibility.

Sample clause

> The Trustees may under sub-clause [   ] apply the whole or any part of the income accumulated as if it were income arising in the then current year.

The effect of this clause is that during the accumulation period any income retained from previous years can be made available to increase the income available in the current year.

Example

Property is settled on discretionary trusts for Gail and Martin. The accumulation period is 21 years and the annual income £100 net.

	Gail	Martin	Accumulate	Total of accumulated income
Year 1	75	25	–	nil
Year 2	–	–	100	100
Year 3	90	–	10	110
Year 4	60	60	–	90
etc				

7.3.1.4 Accumulated income at the end of the accumulation period

Where the trustees are given a discretion over the accumulated income, the settlement must direct what is to happen to any undistributed income at the end of the accumulation period.

Extract from clause

> ... and subject to sub-clause [ ] shall hold such accumulations as an accretion to capital

The power to accumulate and to use accumulated income to increase the available annual income can last only for the accumulation period. Any accumulated income which has not been spent by the end of the accumulation period is added to the capital of the trust fund.

Example

£5,000 is held on discretionary trusts for Penny and Nick. The accumulation period is 21 years and the annual income £100 net.

	Penny	Nick	Total of accumulated income	Capital
Year 20	90	–	320	5,000
Year 21	100	100	<u>220</u>	5,000
Year 22	60	40		5,220
Year 23	50	50		5,220
etc				

7.3.2 Discretionary trusts of capital

The trusts over capital enable the trustees to decide how, when and to which beneficiaries to distribute the capital of the trust fund. The trustees will give effect to their decision by the exercise of a power of appointment.

7.3.2.1 The primary trust

Sample clause

> The Trustees may pay or apply the whole or any part of the capital of the Trust Fund to or for the benefit of all or such of the Beneficiaries, eg, in such shares and in such manner generally as the Trustees shall in their discretion think fit

Example

£10,000 is settled on discretionary trusts for Alice and Bertram. Each year, the trustees pay all available income to the beneficiaries. So far as capital is concerned:

Year 1:   Trustees decide not to pay out any capital.

Year 2:   Bertram is buying a car and the trustees decide to give him £2,000.

Year 15:   For 13 years the trustees exercised their power by not distributing any capital but this year gave £1,000 to Alice to help towards the cost of looking after her new baby and £5,000 to Bertram for alterations to his house.

Year 16:   The trustees decide that the costs of running the settlement outweigh its benefits and so bring it to an end by giving £1,000 each to Alice and Bertram.

7.3.2.2 Transfers on to other trusts

Sample clause

> The Trustees may, subject to the application (if any) of the rule against perpetuities pay or transfer any income or capital of the Trust Fund to the trustees of any other trust, wherever established or existing, under which any Beneficiary is interested (whether or not such Beneficiary is the only object or person interested or capable of benefiting under such other trust) if the

> Trustees in their discretion consider such payment or transfer to be for the benefit of such Beneficiary

The trustees may feel it appropriate to benefit a particular beneficiary by 'resettling' property on new trusts of which he is a beneficiary. This clause enables them to do so. The exercise of such a power is considered in **Chapter 10**.

7.4 Ultimate default trusts

All the capital and income of the trust fund must be fully distributed or be subject to vested interests by the end of the trust (perpetuity) period so that the trusts are not void for perpetuity. If for any reason the trustees have not distributed everything, the property remaining in the trust fund will revert back to the settlor. Even though in practice this never happens because the trustees do distribute fully, the fact that it could happen means that the settlor has an interest in the settlement and suffers adverse tax consequences (see **6.2.11**).

To ensure that 'reverter to settlor' can never happen, the settlement should contain an ultimate default trust, ie, a clause directing who should receive any surplus left in the trust at the end of the trust (perpetuity) period.

This ultimate beneficiary must be living or in existence (eg, a charity) and be given a vested interest in the trust fund at the date of the settlement. A settlor will often choose a charity as the ultimate default beneficiary.

Sample clause

> Subject as above and if and so far as not wholly disposed of for any reason whatever by the above provisions, the capital and income of the Trust Fund shall be held in trust for [name] absolutely

Example

Many years ago, property was settled on discretionary trusts for the settlor's children and remoter issue with a charity as ultimate default beneficiary. The trust (perpetuity) period is 80 years. The settlor had one child (Tracy) when the trust was set up. Tracy had two sons Wayne and Calvin.

Since the settlement was created the trustees have distributed £170,000 of the trust fund but Wayne died when he was 6 years old, Tracy died three years ago and Calvin has just died having never had any children.

There is no other issue of the settlor and a surplus of £30,000 remains within the trust. The trustees must transfer this to the charity and bring the trust to an end.

Chapter 8

Drafting Accumulation and Maintenance Trusts

8.1 What are accumulation and maintenance trusts?

Settlors and testators often wish to settle property on contingent trusts, for example, 'on trust for X if he attains 25' or 'on trust for such of my grandchildren X, Y and Z as attain 21 and if more than one equally between them'. Until the beneficiaries fulfil the contingency, such a trust is a trust without an interest in possession.

Trusts without an interest in possession are normally subject to the periodic charge and the distribution (exit) charges. Trusts without an interest in possession which fulfil the statutory requirements of IHTA 1984, s 71 are singled out for special IHT treatment. They are not subject to the periodic and distribution charges. Lifetime transfers of property to such trusts are PETs rather than LCTs. There is no special treatment for income tax and CGT so that ordinary principles of liability will apply (see **14.5**).

8.1.1 The statutory straitjacket: IHTA 1984, s 71

The structure of an A & M settlement is not dissimilar from a discretionary settlement (see **Chapters 5** and **7**), but the particular skill required by the draftsman is to ensure that the settlement complies with the three requirements of IHTA 1984, s 71:

(a) One or more beneficiaries will, on or before attaining a specified age not exceeding 25, become beneficially entitled to, or to an interest in possession in, the settled property.

(b) No interest in possession subsists in the settled property and the income in it is to be accumulated so far as it is not applied for the maintenance, education or benefit of such a beneficiary.

(c) Either:

(i) not more than 25 years have elapsed since the day on which the settlement was made; or

(ii) all the beneficiaries are children of a common grandparent or are children, widows or widowers of such grandchildren who were themselves beneficiaries but died before becoming entitled as in (a) above.

These requirements impose a discipline on the draftsman not present when drafting interest in possession settlements or discretionary settlements. If the settlement is to qualify as an A & M settlement, it must comply with all three requirements from the outset. It is irrelevant whether it is created on death or by lifetime transfer. If there is any possibility that the settlement may fail to comply with the requirements in the future, it will not qualify as an A & M trust. Particular care is needed when drafting powers for the trustees. If any power is capable of exercise in a manner which is in breach of the requirements of s 71, an A & M settlement will not be created; the fact that the power is not actually exercised by the trustees does not matter. It is common to include restrictions on the manner in which trustees can exercise their powers to avoid prejudicing the A & M status of the trust.

Sample clause

> The Trustees shall not exercise any power in such a way as to prevent the conditions of IHTA 1984, s 71(1) from applying to the Trust Property.

8.1.2   Trustee Act 1925, s 31

It appears that the parliamentary draftsman had the provisions of TA 1925, s 31 in mind when drafting the provisions of s 71 of IHTA 1984. In the case of the most basic A & M trust, the provisions of TA 1925 automatically satisfy the requirements of IHTA 1984. The consequence is that many contingent gifts on death, by will or under the intestacy law, to minor children and/or grandchildren are A & M trusts. The relevance of s 31 to contingent gifts by will to minors in the context of s 71 is considered in **12.6.2.2**.

8.1.3   Lifetime A & M settlements

Clearly, the draftsman of a lifetime A & M settlement must ensure that its trusts comply with the provisions of s 71 of IHTA 1984. He may do so by drafting provisions as illustrated in **5.4** and by placing reliance upon s 31 of TA 1925.

The trust mentioned earlier 'on trust for such of my grandchildren X, Y and Z as attain 21 and if more then equally between them' satisfies the three requirements of s 71 since:

(a)   self-evidently the capital entitlement arises at 21 but income entitlement arises earlier at 18 (s 31), ie, the beneficiary becomes entitled on or before 25; and

(b)   income not applied by the trustees for maintenance, education or benefit must be accumulated (s 31), ie, there is no subsisting interest in possession; and

(c)   again self-evidently all the beneficiaries have a common grandparent.

A settlement drafted in this manner provides the trustees with some discretion and flexibility (through the provisions of TA 1925, ss 31 and 32). Many settlors want greater flexibility. The challenge is then to draft a settlement which complies with s 71 but which contains wider powers and discretions for the trustees.

8.1.4   The objectives of this chapter

The remainder of this chapter considers drafting A & M trusts containing an added degree of flexibility beyond that contained in the settlement described above. However, before proceeding further with this chapter, the explanation of s 71 of IHTA 1984, and the examples provided in **5.4** should be reconsidered. A precedent for the principal clauses of an A & M settlement is in **Appendix 5**.

8.2 Drafting a lifetime settlement

8.2.1 The date, opening words, etc

The formal parts, ie, the appointment of the original trustees and the recitals will follow the usual pattern (see **Chapter 6**). Within the definitions clause, there will be statements as to the perpetuity period (normally an 80-year period) and the accumulation period (normally a period of 21 years from the date of the settlement); the beneficiaries will also be identified (see **8.2.2**).

8.2.2 The beneficiaries

To comply with s 71 of IHTA 1984, there must be at least one beneficiary in existence at the date the settlement is created.

The trust instrument must clearly identify the beneficiaries. It is normal practice to include each beneficiary's date of birth since this enables the trustees to calculate the beneficiary's age and to know the date when his interest will vest, ie, in the income and capital of the trust fund. This may help the trustees take steps in the future to avoid CGT liabilities (see **10.3.2.2**).

Sample clauses

The 'Primary Beneficiaries' shall mean:

(a)   The existing [grand]children of the Settlor namely

[   ] who was born on [   ];
[   ] who was born on [   ];
[   ] who was born on [   ]; and
[   ] who was born on [   ]; and

(b)   every other [grand]child of the Settlor born after the date of this Deed and before the Closing Date.

The 'Closing Date' shall mean whichever shall be the earlier of:

(a)   the date on which the first Primary Beneficiary to do so attains the age of 25; and

(b)   the date on which the Trust Period shall determine.

References to the children, grandchildren and issue of any person shall include his children, grandchildren and remoter issue, whether legitimate, legitimated [, illegitimate] or adopted [, but shall exclude any illegitimate person and his descendants].

Commentary on the clauses

If a settlor anticipates the possibility of further grandchildren being born after the settlement has been made, he may provide for them to be added to the class of beneficiaries. However, it is important to specify that the class is to close on the date when the first beneficiary attains a vested interest in the capital of the trust fund, ie, when the contingency is first satisfied, or the end of the trust if this is earlier. If the class was to remain open beyond the date when the earliest vesting occurs, and if the trustees had distributed funds to a beneficiary whose interest had vested, the trustees would have paid out settled funds too early, ie, before the class had closed. This would amount to a breach of trust by the trustees.

Example

Property is settled on A & M trusts for the grandchildren of Adam contingent upon them reaching 21 years of age. When the settlement is created Adam has two grandchildren: Belinda (16) and Charles (12). By the time Belinda becomes 21, no further grandchildren have been born. David, a grandson, is born three years later.

Compare the first diagram where, as is usual, the class closes when the first beneficiary attains a vested interest with the second where it remains open until all possible beneficiaries have been ascertained.

The expression 'child or grandchild' etc will normally include adopted and legitimated (grand) children and those whose parents are not married to each other. If the settlor wants to exclude any such person, a clause to that effect (eg, as in the sample clause) should be included.

Where a beneficiary becomes entitled to an interest in possession before becoming entitled to capital (eg, at 18 under TA 1925, s 31), there is a benefit to closing the class at that point. If the class remains open, each time a new beneficiary joins the class the share of the capital in which the beneficiary has an interest in possession will be reduced. The reduction will be treated as a potentially exempt transfer and will carry the risk of a charge to IHT if the transferor dies within seven years.

Where, as here, all beneficiaries are the 'grandchildren of a common grandparent' the settlement complies with the third requirement of s 71. Thus, the IHT advantages of the A & M settlement will not be limited to a 25-year period since the date of its creation (see **5.4.1**); they will remain available for however long the settlement may continue.

8.2.3 The principal trusts

This clause will state the primary intention of the settlor, namely that the trustees will hold the capital of the trust fund for the beneficiaries until they attain the specified age. To comply with s 71, the beneficiaries must, at least, become entitled to an interest in possession in the income on or before 25 years. The entitlement to capital can be deferred.

Sample clause

> The Trust Fund shall be held upon trust for such of the Primary Beneficiaries as:
>
> (a)   attain the age of 25 before the end of the Trust Period; or
>
> (b)   are living and under that age at the end of the Trust Period
>
> and, if more than one, in equal shares absolutely.

Commentary on the clause: capital provision

Perpetuity rules

To comply with the perpetuity rules, the contingent interests created by the A & M trust must vest within the perpetuity period chosen for the trust; this will normally be a period of 80 years.

This trust provides contingent gifts which are to vest in beneficiaries at the age of 25 years. Any beneficiary attaining that age within the trust period, ie, the perpetuity period of the trust, will have a vested entitlement. Any beneficiary who is still under the age of 25 years when the trust period ends will immediately acquire a vested entitlement to a share of the trust fund. The perpetuity period is, therefore, complied with and the trusts are not void for perpetuity.

Example

Georgina settled property on A & M trusts for her grandchildren contingent upon them attaining 25 years of age. The perpetuity period was stated as 30 years. When the settlement was created there were two grandchildren in existence: Clara aged 10 years and Sara aged 3 years. A third grandchild, Petra, was born six years later.

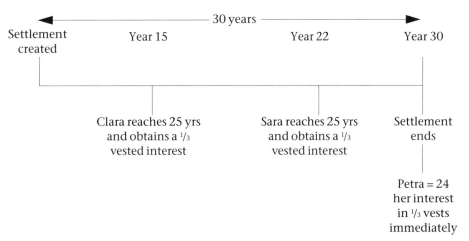

Capital to vest at 25 years (or sooner)

The sample clause above provides that a beneficiary's entitlement to capital will vest at or before the age of 25 and clearly complies with the age requirement of s 71. However, it is possible to delay entitlement to capital beyond the age of 25 and still comply with s 71.

Delaying entitlement to capital beyond the age of 25

Section 71 provides that beneficiaries must become entitled to the settled property capital or 'an interest in possession in it' at or before the age of 25. It is therefore sufficient for a beneficiary to become entitled to the income from the settled property at or before the age of 25 (see below).

Delaying the right to capital beyond 25 years

If he chooses, a settlor may delay the age at which the beneficiary's capital entitlement is to vest. If he does so, the draftsman must then insert the appropriate age within the sample clause. Where capital entitlement is to vest beyond 25 years, the settlement can still qualify as an A & M settlement. To do so, it must give an entitlement to income on or before the beneficiary's 25th birthday (see below).

Trustee Act 1925, s 32

Section 32 of TA 1925 gives the trustees power to apply capital for the advancement or benefit of a beneficiary who has an interest in the capital of the settlement. The power may be exercised where the beneficiary has a contingent interest even though the beneficiary may never satisfy the contingency, for example, because he dies before the age stipulated for the vesting of the capital. In the absence of contrary provision, s 32 will automatically apply to an A & M settlement to enable the trustees to advance up to one half of a beneficiary's presumptive, ie, contingent entitlement to capital irrespective of the age to which the right to the capital has been delayed by the terms of the settlement. Section 32 does not prejudice the A & M status of the settlement.

The implied power may be modified when drafting the A & M settlement to enable the trustees to advance up to the whole of a beneficiary's presumptive entitlement in the same way as the power is often extended when drafting a will. This extension of s 32 does not prejudice the A & M status of the settlement.

Commentary on the clause: income provision

Income entitlement at 18 years

This clause contains no express reference to income. In particular, the clause does not vary the implied provisions of s 31 of TA 1925 by substituting a later age of up to 25 years for the statutory age of 18 years. Income entitlement of the primary beneficiaries and the trustees' duty to accumulate surplus income is, therefore, determined in accordance with s 31 of TA 1925.

Trustee Act 1925, s 31

Unless expressly excluded, s 31 of TA 1925 will automatically apply to the settlement. It serves a twofold purpose in the context of an A & M settlement.

(a)   It ensures an income entitlement on attaining the age of 18 years, ie, the beneficiary has an interest in possession on or before the age of 25 years as required by s 71 of IHTA 1984 (see **5.4.1**); and

(b)   Until the age of 18 years is reached the trustees have discretion to apply the income of the beneficiary's share for his maintenance, education or benefit and they are directed by the section to accumulate (by addition to the capital) any income which they have not applied. This direction to accumulate satisfies a further requirement of s 71 (see **5.4.1**).

The implied power may be modified when drafting the A & M settlement to defer the entitlement to income to any age not exceeding 25. The trustees' discretion will continue until the specified age. This extension of s 31 does not prejudice the A & M status of the settlement.

Conclusion

The effect of the principal trusts considered above is to give the beneficiaries an entitlement to capital at an age which may exceed 25 years but an entitlement to income at 18 years. Until the age at which the income entitlement arises, the trustees have discretion to apply income for the maintenance, education or benefit of a beneficiary and a duty to accumulate any unapplied income (TA 1925, s 31). Accumulated income can be used as income in future years while the interest in capital is contingent. Any undistributed accumulations thereafter are added to the capital (TA 1925, s 31(2)). In addition, the trustees may apply capital under TA 1925, s 32.

8.3 Widening the principal trusts

An A & M settlement will frequently be drafted so that it provides the trustees with a greater degree of flexibility than the trust described above but which at the same time continues to satisfy the requirements of s 71 of IHTA 1984. This can be achieved by widening the principal trusts which apply to the income and capital of the beneficiary's contingent share in the trust fund. In the sample clause which follows, the principal trust discussed at **8.2.3** is repeated (sub-clause (1)) and is extended by sub-clause (2).

Sample clauses

(1)   The Trust Fund shall be held upon trust for such of the Primary Beneficiaries as:

  (a)   attain the age of 25 before the end of the Trust Period; or

  (b)   are living and under the age at the end of the Trust Period

  and, if more than one, in equal shares absolutely.

(2)   The provisions of clause [   ] shall apply to the share of the Trust Fund to which any of the Primary Beneficiaries is or may become entitled under sub-clause [   ]. In those provisions, such share is called the 'Share' and that one of the Primary Beneficiaries who is primarily interested in the Share is called the 'Primary Beneficiary'.

Commentary on the clauses

Sub-clause (1) gives a beneficiary a contingent interest in the trust capital and the income which it generates. The wording ensures that beneficiaries will have a right to the income at 18 years (TA 1925, s 31) and the capital at 25 years and, therefore, satisfies s 71 of IHTA 1984.

Sub-clause (2) establishes that a beneficiary's share of the trust fund is subject to further trusts (set out in later clauses of the trust instrument) which are exercisable by the trustees until the beneficiary's interest vests. The nature of these additional trusts over income and capital are considered below. In this way the trustees can be given additional flexibility over the trust income and its capital similar to the powers of the trustees of discretionary settlements (see **Chapter 7**).

Example

Property has been settled on A & M trusts for Sheila (16) and Ruth (14) contingent upon their attaining 25 years. Sheila will be absolutely entitled to half the property when she attains her 25th birthday. Until then, her interest in both the trust capital and any income it generates is contingent (see sub-clause (1)).

In the language of sub-clause (2), Sheila is the primary beneficiary of half of the trust fund, ie, the 'Share' and so sub-clause (2) applies to create additional trusts over Sheila's contingent interest in half of the trust fund (see below).

8.3.1   Additional trusts applying to income

Sample clauses

(1)   During the Accumulation Period the Trustees may pay or apply any income of the Share to or for the maintenance or education or otherwise for the benefit of the Primary Beneficiary, or any other Primary Beneficiaries who are for the time being living and under the age 25.

(2)   ... [applies to capital, see **8.3.2**]

(3)   Subject as above, the income of the Share shall, during the Accumulation Period, be accumulated as an accretion to the capital of the Share. Any such accumulations may, at any time, be paid or applied in the manner set out in sub-clause [   ] as if they were income of the Share arising in the then current year.

(4)   Subject as above, section 31 of the Trustee Act 1925 (as modified below) shall apply to the income of the Share.

Commentary on the clauses

By sub-clause (1), the trustees may, during the Accumulation Period, at their discretion apply income of a share of the trust fund for any primary beneficiary, ie, they are not limited to applying the income for any particular primary beneficiary. The trustees have, in effect, a discretion to apply the income (for the stated purposes) for any of the beneficiaries.

In so far as income is not applied, sub-clause (3) directs accumulation of the surplus income as an accretion to the share of the primary beneficiary, ie, it is to be treated as part of the capital of that share and not of the whole trust fund. This sub-clause provides a duty to accumulate surplus income and so satisfies the requirement of s 71 of IHTA 1984.

Sub-clause (4) merely reminds the trustees that s 31 of TA 1925 applies to the trusts of the settlement, but that where its effects are contrary to the express income provisions included in the settlement, ie sub-clauses (1) and (3), the express provisions take precedence. However, sub-clauses (1) and (3) apply only during the Accumulation Period. Once this period ends, s 31 operates rather than sub-clauses (1) and (3).

Example 1

The trust fund in Sheila and Ruth's settlement consists of quoted shares and some cash on deposit with the bank. Trust income consists of dividends paid on the shares and interest on the deposit account. The net income of the trust fund in year 1 is £200. Sheila has the chance to go on a school activity holiday costing £80.

Her share of the trust fund is one half, so the trustees can apply up to £100 for her education.

Example 2

The income of the trust fund in year 2 is £100 net. Sheila and Ruth's interests are still contingent. Ruth would like music lessons which will cost £90. This is more than one half of the annual income. The clause allows the trustees to pay the income from Sheila's share for Ruth so that this year they may pay for Ruth's music lessons.

Example 3

Income of the trust fund in year 3 is £150 net. No income is applied by the trustees who must, therefore, accumulate it by adding £75 to each share of the trust fund still held for Sheila and Ruth.

8.3.2 Additional trusts applying to capital

Sample clause

> The Trustees may also pay or apply any capital of the Share to or for the maintenance, education, advancement or otherwise for the benefit of the Primary Beneficiary. No capital may be so applied in a way which would or might prevent the Primary Beneficiary from becoming entitled to it, or to an interest in possession in it, on or before attaining the age of 25 ...

Commentary on the clause

The trustees may use some or all of the capital of the beneficiary's share of the trust fund before he satisfies the contingency. Unlike the additional trusts which apply to the income, the capital which can be made available is limited to the share, ie, the capital of the share of other primary beneficiaries is not available. The effect of the implied power in s 32 of TA 1925 is modified by this clause since the trustees may advance up to the whole of the capital.

The purpose of the limitation in the second sentence of the clause is to ensure that the trustees are not able to exercise their discretionary powers over the capital of the trust fund in such a way as to prevent a beneficiary's interest in the income or capital arising at or before his 25th birthday. The mere possibility of this happening would mean the settlement would not satisfy s 71 of IHTA 1984, and so it would not be an A & M settlement.

The trustees may 'apply any capital of the Share for the ... benefit of the Primary Beneficiary'. The trustees may consider it appropriate to exercise this power by resettling the beneficiary's share of the trust fund. They can do this provided the 'new' settlement does not infringe s 71 (see above and see further **Chapter 10**).

Example 1

Property is settled on Sylvie and Alison contingent upon them attaining 25 years of age. When Sylvie attains 22 years of age, she decides to buy a flat for £50,000. The trust fund is currently valued at £120,000.

Sylvie's contingent share is one half, ie, £60,000 and so the trustees could apply £50,000 now. She would receive a further £10,000 when she attains 25 years.

Had the flat cost £80,000, the maximum the trustees could have applied would have been £60,000, and if they had given this amount to Sylvie it would have extinguished her right to any further capital.

Example 2

£10,000 has been settled on Ken (15) and Wayne (13) contingent on their attaining 18 years and, if they both attain that age, equally between them. Just before Ken's 18th birthday the trustees decide that he is too immature to be able to handle his share of the trust fund. Therefore, the trustees transfer £5,000 to the trustees of a new trust, the terms of which are that the capital and income of the trust fund are to be held on trust for Ken until he attains 25 years of age.

8.4 Ultimate default trusts

It is essential for tax reasons that the trust property can never revert to the settlor (see **Chapter 6**). The trust instrument must include a clause which gives the capital (including accumulated income) to a named individual (or charity) absolutely. Such a clause would take effect only if the principal trusts fail for some reason, ie, the trust property is not fully distributed to the intended beneficiaries.

Example

Property is settled on trust for Adam (14) and Lucinda (12) until they attain 18 years of age and, if they both attain that age, in equal shares.

Adam and Lucinda are killed in a car crash two years later. The trust property will revert back to the settlor unless a settlement contains a default trust.

Sample clause

In the event of the failure or determination of the above trusts, the capital and income of the Trust Fund shall be held upon trust for [such of the Primary Beneficiaries as are living at the date of this Deed, and if more than one, in equal shares] absolutely.

8.5 Restrictions on powers of trustees

The trustees have wide powers which they can exercise over the settled property. They are given these by the settlement, by the general law or (commonly) by a combination of the two. There is the risk that the width of these powers could prevent the settlement from complying with s 71 of IHTA 1984 and so never become an A & M settlement. In an attempt to prevent this, a clause placing restrictions on the trustees' powers is always inserted in the settlement deed.

Sample clause

In this clause, 'qualifying property' means any part of the Trust Fund which is for the time being property to which section 71 of the Inheritance Tax Act 1984 (or any statutory modification or re-enactment of such section) applies.

Where the Trust Fund or any part of it would (in the absence of the restrictions imposed by this sub-clause) fail to be qualifying property by reason only of powers conferred on the Trustees by this Deed or by law, those powers shall be capable of being exercised only in a manner which does not prevent the Trust Fund or that part of it from being qualifying property.

8.6 Summary

Drafting an A & M settlement calls for continuous attention to the requirements of s 71 of the IHTA. Any clause which the draftsman uses should be very closely examined to ensure that its terms do not prevent the settlement from declaring A & M trusts. This is particularly important when the settlor requires as much flexibility as possible for his trustees.

Chapter 9

Trust Advances and Appointments

9.1 What are advances and appointments?

Whether the trustees exercise a power of advancement or a power of appointment, the result is generally the same. The trust property, or some part of it, will become subject to different beneficial interests. The property will either become the absolute property of a beneficiary, ie, it ceases to be subject to the trusts of the settlement, or it will remain settled property subject to the trusts of the original settlement or of a new settlement. The trustees' powers may be sufficiently wide for them to 'declare new trusts' over some part of the trust property. The manner of the exercise of these powers is discussed further in **Chapter 10**.

A power of advancement may be available to the trustees as a statutory power (ie, the power to advance trust capital under TA 1925, s 32) or as an express power through provision in the trust instrument. Powers of appointment can exist only as express powers. Modifying the statutory power of advancement by express provision and the drafting of express powers are considered at **9.4.3** and **9.5**.

9.2 Legal similarities and differences

9.2.1 Similarities

Both types of power are fiduciary and are dispositive in nature. Either can be exercised to create new beneficial interests for the beneficiaries of the trust. Generally, the powers are exercisable by the trustees for the benefit of beneficiaries who have been selected by the settlor of the settlement.

9.2.2 Differences

There are differences which relate to the existence of the powers and the manner of their exercise.

9.2.2.1 Existence of the powers

Only the power of advancement is statutory. Section 32 of TA 1925 will be implied into every settlement but its effect may be extended or restricted by express provision in the settlement depending on the instructions given by the settlor at the time the settlement was created. Section 32 of TA 1925, and its possible modification, are considered at **9.4.3**.

A power of appointment can exist only if there is an express provision in the trust instrument creating it. A power which is widely drafted may permit advancements of the type permitted by s 32 and so render that provision superfluous. Drafting powers of appointment is considered further at **9.5**.

9.2.2.2 Exercise of the powers

Power of advancement

When trustees exercise a power of advancement, they bring forward the beneficiary's entitlement under the settlement. For example, they may hold the trust property for a beneficiary contingently on his attaining 25 years. If the trustees exercise the power in TA 1925, s 32 (or an equivalent express power) and advance capital to the beneficiary when he is aged 21, they bring forward the time when he becomes absolutely entitled to the property.

Power of appointment

A power of appointment in a discretionary settlement allows trustees to grant a beneficiary income or capital from the settlement. Such powers are typically (but not exclusively) found in discretionary settlements. For an example of this in a will creating interest in possession trusts, see **12.7.2**.

The exercise of a power of appointment may have an effect similar to the exercise of a power of advancement. Alternatively, the exercise of the power of appointment may change the beneficial entitlement to the trust property while leaving the property subject to trusts. Those trusts may be the trusts established in the original trust instrument or they may be new trusts specifically created by the instrument which exercises the power.

Example

Trustees are holding property on trust for the settlor's grandchildren. There is a wide power of appointment over the settled property and its income enabling the trustees to appoint the property among the beneficiaries at such times and in such proportions and for such purposes as they think fit. In default of appointment, the trust property will pass equally to such of the settlor's grandchildren living at the date of the settlement who attain 18.

The trustees may exercise a power of this nature:

(a)   To provide capital for the absolute benefit of any single beneficiary, or group of beneficiaries, even before the age of 18 years. They must exercise their powers in proper manner having regard to their fiduciary nature.

(b)   To provide capital for one or more of the beneficiaries on their attaining 21 years, ie, the power of appointment is executed to create new trusts in favour of beneficiaries selected from the class beneficiaries. If the power is exercised in this way, care must be taken to observe the perpetuity period applicable to the original settlement (see **6.2.7**).

9.2.3 General and special powers of appointment

Powers of appointment are generally characterised as either special or general powers of appointment.

9.2.3.1 General powers

These powers permit the trustees to appoint to any person they may choose and are, therefore, uncommon. The settlor will generally wish to select the class of beneficiaries among whom the trustees may exercise the power. For this reason most settlements contain special powers of appointment.

9.2.3.2 Special powers

These permit the trustees to appoint to beneficiaries within a class chosen by the settlor. Two areas in particular require prior consideration before the trustees exercise a special power of appointment.

The objects of the power

No power may be exercised in a manner which exceeds any limitations laid down by the settlor in the settlement. The exercise of the power of appointment must, therefore, be for the benefit of a member or members of a class of beneficiaries selected by the settlor. Although the settlor and his spouse may be within the class of beneficiaries, generally they will be excluded for tax reasons (see **6.2.11**).

The perpetuity period

The property must vest in interest in the beneficiary in whose favour the power is to be exercised before the perpetuity period relevant to the settlement expires. In the case of special powers, this period is the period established by the settlement and which starts to run from the date of creation of the settlement (see **6.2.7**).

Example

The facts are the same as in the example at **9.2.2.** The perpetuity period is 80 years. Fifteen years after the settlement is created, the trustees appoint one quarter of the trust funds on trusts for the settlor's grandchild, Millie (aged 1) if she attains 21 years. There is an ultimate gift over to charity.

As the property appointed by the trustees vests within the perpetuity period, the power is properly exercised.

9.3 Practical similarities

The exercise of a power will require the execution by the trustees of a deed of advancement or a deed of appointment depending on the method selected by the trustees.

The initiative for the exercise of the power will generally come from one or more of the beneficiaries, normally because they need money. The trustees must, on each occasion, consider whether they have adequate powers to satisfy the beneficiary's request and, if so, whether they wish to exercise those powers.

Any exercise of a power pursuant to such a request will have taxation implications. These should be fully considered before any power is exercised. Taxation aspects of the exercise of powers are considered in **Chapter 10**.

Sometimes, the trustees rather than the beneficiaries will take the initiative as to the need to exercise a power and begin discussion with the beneficiaries on the manner and method of exercise of the power. This often happens where the trustees foresee a tax problem which they can avoid by using their powers. These aspects of the use of the trustees' powers are considered further in **Chapter 10**.

The exercise of either power may cause settled property to cease to be subject to trusts. In such cases the trustees will need to transfer the trust property to the beneficiary. Similarly, if property becomes subject to new trusts, the trustees of the original settlement may need to transfer the property to the trustees of the new settlement. The manner of vesting trust property in beneficiaries or new trustees is considered at **14.4.3**.

9.4   The statutory power of advancement

9.4.1   The power of advancement

Section 32 of TA 1925 states:

(1)   Trustees may at any time or times pay or apply any capital money subject to a trust, for the advancement or benefit, in such manner as they may, in their absolute discretion, think fit, of any person entitled to the capital of the trust property or of any share thereof, whether absolutely or contingently on his attaining any specified age or on the occurrence of any other event, or subject to a gift over on his death under any specified age or on the occurrence of any other event, and whether in possession or in remainder or reversion, and such payment or application may be made notwithstanding that the interest of such person is liable to be defeated by the exercise of a power of appointment or revocation, or to be diminished by the increase of the class to which he belongs:

Provided that—

(a)   the money so paid or applied for the advancement or benefit of any person shall not exceed altogether in amount one half of the presumptive or vested share or interest of that person in the trust property; and

(b)   if that person is or becomes absolutely and indefeasibly entitled to a share in the trust property the money so paid or applied shall be brought into account as part of such share; and

(c)   no such payment or application shall be made so as to prejudice any person entitled to any prior life or other interest, whether vested or contingent, in the money paid or applied unless such person is in existence and of full age and consents in writing to such payment or application.

(2)   This section applies only where the trust property consists of money or securities or of property held upon trust for sale calling in and conversion, and such money or securities, or the proceeds of such sale calling in and conversion are not by statute or in equity considered as land, or applicable as capital money for the purposes of the Settled Land Act 1925.

(3)   This section does not apply to trusts constituted or created before the commencement of this Act.

9.4.2   Commentary on the statutory power

9.4.2.1   The power is discretionary: the trustees 'may'

Beneficiaries cannot compel trustees to exercise the power. Before exercising this power, the trustees must ensure their intended use of the power is for a legitimate purpose. If not, it will be an improper exercise of the power which will be invalid and which may cause the trustees personal liability for loss suffered by the trust fund.

9.4.2.2 Interest in capital of the trust fund (or part)

Only beneficiaries with an interest in the capital may benefit from exercise of the power. However, the interest may be any of the following:

(a) absolute or contingent (on attaining any age or on any other event occurring);

(b) in possession, remainder or reversion.

It does not matter that a beneficiary's interest is liable to be defeated or diminished by the occurrence of a future event, for example, because the beneficiary may die at a young age and never reach the age at which the interest vests.

Example

Trustees are holding £10,000 on trust for Saul contingent upon his attaining the age of 25 years (if he dies under the age of 25 the money is to go to charity). On his 18th birthday, the trustees advance £2,500 to enable Saul to go to university. This is a proper exercise of the power even though Saul may die before his 25th birthday.

Beneficiaries of a discretionary trust do not have an interest in the capital of the settlement. They have a mere hope of benefiting if the trustees exercise their discretion in their favour. While their interest is discretionary, they cannot benefit from s 32.

9.4.2.3 Limitations on the exercise of the power

The trustees may exercise their power only where it is for 'the advancement or benefit' of the beneficiary. 'Advancement' is normally considered to cover capital payments designed to 'set the beneficiary up in life (often in a business)' or payments made on the occasion of marriage. 'Benefit' has a particularly wide meaning. It has been held *Pilkington and Another v Inland Revenue Commissioners and Others* [1964] AC 612 to have a meaning wide enough to permit the trustees to exercise their power of advancement by creating new trusts in relation to settled property if such is for the benefit of the beneficiary (a *'Pilkington* advance').

Example

Trustees are holding £100,000 on A & M trusts for Martha when she attains 25 years. She is now aged 24, is wealthy and has two children aged 1 and 3 years. She would prefer the funds transferred to trustees for her children so that IHT may be avoided if she should die soon after her 25th birthday. The trustees may exercise their power and advance some of the settled funds onto accumulation and maintenance trusts for Martha's children.

The statutory power limits the trustees to paying or applying 'not more than one half' of a beneficiary's presumptive or vested share. If the power is exercised, the amount paid or applied must be 'brought into account' if the beneficiary later becomes entitled to a share in the trust property.

9.4.2.4 Prior life or other interests

The statutory power can be exercised only if consent is obtained from a beneficiary with a prior interest. For example, if property is held on trust for a beneficiary for life and then for other beneficiaries in remainder, the trustees could not exercise their power in favour of the remaindermen without the consent of the life tenant.

9.4.3 Modifying the statutory power

Normally, only minor amendments, as discussed below, need to be made to the statutory form of the power. They are similar to those made when drafting a will for a testator. As mentioned at **9.2.2**, it is often the case that a settlement contains a wide power of appointment. If so, the trustees may prefer to exercise this power rather than the statutory power, even in modified form.

The alterations made by express provision to the statutory power of advancement are normally:

(a)   to permit the trustees to pay or apply up to the whole (not merely one half) of a beneficiary's presumptive or vested share;

(b)   to remove the requirement that the distribution has to be brought into account;

(c)   to remove the requirement for a person with a prior interest to consent to the advance.

It is unnecessary to consider extending the circumstances in which the statutory power can be exercised by the trustees. The phrase 'advancement or benefit' is generally considered sufficiently wide, especially in view of the particularly wide meaning of the word 'benefit'.

9.5 Drafting powers of appointment

As there is no statutory power of appointment, all powers must be drafted as express powers in a trust instrument. The precise form which the power takes will depend upon the particular settlement which is to be drafted. Powers of appointment are considered at **7.3.2** and **8.3** in connection with drafting discretionary settlements and accumulation and maintenance settlements.

9.6 Taxation aspects of the exercise of powers of advancement and appointment

As each power is exercisable in relation to the trust capital, ie, the property in the settlement, it follows that the IHT and CGT aspects of the exercise of the power need be considered by the trustees before the power is actually exercised. These are discussed in **Chapter 10**.

Chapter 10

The Exercise of Powers of Advancement and Appointment

10.1 Interest in possession settlements

10.1.1 The nature of the trusts and the powers

Settlements with an interest in possession are usually created because the settlor or the testator is seeking to provide one person (often a spouse) with an income for life while controlling the ultimate devolution of the capital. It is relatively unusual to create such settlements during the settlor's lifetime. They are much more commonly created by will.

After the trust comes into effect, the trustees may be asked by beneficiaries to exercise their powers to apply capital.

Since the introduction of TLATA 1996, it is usual for trustees of interest in possession settlements to hold the settled property 'on trust' and have an appropriate power of sale among the administrative provisions of the settlement. The beneficial trusts provide the life tenant with an income for life and the remainderman with an interest which vests in possession on the life tenant's death. Until then, it is vested in interest only.

> Example
>
> Trustees hold settled property worth £200,000 on trust to pay the income to Aida for life, thereafter for Carmen in remainder. Aida has an interest in possession, ie, the right to income produced by the trust property. Carmen has the right to receive the trust property when Aida dies.

Carmen's interest in the example, is an interest in remainder but is often called (albeit incorrectly) 'a reversionary interest'. It is an asset which can be professionally valued, ie, a value can be placed on Carmen's right to receive the trust property when Aida dies. Since Carmen has the right to receive the trust property only when Aida dies, the value of the interest in remainder may be significantly less than the current value of the settled property. The value will be influenced (inter alia) by the prospective life expectancy of Aida. Carmen's interest in remainder is an asset which she may consider selling or possibly giving away as part of her estate planning arrangements (see **4.6.2**).

> Example
>
> If Carmen waits until Aida dies, she will receive the full trust fund (currently valued at £200,000). Carmen, however, is in need of some money immediately and decides to sell her interest in remainder to David.
>
> (a)   assuming Aida is 84 years old, David might pay Carmen £175,000 for the right to receive the trust fund when Aida dies;
>
> (b)   assuming Aida is 35 years old, David might pay Carmen £40,000 for that right.

If Carmen's sale is for full value, no IHT nor CGT would be payable by her. If, instead, she gave her interest in remainder to David, no tax would be payable (see **4.6.2**) because:

(a) her interest in remainder is 'excluded property' for IHT purposes, ie, it is not in Carmen's 'estate' and so may be given away free of IHT; and

(b) as a beneficial interest in settled property acquired without any payment by Carmen, it is exempt from CGT on a disposal whether by sale or gift.

The trustees' power to advance capital to the remainderman in s 32 of TA 1925 applies to an interest in possession settlement although it may have been modified by express provision in the trust instrument. Any exercise of the statutory power to pay or apply trust property would, unless also suitably modified, require the prior consent of the life tenant.

10.1.2 Provision of capital for the beneficiaries of an interest in possession settlement

Apart from capitalisation of a life interest on an intestacy, there are three methods of providing the beneficiaries with capital from the trust.

(a) By the exercise of an express power of advancement or appointment. Only if the trust instrument contains express provision can the trustees apply capital to or for the benefit of the life tenant.

(b) By the exercise of the statutory power in s 32 of TA 1925 in favour of the remainderman (with consent of the life tenant, unless modified).

The decision to exercise either of these powers is a matter for the trustees. Their decision will generally follow an approach by the beneficiary with a request for the advance of some money. The trustees' decision should be formally recorded either:

(i) by a minute in the trustees' minute book for the trust (if any); or

(ii) by signing a separate notice to the effect that, in exercise of a power contained in the settlement or in s 32 of TA 1925 certain property is advanced from the settlement to a named beneficiary. This notice should be retained with the trust instrument and records.

(c) By partitioning the trust fund between the life tenant and the remainderman (see **10.1.3**).

10.1.3 Partitioning the trust fund

In the absence of an express power to advance capital to a life tenant, capital may be provided by 'breaking the trust' under the rule in *Saunders v Vautier* (1841) 4 Beav 115. 'Trust busting' under this rule allows beneficiaries who are of full age and capacity and together entitled to the whole beneficial interest in the trust fund to bring the settlement to an end and to direct the trustees to transfer the property as they wish.

If the beneficiaries decide to end the trust in this way, they will need to reach agreement as to the value of their respective beneficial interests, ie, a value needs to be placed on the life tenant's right to receive income for life and on the remainderman's right to receive the capital of the trust on the life tenant's death. Agreement may be reached informally between the beneficiaries or by formal valuation by an actuary instructed to act on their behalf.

Example

Trustees hold £10,000 on trust for Mary for life, remainder to William. Mary and William agree that their respective interests are worth 40% and 60% of the settled property. They may direct the trustees to sell the trust property and to divide the sale proceeds between them in the agreed proportions.

Instead of directing the trustees to sell the trust property as in the example, the beneficiaries may prefer to direct the trustees to divide the assets between them so that each beneficiary receives the appropriate proportion of the trust fund. This method of division will require each asset to be valued separately. It may be necessary for the trustees to use cash to achieve exactly the correct proportions of the funds for each beneficiary.

Example

The facts are the same as in the previous example. The £10,000 trust fund is made up of shares in A plc valued at £5,000, shares in B plc valued at £4,000 and £1,000 cash.

William will receive:

£3,000 A plc shares;
£2,400 B plc shares;
£600 cash.

Mary will receive:

£2,000 A plc shares;
£1,600 B plc shares;
£400 cash.

Before the settled property is actually distributed among the beneficiaries, the trustees must first consider the taxation implications.

10.1.4 Taxation implications of provision of capital for the beneficiaries

The exercise of the statutory or express power of advancement has capital tax implications which the trustees must consider before releasing the formerly settled property from their control. The trustees will often become personally liable for tax as a result of the exercise of a power. They should retain some of the trust property in their own names until all liabilities have been discharged.

10.1.4.1 Inheritance tax

The 'estate' of an individual is defined (IHTA 1984, s 5) for IHT purposes as 'all the property to which he is beneficially entitled' and this includes property in which he has an interest in possession (s 49). This is the position of a life tenant.

Example

Trustees hold a fund of £50,000 for Leonard for life, remainder to Rachel. Leonard has assets of his own which amount to £100,000. His estate for IHT purposes will be valued at £150,000.

The lifetime termination of an interest in possession is a PET provided the property is then held for, inter alia, one or more of the beneficiaries absolutely, ie, the settlement has come to an end. Tax (calculated in the normal manner where there is a 'failed' PET) will be payable only if the former life tenant dies within seven years of termination of the settlement (IHTA 1984, ss 52(1) and 3A). Inheritance tax may, therefore, become payable where a power is exercised to provide capital to beneficiaries in the three ways mentioned below. If IHT is payable, it is the trustees of the settlement who must pay it to the Revenue and who should therefore reserve funds for the purpose.

If an interest in possession is terminated to create a trust without an interest in possession, there will be a lifetime chargeable transfer.

Express power to appoint capital to life tenant

If the trustees exercise a power to advance all of the capital to the life tenant, his interest in possession will determine in the capital advanced. However, no IHT will be payable. This is because there is no fall in the value of his estate since for IHT purposes he is deemed already to own that property which is actually being advanced (IHTA 1984, s 53(2)).

Example

Assume that in the previous example the trustees advance the whole fund to Leonard.

Before the advance:

Leonard's estate	£100,000	
Trust fund	£ 50,000	£150,000

After the advance:

Leonard's estate £100,000 + £50,000 advanced = £150,000.

Statutory power of advancement to remainderman

If the trustees exercise their power to advance the capital to the remainderman, the life tenant's interest in possession ends in that part of the settled property. The life tenant makes a PET which becomes chargeable only if he dies within seven years of the advance (IHTA 1984, ss 3A and 52(1)).

Example

Assume that the trustees holding the trust property for Leonard for life, remainder to Rachel had advanced £10,000 to Rachel. Leonard is treated as making a PET. If it becomes chargeable, any IHT payable on the £10,000 (ie, the value of the property in which Leonard's interest in possession has ended) is payable by the trustees from the trust fund.

Note: The statutory power requires the life tenant's consent although the need for consent can be removed in the trust instrument.

Partition of the trust fund

If, by agreement, the fund is partitioned, the life tenant's interest in possession ends in the trust property which passes to the remainderman. This too is a PET made by the life tenant. Inheritance tax is payable by the trustees on that portion of the trust fund if the life tenant dies within seven years of the partition (IHTA 1984, s 52(2)).

Example

Assume that Leonard and Rachel in the previous example agreed to partition the £50,000 fund between them in proportions of 30:70. Leonard makes a PET of £35,000 (£50,000 – £15,000 = £35,000). If Leonard dies within seven years of the PET, IHT is payable by the trustees from the partitioned trust fund (which they should remember).

10.1.4.2 Capital gains tax

Liability to CGT occurs only if there is a disposal of chargeable assets. Disposals may be actual or deemed. No actual disposal occurs on the exercise by the trustees of their power of advancement. However, in each case there is a deemed disposal. Actual disposals by trustees are considered in **Chapter 14**.

Deemed disposals (TCGA 1992, s 71, as amended by Finance Act 1999, s 75)

A deemed disposal occurs when an individual becomes 'absolutely entitled' to settled property against the trustees, for example, on any of the occasions mentioned in **10.1.2**. The trustees are deemed to dispose of each item of settled property at its market value and to re-acquire it immediately at the same value as nominees for the beneficiary, ie they continue to hold the property in their names as bare trustees for the beneficiary. The property is no longer settled property but belongs to the beneficiary whose acquisition cost of the property is the market value when the re-acquisition occurred.

Example

Trustees appoint 1,000 ABC plc shares worth £20,000 to Leonard, the life tenant of an interest in possession settlement. The shares were worth £2,000 when the settlement was created. A deemed disposal occurs at the date of the appointment.

Value at deemed disposal	£20,000
Less: acquisition cost	£2,000
	£18,000
indexation allowance (say)	£1,000
Chargeable gain (subject to taper relief based on the trustees' period of ownership)	£17,000

Leonard's acquisition cost of the shares is £20,000.

Reliefs, exemptions and rate of tax

If any tax is due, it is calculated at 40% of the tapered gain and is payable by the settlement trustees. As their deemed disposal gave rise to the gain, any tax is their liability. They pay the tax from the settled funds. If a loss occurs, the trustees can claim relief for it by setting the loss against their gains on other disposals of trust assets in the same or future tax years.

Before calculating their liability to tax, the trustees may deduct an annual exemption of £4,250, ie, one half of the exemption available to individuals.

On the joint election of the trustees and beneficiaries, hold-over relief will be available when assets leave a settlement if:

(a)   the settled property comprises business property (see **4.4.5.2**); or

(b)   the occasion gives rise to an immediate liability to IHT, ie, it is not a PET. This is not the case where property ceases to be subject to an interest in possession settlement (but see **10.2.7** and **10.3.2** for discretionary settlements and accumulation and maintenance settlements).

If they claim hold-over relief, taper relief and the annual exemption will not be available.

Beneficiaries' and trustees' losses

If a loss arises on the deemed disposal, the trustees may claim relief for it by deducting it from:

(a)   gains which accrued to the trustees on disposals earlier in the same tax year as the deemed disposal; or

(b)   gains accruing on the deemed disposal, ie, gains on the assets to which the beneficiary is entitled.

If relief is not available to the trustees (because they have insufficient gains), the loss may be transferred to the beneficiary. He may use the loss to offset future gains made on the disposal of assets received from the settlement only. In other words, the loss is not generally available to offset gains on disposals of his other assets.

10.1.5 Drafting a deed of partition

Heading and date

Sample clause

> DEED OF PARTITION
> DATE: [   ]

Parties

Normally, there will be three parties:

(a)   the life tenant (who gives up the right to income in part of the trust fund); and

(b)   the reversioner (who gives up the right to part of the capital of the trust fund); and

(c)   the trustees.

Sample clause

> (1)   [name and address] ('the Life Tenant');
>
> (2)   [name and address] ('the Reversioners'); and
>
> (3)   [name and address] ('the Trustees')

Recitals

The recitals will explain the background circumstances giving rise to the partition.

Sample clause

> RECITALS
>
> (A) This Deed is supplemental to the settlement ('the Settlement')
> [and to the other documents and events] specified in the First Schedule.
>
> (B) The Trustees are the present trustees of the Settlement.
>
> (C) Under and by virtue of the Settlement and in the events which have happened, the Life Tenant is entitled to the income of the Trust Fund for life and, subject thereto, the capital and income of the Trust Fund is held upon trust for the Reversioners [in equal shares] absolutely.
>
> (D) The Trust Fund presently consists of the property described in Parts 1 and 2 of the Second Schedule.
>
> (E) It has been agreed between the Life Tenant and the Reversioners that the Trust Fund shall be partitioned so that [   ] per centum as described in Part 1 of the Second Schedule ('the Life Tenant's Share') shall be held for the Life Tenant absolutely and the balance remaining being [   ] per centum as described in Part 2 of the Second Schedule ('the Reversioners' Share'), shall be held for the Reversioners in equal shares absolutely.
>
> (F) The Trustees have agreed, following the joint request of the Life Tenant and the Reversioners, to release the Trust Fund to the parties respectively entitled under the above agreement.
>
> [(G) This partition is carried out following and in accordance with actuarial advice.]

The clauses assume that there is more than one reversioner and that the reversioners agree to divide their share equally between them. They will need amendment if there is only one reversioner. If the parties did not obtain actuarial advice, delete clause G.

The operative part

Normally, there will be two clauses, one each for the life tenant and the reversioner, whereby they respectively assign and surrender to the other their interest in the income or capital of the trust fund. The consequence is that the trust property is freed from the trust and may be transferred by the trustees in accordance with the arrangement mentioned in the recitals.

Sample clause

OPERATIVE PROVISIONS

1. Definitions and construction

In this Deed, where the context admits, the definitions and rules of construction contained in the Settlement shall apply.

2. Assignment by Life Tenant

The Life Tenant hereby assigns [his/her] interest in the Reversioners' Share to the Reversioners in equal shares absolutely, to the intent that such interest shall merge and be extinguished in the reversion and that the Reversioners shall become entitled to the Reversioners' Share [in equal shares] absolutely.

3. Assignment by Reversioners

The Reversioners hereby assign their respective interests in the Life Tenant's Share to the Life Tenant absolutely, to the intent that the life interest and the reversion shall merge, the life interest shall be enlarged and the Life Tenant shall become entitled to the Life Tenant's Share absolutely.

4. Payment of tax

Without prejudice to the provisions contained in clause 5, it is hereby agreed and declared that any inheritance tax occasioned by the partition in respect of the Reversioners' Share shall be borne by that share and any capital gains tax occasioned by the partition shall be borne by the Life Tenant and the Reversioners in the same proportions as they become absolutely entitled to the Trust Fund.

5. Trustees' lien

Nothing in this Deed shall prejudice or impair in any way any lien to which the Trustees are entitled in respect of any claim for costs, charges or expenses or in order to protect themselves against any tax liabilities.

Clauses 4 and 5 above deal with liability to IHT and CGT which may arise following the partition and the position of the trustees who are liable for that tax. This was considered at **10.1.4**.

10.1.5.1 Schedules

The First Schedule will give details of the settlement which is to be ended, ie the date and parties to it. A Second Schedule will detail the division of the trust property between the life tenant and the reversioner in accordance with the agreement stated in the recitals.

10.2   Discretionary settlements

10.2.1   The nature of the trusts and the powers

Whereas a life tenant of an interest in possession settlement has a right to enjoy the income of settled property, a person who is among the class of beneficiaries of a discretionary settlement has no such right. As an object of the trustees' discretion, he has no right to capital or income unless and until the trustees exercise their discretion. He has a mere hope of benefiting.

Drafting the dispositive provisions of a discretionary settlement is considered in detail in **Chapter 7**. Generally, the trusts are drafted in as wide a form as possible. Such wording permits maximum possible flexibility for the trustees. They can pick and choose between beneficiaries. They have power to appoint absolute interests or to make trust appointments, ie, to create new trusts in favour of the beneficiaries. Unless and until this power is exercised, the trust fund and its income will be subject to default provisions.

10.2.2   Taxation implications of exercising the power of appointment

The exercise of the power will affect the capital of the settlement. Before exercising it, the trustees must consider the IHT and CGT implications. Having done so, additional clauses may be inserted in the deed of appointment dealing with the payment of the tax (see **10.2.8**).

10.2.3   Inheritance tax

Settlements without an interest in possession (IHTA 1984, ss 58–69) are subject to their own regime. The concept of ownership of the settled property by the beneficiaries is not relevant. The settlement is a taxable entity in its own right. Rates of tax are limited to half the rates applicable on death, ie, a maximum rate of 20% applies, although tax is often charged at rates considerably less than 20% (see **10.2.4**).

The regime charges IHT on 'relevant property', ie, settled property in a settlement in which there is no qualifying interest in possession. A qualifying interest in possession includes one to which an individual is beneficially entitled, for example, the life tenant in an interest in possession settlement.

There are a number of occasions when a discretionary settlement is charged to IHT (in addition to the charge which may have arisen when the settlement was created, see **Chapter 5**). These include the periodic charge and the distribution (exit) charge.

10.2.3.1   The periodic charge

This is an anniversary charge at 10-yearly intervals on relevant property in the settlement immediately before the 10th anniversary. The anniversary is calculated from the date of the settlement (or the date of death if the discretionary settlement was created by will).

> Example
> A discretionary settlement is created on 1 July 1995, the first 10-year anniversary charge falls on 1 July 2005 and the second on 1 July 2015, etc.

10.2.3.2   The distribution (exit) charge

A charge also arises when certain events occur, ie, when property ceases to be 'relevant property'. The most common occasion is when property leaves the settlement, for example, on the exercise of a power of appointment by the trustees. Another occasion is when property ceases to be subject to the discretionary trusts because an interest in possession has arisen in some part of the settled property, ie, there is now a qualifying interest in possession. Such an interest may arise following the exercise by the trustees of a power of appointment whereby a beneficiary is given a right to income but not to capital (see also *Sansom and Another v Peay (Inspector of Taxes)* [1976] 3 All ER 375 – see **4.7.3.5**).

This charge is based on the number of complete quarters (periods of three months) the property has been in the settlement since its creation or the previous periodic charge. There are 40 quarters in a 10-year period. If property has been in the settlement for five years, 20 quarters will be used to calculate the charge.

There is no distribution charge, however, if the date when the property ceases to be relevant property is within three months after the creation of the settlement, or within three months after any 10-year anniversary of the creation of the settlement (IHTA 1984, s 65(4)).

10.2.4 The distribution (exit) charge before the first 10-year anniversary

A special provision operates to calculate the charge when property ceases to be 'relevant property' before the first periodic charge.

To calculate the liability to IHT, it is necessary to calculate the settlement's rate of IHT and then to apply that rate to the fall in the value of the trust fund, for example, the fall in value when property leaves the settlement following the exercise of a power of appointment. The value of the trust fund when the charge arises is not relevant to this calculation. To calculate the exit charge, it is necessary to follow five steps.

Step 1: Ascertain the value of a hypothetical chargeable transfer

This is done by adding together:

(a)   the value of the trust property on creation; and

(b)   the value of property added to the settlement after its creation, if any (using the value when added); and

(c)   the value of property in any related settlement (ie, the value at creation of any other settlement created by the settlor on the same day).

Step 2: Ascertain the tax on this hypothetical transfer

The rate of tax is ascertained from the current table of rates. Tax is calculated at 0% or 20%, ie, half the death rate, even if the discretionary settlement is created by will. Any chargeable transfers made by the settlor in the seven years before the settlement was created will reduce the nil rate band available. However, no account is taken of any transfers made on the same day as the settlement. Thus, if the discretionary settlement is created by a will, no account is taken of the rest of the deceased's estate (although his cumulative total of chargeable transfers will be relevant).

Step 3: Ascertain the settlement rate of tax

The tax calculated in Step 2 is converted to an estate or average rate. The rate at which tax is then charged, 'the settlement rate', is 30% of this rate. Thus the maximum rate is 30% × 20% (Step 2) = 6%.

Step 4: The charge to IHT

Inheritance tax is charged on the fall in value of the trust property, as a result of the exercise of the power of appointment, at the rate of one-fortieth of the settlement rate for each complete quarter (three months) between the setting up of the settlement and the event giving rise to the liability. If an appointment occurs within the first quarter, there is no liability.

Step 5: Paying the IHT

If the tax is paid from the amount to be distributed there is no grossing up and the amount calculated at Step 4 is paid. If the tax is paid from the balance of the trust fund, it is necessary to gross up the distribution to calculate the tax payable.

Example 1

A settlor settles £100,000 on discretionary trusts on 1 July 2003. On 1 February 2006 the trustees appoint £50,000 to a beneficiary.

Assume that at the time the settlement was created the settlor had made no previous transfers, ie, he had no cumulative total, no property has been added and there were no related settlements.

Step 1:	Find value of hypothetical chargeable transfer	
	No property added or related settlements, therefore just the original valued settled	£100,000
Step 2:	Ascertain tax on hypothetical chargeable transfer	
	The settlor made no chargeable transfers in the 7-year period before 1 July 2003 and so there is a full nil rate band available	
	Portion of nil rate band available	£100,000
	IHT	nil
Steps 3–5	Need not to be made	
	The charge to IHT is nil on the £50,000 appointed	

Example 2

As above, but assume that the settlor's cumulative total of chargeable transfers was £185,000 and that he paid the IHT when the settlement was created.

Step 1:	Find value of hypothetical chargeable transfer	
	No property added or related settlements, therefore just the original valued settled	£100,000
Step 2:	Ascertain tax on hypothetical chargeable transfer	
	The settlor has made chargeable transfers totalling £185,000 in the 7-year period before 1 July 2003	
	Balance of nil rate band remaining	£90,000
	Portion of hypothetical chargeable transfer taxed at 20%	£10,000
	IHT @ 20% × £10,000 = £2,000	
Step 3:	Ascertain settlement rate	
	First find the Average Rate of tax by dividing the tax by the value of the hypothetical chargeable transfer:	

$$\frac{£2,000}{£100,000} \times 100 = 2\%$$

Then convert to the Settlement Rate which is 30% of the Average Rate:

$$30\% \times 2\% = 0.6\%$$

Step 4:   Ascertain the charge to IHT

Apply the Settlement Rate to
the number of complete quarters which
have occurred in the period between the date
the settlement was created and the date of the
appointment, divided by 40
(1 July 2003–1 February 2006 = 10 complete quarters)

and apply this to the value by which the trust
property has fallen as a result of the appointment

IHT on the appointment of £50,000 is

$$0.6\% \times \frac{10}{40} \times £50,000 = £75$$

Step 5:   Paying the IHT

If the beneficiary pays, the IHT will be £75

If the trustees pay, grossing up applies.

Example 3

As above but the settlor had a cumulative total of £275,000, ie, his nil rate band was already exhausted when the settlement was created.

Step 1:   Find value of hypothetical chargeable transfer

No property added or related settlements, therefore
just the original valued settled   £100,000

Step 2:   Ascertain tax on hypothetical chargeable transfer

The settlor has made chargeable transfers totalling
£275,000 in the 7-year period before 1 July 2003

As there is no available nil rate band the whole of
the hypothetical chargeable transfer is taxed at 20%

IHT @ 20% × £100,000 = £20,000

Step 3:   Ascertain settlement rate

First find the Average Rate of tax by dividing the tax
by the value of the hypothetical chargeable transfer:

$$\frac{£20,000}{£100,000} \times 100 = 20\%$$

Then convert to the Settlement Rate which is
30% of the Average Rate:

30% × 20% = 6%

Step 4:   Ascertain the charge to IHT

Apply the Settlement Rate to
the number of complete quarters which have
occurred in the period between the date the
settlement was created and the date of the
appointment, divided by 40
(1 July 2003–1 February 2006 = 10 complete
quarters)

and apply this to the value by which the trust
property has fallen as a result of the appointment

IHT on the appointment of £50,000 is

$$6\% \times \frac{10}{40} \times £50,000 = £750$$

Step 5:   Paying the IHT

If the beneficiary pays, the IHT will be £750

If the trustees pay, grossing up applies

The effect of the settlor's cumulative total of chargeable transfers

If the settlor had made no chargeable transfers before making the settlement – as in Example 1 (and had created no related settlement nor added any property to the discretionary settlement) – then a full nil rate band is available to the trustees. Thus, if the hypothetical chargeable transfer in Step 1 (the value of the property at the start of the settlement) does not exceed £275,000, the rate of tax on *all* exit charges before the first 10-year anniversary will be a nil rate as established in Step 3. Increases in the value of the trust fund since the creation of the settlement will not affect the position.

Trustees of a discretionary settlement not yet 10 years old can take advantage of this nil rate to distribute all the settled property without liability to IHT. This is an important planning point for the trustees.

10.2.5 The first 10-year anniversary charge

This charge is on the value of the property in the settlement (including any accumulated income) immediately before the anniversary of the creation of the settlement.

Step 1: Ascertain the value of a hypothetical chargeable transfer

This is done by adding together:

(a)   the current value of the relevant property in the settlement; and

(b)   the value at creation of any property in a related settlement (if any); and

(c)   the value at creation of other property in the settlement (if any).

Items (b) and (c) are anti-avoidance provisions which rarely apply. Thus, any charge will usually relate only to the current value of the settled property. For this purpose income will be included as relevant property once it has been accumulated. Income is accumulated for this purpose when the trustees take an irrevocable decision to accumulate (or perhaps after the lapse of a reasonable period of time in which to distribute). Although this is not clear from the legislation, it is the view adopted by the Revenue (see Inland Revenue Statement of Practice (SP 8/86)).

Step 2: Ascertain the tax on this hypothetical transfer

The tax is ascertained from the table of rates. Two cumulative totals may be relevant to this:

(a)   the settlor's cumulative total of chargeable transfers in the seven years before the settlement was created, and

(b)   the settlement's own cumulative total of chargeable transfers made in the first 10 years must be taken into account.

Tax is calculated at 20%, ie, half the death rate (even if the settlement is created by will).

Step 3: Ascertain the settlement rate of tax

The tax calculated in Step 2 is converted into an estate or average rate. The settlement rate is 30% of this rate.

Step 4: The charge to IHT

IHT is charged at the settlement rate applied to the property in the settlement at the anniversary date.

Step 5: Paying the IHT

The trustees will pay the tax from the trust fund.

Example 1

On 1 July 2003 a settlor settled £100,000 on discretionary trusts. The first 10-year anniversary charge falls on 1 July 2013 when the trust fund is worth £140,000 as a result of sound investment by the trustees. No income has been accumulated.

Assume that the settlor had no cumulative total when he created the settlement and no appointments have been made.

Step 1:	Find value of hypothetical chargeable transfer	
	No related settlements or non-relevant property in this settlement, therefore just the value of relevant property at the date of the first 10-year anniversary	£140,000
Step 2:	Ascertain tax on hypothetical chargeable transfer	
	The settlor made no chargeable transfers in the 7-year period before 1 July 2003 and there have been no chargeable transfers out of the settlement in the 10 years since creation, so there is a full nil rate band available	
	Portion of nil rate band available	£140,000
	IHT	nil

Steps 3–5: Need not be made

Example 2

As above, but assume that in 2003 the settlor had a cumulative total of £185,000 from an earlier transfer of value.

Step 1:	Find value of hypothetical chargeable transfer	
	No related settlements or non-relevant property in this settlement, therefore just the value of relevant property at the date of the first 10-year anniversary	£140,000
Step 2:	Ascertain tax on hypothetical chargeable transfer	
	The settlor has made chargeable transfers totalling £185,000 in the 7-year period before 1 July 2003	
	There have been no chargeable transfers out of the settlement in the 10 years since creation	
	Balance of nil rate band remaining	£90,000
	Portion of hypothetical chargeable transfer taxed at 20%	£50,000
	IHT @ 20% × £50,000 = £10,000	
Step 3:	Ascertain settlement rate	
	First find the Average Rate of tax by dividing the tax by the value of the hypothetical chargeable transfer:	

$$\frac{£10,000}{£140,000} \times 100 = 7.14\%$$

Then convert to the Settlement Rate which is 30% of the Average Rate:

$$30\% \times 7.14\% = 2.14\%$$

Step 4:   Ascertain the charge to IHT

Apply the Settlement Rate to the value of relevant property at the date of the first 10-year anniversary

IHT on the first 10-year anniversary is

2.14% × £140,000 = £2,996

Step 5:   Paying the IHT

The trustees pay the IHT from the trust fund.

Example 3

As above, assume that the settlor had a cumulative total of £185,000 in 2003, but that during the first 10 years of the settlement the trustees made an appointment of £50,000 to a beneficiary.

Step 1:   Find value of hypothetical chargeable transfer

No related settlements or non-relevant property in this settlement, therefore just the value of relevant property at the date of the first 10-year anniversary   £140,000

Step 2:   Ascertain tax on hypothetical chargeable transfer

The settlor has made chargeable transfers totalling £185,000 in the 7-year period before 1 July 2003

There has been a chargeable transfer of £50,000 out of the settlement in the 10 years since creation

The cumulative totals of the settlor and the settlement are together £185,000 + £50,000 = £235,000

Balance of nil rate band remaining   £40,000

Portion of hypothetical chargeable transfer taxed at 20%   £100,000

IHT @ 20% × £100,000 = £20,000

Step 3:   Ascertain settlement rate

First find the Average Rate of tax by dividing the tax by the value of the hypothetical chargeable transfer:

$\frac{£20,000}{£140,000} \times 100 = 14.29\%$

Then convert to the Settlement Rate which is 30% of the Average Rate:

30% × 14.29% = 4.29%

Step 4:   Ascertain the charge to IHT

Apply the Settlement Rate to the value of relevant property at the date of the first 10-year anniversary

IHT on the first 10-year anniversary is 4.29% × £140,000 = £6,006

Step 5:   Paying the IHT

The trustees pay the IHT from the trust fund.

The effect of cumulative totals of chargeable transfers of the settlor and the settlement

Each of these has the effect of reducing, or extinguishing, the nil rate band available to the settlement on the occasion of the anniversary charge. Uniquely, the settlor's own cumulative total at the time he made the settlement remains relevant to IHT calculations for as long as the settlement continues. It does not 'drop out' in the way it does for an individual after seven years.

The settlement's own cumulative total ceases to be relevant once an anniversary has passed, although subsequent exit charges will cause the settlement to acquire another cumulative total which will remain relevant until the next 10-year anniversary charge and so on. These factors are particularly relevant to the trustees when considering whether to make distributions, ie, appointments of settled property or to 'break' the settlement.

10.2.6 Subsequent distribution and anniversary charges

Later distribution (exit) charges are brought about by the same events as discussed previously (see **10.2.3**). IHT is charged on the fall in the value of the settled property at a rate based on the rate at the previous 10-year anniversary charge. The number of quarters (periods of three months since then) will be relevant.

Example 3 (continued) – Exit charge

A discretionary settlement created on 1 July 2003 had a settlement rate of 4.29% on its first 10-year anniversary (1 July 2013). On 1 January 2016 (10 quarters later) the trustees appoint £40,000 to a beneficiary. The rate will be one-fortieth of the settlement rate for each complete quarter since the first 10-year anniversary.

The rate of IHT will be $4.29\% \times \dfrac{10}{40} = 1.07\%$

IHT payable will be £40,000 × 1.07% = £428

Later anniversary charges are calculated in the same way as the first anniversary charge. Any cumulative total of chargeable transfers of the settlor before he created the discretionary settlement are taken into account but only exit charges since the last anniversary charge will be relevant.

Example 3 (continued) – Anniversary charge

The facts are the same as in the previous example. Calculate the anniversary charge in 2023 when the value of the trust fund has increased to £190,000 and no further distributions have been made.

Step 1:	Find value of hypothetical chargeable transfer	
	No related settlements or non-relevant property in this settlement, therefore just the value of relevant property at the date of the second 10-year anniversary	£190,000
Step 2:	Ascertain tax on hypothetical chargeable transfer	
	The settlor has made chargeable transfers totalling £185,000 in the 7-year period before 1 July 2003	
	There has been a chargeable transfer of £40,000 out of the settlement in the 10 years since the previous 10-year anniversary	
	The cumulative totals of the settlor and the settlement are together £185,000 + £40,000 = £225,000	
	Balance of nil rate band remaining	£50,000
	Portion of hypothetical chargeable transfer taxed at 20%	£140,000
	IHT @ 20% × £140,000 = £28,000	
Step 3:	Ascertain settlement rate	
	First find the Average Rate of tax by dividing the tax by the value of the hypothetical chargeable transfer:	
	$\dfrac{£28,000}{£190,000} \times 100 = 14.74\%$	
	Then convert to the Settlement Rate which is 30% of the Average Rate:	
	30% × 14.74% = 4.42%	

Step 4:   Ascertain the charge to IHT

Apply the Settlement Rate to the value of relevant property at the date of the second 10-year anniversary

IHT on the second 10-year anniversary is
$4.42\% \times £190,000 = £8,398$

Step 5:   Paying the IHT

The trustees pay the IHT from the trust fund.

10.2.7 Capital gains tax

As in the case of interest in possession settlements, a deemed disposal by the trustees will occur on their exercise of a power of appointment whereby someone becomes 'absolutely entitled' to the settled property against the trustees.

10.2.7.1 Deemed disposals

Deemed disposals have been considered at **10.1.4.1** in relation to interest in possession settlements. The principles discussed apply equally to appointments by trustees from discretionary trusts in favour of individuals.

If the appointment by the trustees creates new trusts of which there are new trustees, these new trustees may become absolutely entitled to the settled property as against the 'old' trustees. If so, the old trustees will make a deemed disposal to the new trustees. However, if the property appointed remains subject to some of the original trusts and trust instrument, there will be no deemed disposal.

There is often a fine line between the two situations. This is considered further at **10.4**.

10.2.7.2 Reliefs, exemptions and rates

The rate of CGT for discretionary trustees is 40% of the net chargeable gain. An annual exemption of £4,250 is available to the trustees.

Hold-over relief will generally be available when assets leave a discretionary settlement (see **10.1.4**). The relief can be claimed, inter alia, if the occasion which gives rise to the disposal is also an occasion of immediate liability to IHT. The relief will be available even if the rate at which IHT is charged is at 0% – for example, because the transfer is within the nil rate band.

However, because s 65(4) of IHTA 1984 provides that there is no charge to IHT if assets leave the discretionary trust within three months after the date of creation, or three months after the date of any 10-year anniversary, hold-over relief is not available if the exit occurs during this time (unless the assets qualified as business assets under s 165 of TCGA 1992).

If the trustees and the beneficiaries agree to claim hold-over relief, it is convenient to add an appropriate clause to the deed of appointment containing their hold-over election. As a joint election of the beneficiaries and the trustees is required, they should all be made parties to the deed of appointment. If preferred, the election can be contained in a separate document.

Example

Trustees of a discretionary settlement appoint 5,000 DEF plc shares worth £20,000 to Johan. The shares were worth £5,000 when they were acquired.

Disposal consideration	£20,000
Less: Acquisition cost	£5,000
	£15,000
Indexation allowance (say)	£750
Chargeable gain (subject to taper relief based on the trustees' period of ownership)	£14,250

(a)   No hold-over relief election:

Trustees pay tax on £14,250 – £4,250 (annual exemption) = £10,000 @ 40% = £4,000. Johan acquires the shares at a cost of £20,000.

(b)   Hold-over relief election:

There are two consequences:

(i)   the trustees pay no CGT

(ii)   Johan's acquisition cost is reduced

Market value of shares at appointment	£20,000
Less: held-over gain	£14,250
Johan's acquisition cost	£5,750

Johan benefits from the trustees' indexation allowance but not from their annual exemption or from their period of ownership for the purposes of taper relief.

10.2.8   Drafting a deed of appointment

A deed should always be used even though an absolute appointment may be made less formally and could merely be recorded by the trustees making a memorandum note in their records.

Heading and date

Sample clause

DEED OF APPOINTMENT

DATE: [   ]

Parties

There will be two parties to a deed if an absolute appointment is intended:

(a)   the appointors, sometimes defined as 'the trustees'; and

(b)   the beneficiary.

If an appointment on further trusts with the same trustees is to be made, the deed will normally be made by the appointors alone.

Sample clause

BETWEEN

(1)   [name and address] ('the Appointors')

(2)   [name and address] ('the Beneficiary')

Recitals

The recitals should explain the circumstances surrounding the exercise of the power. They will be confined to a brief statement that the trustees intend to exercise their power of appointment under the settlement in the manner indicated in the operative part of the deed.

Sample clause

RECITALS

(A) This Deed is supplemental to the settlement ('the Settlement')

[and to the other documents and events] specified in the [First] Schedule.

(B) The Appointors are the present Trustees of the Settlement.

(C) [   ] is a member of the class of Beneficiaries.

(D) The Appointors wish to exercise their power of appointment under clause

[   ] of the Settlement in the following manner.

The operative part

Sample clause

OPERATIVE PROVISIONS

1.   Definitions and construction

In this Deed:

1.1   'the Appointed Fund' shall mean [that part of] the Trust Fund [specified in the Second Schedule]; and subject thereto,

1.2   where the context admits, the definitions and rules of construction contained in the Settlement shall apply.

2. Appointment

The Appointors, in exercise of the power of appointment conferred by clause [ ] of the Settlement and of all other relevant powers, hereby [ir]revocably appoint and declare that the Appointed Fund shall henceforth be held upon trust for [ ] absolutely.

[3. Application of Settlement provisions

The trusts, powers and provisions contained in the Settlement shall continue to be applicable to the Appointed Fund so far as consistent with the provisions of this Deed.]

[4. Payment of tax and expenses

Any inheritance tax or capital gains tax and all other costs, expenses and other liabilities occasioned by the appointment contained in this Deed shall be borne by [the Appointed Fund] [the balance of the Trust Fund.]

5. Trustees' lien

Nothing in this Deed shall prejudice or impair in any way any lien or charge to which the Trustees are entitled in respect of any tax and other liabilities whatever for which they are or may become accountable.

[6. Capital gains tax hold-over relief

The parties claim relief under the provisions of s [165] [260] of the Taxation of Chargeable Gains Act 1992 in respect of the appointment contained in this Deed.]

[7. Power of revocation

The Trustees shall have power, at any time during the Trust Period, by deed or deeds wholly or partly to revoke the appointment contained in this Deed.]

Clause 3 will not be required if the appointment is both irrevocable and gives the beneficiary an absolute interest. If the appointment is onto trusts, clause 3 can be used to indicate that the powers under the original settlement are to apply to the Appointed Fund (where those powers are considered suitable). Clause 3 will also be required where the appointment is revocable. Clause 4 deals with the division of capital tax liability where part only of the trust fund is appointed. If the whole fund is appointed, it can be omitted.

Clause 6 is a claim by the parties for hold-over relief on the basis that the appointment is an occasion of charge to IHT (s 260). An equivalent claim could be made under TCGA 1992, s 165 if the assets appointed from the settlement were business assets. Hold-over relief is considered at **4.4.5.2** and see **10.1.4.** Clause 7 will not be required if, as is usual, the appointment is irrevocable.

Schedules

Schedules will give details of the settlement under which the appointment is made and of the trust fund (or part) which is being appointed.

10.3 Accumulation and maintenance settlements

10.3.1 The nature of the trusts and the powers

As we saw in **Chapter 8**, A & M settlements are a particular type of settlement without an interest in possession. They enjoy privileged treatment for IHT purposes but will only qualify as A & M settlements if the requirements of IHTA 1984, s 71(1) are fulfilled.

A power of appointment may be inserted in an A & M settlement. However, considerable care is needed to ensure that neither the wording of the power, nor the manner in which it may be exercised, cause the settlement to fail to qualify from the outset as an A & M settlement and so lose the IHT advantages. If, through the existence of the power, there is any possibility, however remote, that an entitlement to income or capital will not be acquired on or before the beneficiary attains 25 years of age, the settlement will not qualify as an A & M settlement. Drafting the power so that it is not capable of exercise by the trustees in a way which could infringe the conditions was considered in **Chapter 8**.

10.3.2 Taxation implications of exercising the power of appointment

The exercise of the power by the trustees will affect the capital of the trust. Thus, before its exercise the trustees must consider the IHT and CGT implications as well as making provision for any tax for which they may become liable.

10.3.2.1 Inheritance tax

The exercise of the power of appointment shows the advantages of the A & M settlement.

Normally, the effect of the exercise of the power is that the property in the settlement is no longer held in a 'no interest in possession settlement'. If the trustees give a beneficiary a right to income, they create an interest in possession settlement. If the trustees give a beneficiary an absolute right to trust property, it leaves the settlement completely. Under the normal discretionary settlement charging regime, a distribution (exit) charge would arise in both cases (see **10.2.3.2**) but this is not so for A & M settlements.

Provided the A & M settlement is drafted to comply with the basic conditions, the exercise of a power of appointment will not give rise to an IHT liability. The IHTA 1984, s 71(4) provides that tax shall not be charged under this section:

(a)   on a beneficiary becoming beneficially entitled to, or to an interest in possession in, settled property on or before attaining the specified age; or

(b)   on the death of the beneficiary before attaining the specified age (the specified age is an age not exceeding 25 years, as required by s 71(1)(a)).

Example

£100,000 is held by trustees on A & M trusts for such of Sanjay's grandchildren as attain 21 years. The trustees exercise a power to appoint £50,000 on interest in possession trusts for the benefit of the eldest grandchild. No IHT is payable. The grandchild has an interest in possession on or before 25 years as required by s 71 of the IHTA 1984. The property remains settled property subject to interest in possession trusts. The A & M settlement has ended in relation to the £50,000.

Exit charges and accumulation and maintenance settlements

An A & M settlement will end when the conditions in IHTA 1984, s 71 are no longer satisfied. Often this will occur following the exercise of a power of appointment. This occurred in the previous example where an interest in possession was created; a similar result would occur if an absolute entitlement was granted by the exercise of the power.

An A & M settlement will also end where the beneficiary satisfies the conditions for the vesting of income and/or capital contained in the settlement. For example, a settlement giving the right to income at 18 years (TA 1925, s 31 applies) and capital at 25 years will end once the beneficiary attains majority (condition (b) in **5.4.1** is no longer satisfied). Likewise, a settlement giving the right to income and capital at 25 years (TA 1925, s 31 modified appropriately) will end once the beneficiary attains 25 years.

No liability to IHT will arise in either of these circumstances (IHTA 1984, s 71(4)(a)), nor will liability arise on the death of a beneficiary before reaching a specified age (s 71(4)(b)). However, if the settlement ends in other circumstances, an exit charge can arise.

Example 1

Property is held by trustees on A & M trusts for the settlor's only grandchild, Helen, contingent on her reaching 18 and in default to her father, Tom, the settlor's only child. If Helen reaches 18 and takes the property, there is no charge to IHT. If she dies at 16 and the property passes to Tom, there is no charge to IHT, because the settlement ends when Helen, the only beneficiary, dies under the specified age of 18.

Example 2

Property is held by trustees on A & M trusts for the settlor's grandchildren. The settlor is dead. In default the property will pass to Jack, the only child of the settlor. The settlor's only grandchild dies in a road accident. The trust continues for the benefit of any future born grandchildren of the settlor. Later, Jack dies having had no other children. The trust ends at this point and the property passes to Jack's estate. No IHT is payable on the value of the property in the settlement as a result of the grandchild's death. However, as the settlement did not end at this point, there will be an exit charge on the distribution to Jack's estate based on the value of the fund and the length of time it has been in the settlement.

A liability may also arise where the period of 25 years for the duration of the settlement expires (condition (c) in **5.4.1**) in a settlement where the common grandparent test was not used.

10.3.2.2   Capital gains tax

As in the case of interest in possession settlements and discretionary settlements, a 'deemed' disposal will occur when someone becomes 'absolutely entitled' to the trust property against the trustees.

Deemed disposals

The principles discussed in **10.2.7** in relation to discretionary settlements apply equally to appointments by trustees from A & M settlements.

Reliefs, exemptions and rates

The rate of tax for A & M trustees is 40% of any net chargeable gain. An annual exemption of £4,250 is available to the trustees.

Hold-over relief is available if the settlement qualifies as an A & M settlement at the time of the deemed disposal (TCGA 1992, s 260) or if the assets disposed of are business assets (TCGA 1992, s 165) – see **4.4.5.2**.

If the A & M settlement has ended before the deemed disposal occurs, relief will not be available. Perhaps the most common example of this is where the beneficiary of an A & M settlement becomes absolutely entitled to an interest in possession and then becomes absolutely entitled as against the trustees. The A & M settlement ended when the interest in possession was acquired.

If the settled property is 'business assets', the relief will always be available (TCGA 1992, s 165) regardless of the type of settlement. In the following examples, there are no business assets.

Example 1

Trustees of an A & M settlement hold property on trust for Rajid if he attains the age of 18 years. When he does so, the A & M settlement ends and Rajid becomes absolutely entitled to the settled property. Any gain made by the trustees on the deemed disposal on Rajid's 18th birthday may be held over on an election being made by the trustees and Rajid.

Example 2

Trustees of an A & M settlement hold property on trust for Amy contingently on her attaining the age of 25 years. At 18, Amy becomes entitled to the income of the settled property under s 31 of the TA 1925. The A & M settlement ends (because Amy now has a right to the income) but no deemed disposal occurs. This is not an event which affects the capital of the settlement.

At 25, Amy becomes absolutely entitled to the settled property. A deemed disposal occurs and hold-over relief is not available since the A & M settlement ended when the interest in possession arose on Amy's 18th birthday.

Example 3

Assume the facts are as in Example 2, but Amy is entitled to both the capital and the income at the age of 25 (TA 1925 is modified suitably). When the deemed disposal occurs on her 25th birthday, the A & M settlement ends. Any gain on the deemed disposal by the trustees may be held over on an election being made by Amy and the trustees since the A & M settlement continued until her 25th birthday.

Hold-over relief planning

By planning ahead the trustees may be able to overcome the potential loss of hold-over relief. If they consider it appropriate, they may be able to exercise either the statutory power of advancement (under TA 1925, s 32) or an express power of appointment to coincide with the time when the beneficiary is to obtain an interest in possession. If the statutory power is exercised, only one half of the beneficiary's entitlement can be advanced to him (with the benefit of hold-over relief) leaving the beneficiary to become entitled to the remaining half of the entitlement on the vesting date provided by the settlement.

10.3.3 Drafting a deed of appointment

As the beneficial interests under an A & M settlement are similar to those under a discretionary settlement, a power of appointment by the trustees will be drafted in a similar manner to the deed discussed in **10.2.8**. As in that case, the trustees may create by appointment absolute interests or interests under new trusts.

However, the terms of the power must be limited so as not to infringe the s 71 requirements for A & M status.

When the trustees propose exercising a power, they must remember the requirements of s 71 and ensure that the appointment does not infringe them (for example, by making an appointment which will vest after the age of 25).

10.4 Resettlements

10.4.1 Absolute entitlement for CGT?

So far, this chapter has concentrated upon deemed disposals where an individual has become absolutely entitled to settled property against the trustees. Modern settlements, in particular discretionary settlements but also accumulation and maintenance trusts, are drafted in flexible form and usually include fiduciary powers for the trustees to 'declare new trusts' in relation to some or all of the settled property. The possibility of exercising either a power of advancement or appointment in this way is mentioned in **Chapter 9** (see **9.1**). Although the statutory power of advancement (TA 1925, s 32) is generally used to give an individual absolute entitlement to property freed from any continuing trusts, it has been held that the section may also be used to create trust advances, ie, to advance property in such a way that it is to be held in trust for a beneficiary, see *Pilkington and Another v Inland Revenue Commissioners and Others* [1964] AC 612 where a settled advance was for a beneficiary's 'benefit' within s 32 (see **9.4.2.3**).

The phrase 'absolutely entitled against the trustees' does not mean 'absolutely and beneficially entitled'. It is therefore possible that one set of trustees (whether they are the same people or not) may, following the exercise of a fiduciary power, become absolutely entitled against another set of trustees. However, this does not necessarily mean that there will be a separate settlement. If there is not, then the usual rule in TCGA 1992, s 69 that the trustees are a single and continuing body of persons will apply, ie, there will be no deemed disposal and so there can be no question of liability to CGT arising.

If trustees propose exercising their power to declare new trusts, they need to consider whether or not the exercise of the power will amount to a deemed disposal. This is an area of some uncertainty although clarification has been provided through the Inland Revenue Statement of Practice (SP 7/84) following the decision in *Bond (Inspector of Taxes) v Pickford* [1983] STC 517 (see **10.4.2** and **10.4.3**).

10.4.2 A separate settlement or not?

In *Roome and Another v Edwards (Inspector of Taxes)* [1982] AC 279, the leading case in this area, Lord Wilberforce suggested that the existence of separate trustees, trusts and trust property was not necessarily conclusive as to the existence of a separate settlement. In the following extracts from the judgment, he draws a distinction between a special power of appointment (its exercise being unlikely to create a separate settlement) and the exercise of a wider form power which is more likely to create a separate settlement because property may be removed from the original settlement and subjected to other trusts:

> ... trusts declared by a ... special power of appointment are to be read into the original settlement ... If such a power is exercised, whether or not separate trustees are appointed, I do not think that it would be natural ... to say that a separate settlement had been created, still less so if it were found that provisions of the original settlement continued to apply to the appointed fund, or that the appointed fund were liable, in certain events, to fall back into the rest of the settled property.

> If such a [wider form] power is exercised, the natural conclusion might be that a separate settlement was created, all the more so if a complete new set of trusts were declared as to the appropriated property, and if it would be said that the trusts of the original settlement ceased to apply to it. There can be many variations on these cases each of which will have to be judged on its facts.

In *Bond (Inspector of Taxes) v Pickford,* there were three relevant powers in the settlement whereby the trustees could:

(a)   pay or apply funds to or for the benefit of the beneficiaries;

(b)   allocate funds to beneficiaries either absolutely or contingently on attaining a specified age;

(c)   resettle funds for the benefit of the beneficiaries.

What was the effect of an allocation of funds for named beneficiaries on attaining 22 years of age under (b) above: did it create a separate settlement? The Court of Appeal held that a new settlement had not been created and in doing so distinguished between powers in the 'narrower form' and powers in the 'wider form'. The former do not permit property to be freed from the original settlement; the latter do permit this. It is not so much the description given to the power in the trust instrument which is significant, it is what it permits the trustees to do. The Court of Appeal held that the power in (b) above was a narrower form power in that it permitted a reorganisation internally within the original settlement and not the removal of funds from the settlement.

The manner of exercise of any given power is crucial. The mere fact that a wider form power may be exercised to free property from the original settlement does not necessarily mean it has been exercised in this way. It will be a matter of intention; the trustees may decide to exercise it in a narrower form way. If they wish to avoid a separate settlement, and the associated deemed disposal for CGT, they will exercise the power in a narrower way; the property will remain subject to the original trusts.

10.4.3   Inland Revenue Statement of Practice (SP 7/84)

This Statement of Practice followed the Court of Appeal decision in *Bond (Inspector of Taxes) v Pickford* and contains the following:

> ... the Board considers that a deemed disposal will not arise when ... [powers in the wider form, which may be powers of advancement or certain powers of appointment, are] ... exercised and trusts are declared in circumstances where:
>
> (a)   the appointment is revocable, or
>
> (b)   the trusts declared of the advanced or appointed funds are not exhaustive so that there exists a possibility at the time when the advancement or appointment is made that the funds covered by it will on the occasion of some event cease to be held upon such trusts and once again come to be held upon the original trusts of the settlement.

Further, when such a power is exercised the Board considers it unlikely that a deemed disposal will arise when trusts are declared if duties in regard to the appointed assets still fall to the trustees of the original settlement in their capacity as trustees of that settlement ... Finally, the Board accepts that a power of appointment or advancement can be exercised over only part of the settled property and that the above consequences would apply to that part.

By this Statement of Practice, the Revenue accepts that a new settlement can be created only if a wider form power is exercised. There are, however, limitations when a new settlement would not be created, ie, where the exercise is revocable, the trusts are not exhaustive in the sense that some of the property could again become subject to the original trusts and where the trustees of the original settlement have continuing duties in relation to the settled property.

10.4.4 Drafting the trustees' power of appointment

Powers of appointment given to trustees should be drafted as separate clauses in such a way as to make it abundantly clear whether they are wider form or narrower form powers. Trustees, having considered the effect of the exercise of their powers fully (including the CGT consequences) can then specifically exercise by deed a narrower or a wider form power. By so doing, difficulty of construction and effect for CGT of the deed of appointment should be avoided.

10.4.5 The CGT consequences of a separate settlement

If a separate settlement is created by the exercise of the power of appointment, the new trustees become absolutely entitled against the old (whether they are the same people or not) so that there is a deemed disposal for CGT. The calculation of the gain (or loss) follows normal principles (including the deductions for the indexation allowance, taper relief and the trustees' annual exemption of £4,250). The trustees pay any tax due from the settled property.

If cash is appointed, no liability to CGT will arise. Otherwise, hold-over relief may be available to the trustees under TCGA 1992, s 165 or s 260 depending on the circumstances but, in this case, the annual exemption and taper relief will not be available.

10.4.6 The documentation if a separate settlement

In addition to a deed of appointment drafted in the manner discussed earlier, the trustees of the old settlement will need to sign stock transfer forms to transfer the settled stocks and shares to the new trustees. If they are the same people, stock transfer forms will still be required but it may be sensible specifically to designate the transferees as trustees of the newly created settlement so as to avoid confusing the share certificates in their own names for the investments in the new settlement with those belonging to them as trustees of the original settlement.

10.4.7 Summary

Tax on exercise of powers of appointment and advancement.

Settlement	IHT	CGT
Interest in possession	PET (except to the extent the life tenant benefits)	Deemed disposal No hold-over relief (unless business assets)

Discretionary	Exit or periodic charge	Deemed disposal (if absolute entitlement)
		Hold-over relief available
Accumulation and maintenance	No exit or periodic charge	Deemed disposal (if absolute entitlement)
		Hold-over relief available provided IHTA 1984, s 71 satisfied (or if business assets)

Chapter 11

Basic Will Drafting

This chapter deals with the basic content of a will, and the typical provisions likely to appear in all types of will. The next chapter deals with the special provisions required for the creation of different types of trust within a will. For further exploration of the subject, refer to practitioners' books such as Withers, *Practical Will Precedents* (Sweet & Maxwell), *Williams on Wills, Wills Probate and Administration* (Butterworths).

It is important to be aware that since the House of Lords' decision in *White v Jones* [1995] 1 All ER 691, will drafting is the fastest growing area for negligence claims against solicitors. Many firms prohibit anyone who is not a specialist from attempting it.

11.1 Preliminary matters

A solicitor taking instructions for a will should be aware of the need for the testator to have the requisite capacity and intention. This is considered in LPC Guide, *Pervasive and Core Topics*, para 31.2.

The solicitor should also be aware of the tax consequences of the testator's instructions, and be able to advise on tax savings where possible. Inheritance tax on death is considered in LPC Guide, *Pervasive and Core Topics*, para 4.3, and general tax planning is considered in **Chapter 4** above.

The solicitor should also be aware of relevant issues of professional conduct. For example, instructions must be taken from the client and not from an intermediary. The solicitor must not draft a will giving a significant amount to him/herself, a partner or member of the solicitor's family unless the client has obtained independent advice.

At the time of writing the Civil Partnership Act (CPA) 2004 is due to become effective in December 2005. Once it is in effect it will have important implications for will drafting. The CPA 2004 allows same sex couples who are not closely related to each other to register a civil partnership.

Persons who have registered a civil partnership will, in effect, be treated as spouses for the purposes of succession to property. Basically the provisions of the Married Women's Property Act 1882, s 11 and enactments relating to wills and administration of estates, and the Inheritance (Provision for Family and Dependants) Act 1975 are amended to apply in relation to civil partnerships as they do to marriages.

The main provisions relating to wills and administration that are amended are:

(a) revocation by marriage/civil partnership unless a will is made in expectation of marriage or civil partnership;

(b)   gift in will to former spouse/civil partner treated as lapsed where divorce/ dissolution of civil partnership occurs;

(c)   avoidance of gifts attested by spouse/civil partner;

(d)   entitlement on intestacy including rights to take 'matrimonial home' in or toward satisfaction of absolute entitlement on intestacy; and

(e)   civil partners have same rights as spouses to make applications under the Inheritance (Provision for Family and Dependants) Act 1975.

In this chapter we have included references to civil partner where appropriate.

11.2   Basic content of a will

All wills should contain the following:

(a)   opening words or commencement;

(b)   revocation clause;

(c)   date;

(d)   appointment of executors;

(e)   legacies and/or gift of residue;

(f)   attestation clause.

Although these provisions may be sufficient for a very simple will, most wills require additional provisions. For example, if any of the legacies is to a charity, it is desirable to make provision for the possibility that the charity may amalgamate or cease to exist. If any of the legacies give rise to a continuing trust, it may be necessary to supply express trust administration powers for the trustees.

11.2.1   Opening words or commencement

The main purpose of this clause is to identify the testator and the nature of the document.

The full name and address of the testator should be stated. If the testator holds property in any other name, it will be helpful when the application for the grant of representation is later made if the will also states this other name and indicates that the testator is also known by it. Details of the testator's occupation may also be included as further identification.

A statement that the document is the 'last will' or 'last will and testament' (there is no legal difference between these phrases) should be included. This helps demonstrate that the testator had an intention to make a will, which is a legal requirement.

The date may appear within the commencement or at the end of the will. A space should be left as the will is dated on execution.

If the testator intends to marry in the near future he should state that the will is made in expectation of that marriage and that he does not wish the marriage to revoke the will. In the absence of such a statement the will is automatically revoked by subsequent marriage. Civil partnership will have the same effect.

11.2.2   Revocation clause

The purpose of this clause is to indicate that all earlier wills and codicils are expressly revoked. Any later will impliedly revokes earlier wills and codicils but only to the extent that the later will is inconsistent with the earlier provisions. An express revocation avoids the risk of an earlier will or codicil not being wholly revoked by the implied revocation.

The revocation clause may appear by itself, but it is also commonly incorporated into the commencement. It should appear near the beginning of the will.

11.2.3 Appointment of executors (and trustees)

The purpose of this clause is to appoint the persons that the testator has chosen to administer his estate (the executor(s)). If the testator does not take the opportunity to name his own choice, the Non-contentious Probate Rules 1987 (SI 1987/2024) will govern who may act as administrator (see LPC Guide, *Pervasive and Core Topics*, para 32.10.2).

It is sometimes sensible to create an express trust of the estate (see below for where this is the case). Where this happens, the testator should appoint persons to be trustees. It is often convenient to name the same people as both executors and trustees, although it is not essential. Such people will act as executors while they collect in the estate, pay debts and distribute the estate. When they have completed that stage, they will transfer the property that is to be held on trust to themselves to hold in the new capacity of trustee.

11.2.3.1 How many executors?

In principle there is no maximum number of executors that can be named in the will. However, as only a maximum of four can apply for the grant of probate to the same assets, there is little point in naming more than four.

It is possible to limit the appointment of executors to particular parts of the estate. For example, a testator may appoint specialists to deal with his business assets or literary effects and members of his family to deal with his general assets. In such a case each appointment can be of up to four people.

The minimum number is one, and this will often be sufficient for a small, simple estate where the executor is the sole or main beneficiary. (A sole executor can give a good receipt for the proceeds of sale of land held in the estate.) However, there is a risk that the sole executor may pre-decease the testator or be unable to act for some other reason. For example, the effect of a divorce on a will is that the spouse is deemed to have died at the date of the divorce, so that any appointment of the spouse as executor will not take effect (Wills Act 1837, s 18A). (The dissolution of a civil partnership will have the same effect.) It is therefore prudent to appoint at least two persons, or name a substitute for a sole executor.

If the executors will also be trustees it is sensible to appoint at least two so that they can give a good receipt for the proceeds of sale of any land held in the trust.

11.2.3.2 Whom to choose?

The testator may appoint any combination of:

(a) individuals who are not professionals (eg, family or friends);

(b) solicitors or other professionals (as individuals or as a firm);

(c) banks or other trust corporations.

A testator may ask for advice on the type of person he should appoint and the solicitor should therefore be able to discuss the relevant considerations allowing the testator to make an informed choice.

11.2.3.3   Non-professional individuals

Choosing family members or close friends whom the testator can trust will have the advantage of ensuring that persons familiar with the testator and his affairs will deal with the estate. A further advantage is that such persons are unlikely to want to charge the estate for their time spent in dealing with it. However, this advantage may be more apparent than real. If the estate is other than straightforward, it is likely that the individuals will lack the expertise necessary to complete the administration and will have to employ a solicitor. The costs of this will be paid from the estate.

Naturally the testator should only choose those responsible enough to deal with the estate, and should not appoint anyone barred from taking out a grant of probate (such as a minor or a convicted criminal).

11.2.3.4   Solicitors or other professionals

Choosing a solicitor or other professional will mean that the executor will have the necessary expertise to administer the estate. Family and friends will be spared the burden at a time when they may be grieving. However, the professional executor will expect to be paid not just for expenses incurred but also for the time spent doing the work.

An individual solicitor may be appointed, but there is a risk that this person may die or retire. To avoid this possibility the firm of solicitors can be appointed.

If the testator decides to appoint a firm of solicitors there are some drafting considerations:

(a)   The firm, being a partnership, has no legal identity and so cannot be appointed. Instead the appointment is of the partners in the named firm. As these will change from time to time it is important to specify that it is the partners in the firm at the date of death who are appointed. Otherwise the appointment will be of those at the date of the will. It is usual to express the wish that only two partners will take the grant and act in the administration.

(b)   The firm may change its name or amalgamate between the date of the will and the date of death, and it is sensible to provide for this. Usually the testator will indicate that the appointment is of the partners in the new or amalgamated firm.

11.2.3.5   Banks or other trust corporations

A testator may consider appointing a bank as executor. Most high street banks have a trustee department, and it is able to act via the mechanism of a trust corporation. Appointing this type of executor has some similar advantages to appointing a firm of solicitors: the corporation will not die or retire, and there should be financial and some legal expertise. Disadvantages include the fact that the corporation may seem large and impersonal to the family. The charging methods of banks may also be disadvantageous, as they usually charge a percentage of the value of the estate, which can be a significant expense.

11.2.3.6   Charging provisions

Whether it is an individual professional or a firm appointed, there will be a need to consider the charging arrangements. An executor or trustee is a fiduciary and unable to profit from his position, unless authorised. The Trustee Act (TA) 2000, s 29 allows the payment of reasonable remuneration to a trustee for time spent and work done (even if such work could have been done by a lay person), but only if the trustee is either:

(a)   a trust corporation; or

(b)   a trustee 'acting in a professional capacity', but who is not a sole trustee and who has got the written consent of all his co-trustees.

'Acting in a professional capacity' means acting in the course of a profession or business which involves providing relevant services to trusts.

Trustees may only charge for services carried out after 1 February 2001, although the provision applies to all trusts unless excluded.

An express charging provision will always be required to allow any trustee who does not fall within s 29 to charge for time spent and work done. It may also be desirable to include express provisions allowing:

(a)   a trust corporation to be paid in accordance with its standard terms and conditions; and/or

(b)   a trustee to retain remuneration he has received for services given as a director of a company in which the trust holds shares.

It is usual in any express charging clause to state that the solicitor or other professional may charge for work done, even though it could have been done by a non-professional. Again, although the TA 2000 now provides for this, it is better to have clear express drafting within the will.

Where an express charging provision is included it may appear early on together with the clause appointing the executors, or later among the administrative provisions. It does not matter which approach is used.

Until the TA 2000 came into force, a charging clause was treated as a legacy in the will. Under s 15 of the Wills Act 1837, a beneficiary loses his benefit if he or his spouse (or civil partner) witnesses the will. Therefore, in the past if a will had a charging clause, it could not be witnessed by the individual solicitor appointed or any of the partners in the firm appointed, or any spouses or civil partners. The TA 2000 now provides that a charging clause does not qualify as a legacy for these purposes. (However, the TA 2000 only operates for this purpose on wills where death occurred after 1 February 2001.)

11.2.4   Non-residuary gifts

A testator may wish to make gifts of specific assets or of money. Traditionally a legacy is a gift of personalty and a devise is a gift of land. The term 'gift' applies to either. There are various types of gift.

11.2.4.1   Specific gifts

This is a gift of a specific item or items or specific piece of land which the testator owns, for example, 'I give my diamond engagement ring to my daughter'. If the testator does not own the specific item or property at death, the gift fails ('adeems'). The beneficiary gets nothing in place of the gifted item unless the will expressly provides for substitution.

11.2.4.2   General gifts

This is a gift of an item corresponding to a description. If the testator does not own this item at death, it must be obtained using funds from the estate, for example, 'I give 100 shares in Z plc to my son'. If the testator does not own 100 such shares then they must be purchased.

11.2.4.3 Demonstrative gift

This is a gift that is general in nature but is directed to be paid from a specific fund, for example, 'I give £500 to X to be paid from my Nationwide savings account'. If the account exists at the date of the death and contains £500 or more, the legacy is paid from the account and is classified as specific. If there is no account (or if it contains less than £500), the legacy is paid, in whole or in part, from the rest of the estate and to that extent is classified as general.

11.2.4.4 Pecuniary gift

This is a gift of money. This gift will usually be general, but could be demonstrative, or possibly even specific, for example, 'I give the £100 held in the safe in the study'.

Note: Where there are insufficient assets in an estate to pay all debts and expenses and pay the legacies in full, legacies will be reduced ('abate') proportionately. General legacies will be reduced first and only if they are insufficient will specific legacies be taken.

Where a testator wishes to include non-residuary gifts, there are a number of matters to consider and upon which instructions should be obtained.

11.2.4.5 The beneficiary

Identification

This person must be clearly identified in the will, otherwise the gift will fail for uncertainty. Accurately stating the name and address is important, and including the relationship to the testator will also help. Where the gift is to a person, rather than a group, it is unwise only to describe that person by relationship, for example, to 'my nephew' because there may be more than one person answering that description. A gift to 'my nephews', though will not suffer this problem.

Where the identity of the person who fits the description changes, it is the person who fits that description at the date of the will who is construed as the beneficiary. For example, a gift to 'my son's wife' will mean his wife at the date of the will, even if by the date of death he is married to someone else.

Vested or contingent?

Where the testator wishes to benefit persons who may be minors, or relatively young, he should consider whether he wishes to make outright or contingent gifts.

A vested gift imposes no conditions, and the beneficiary will be immediately entitled to it merely by outliving the testator. For example, 'I give £10,000 to my grandson, Oliver'. If the beneficiary is under 18 then he will be unable to give a good receipt to the executors (unless the will permits it) and there will be a trust of the gift until he is 18. Here, therefore if Oliver were over 18 at his grandfather's death he would receive his gift straight away. If he were under 18, he would receive his gift as soon as he became 18. If he were to die under 18 the money would form part of his estate.

A contingent gift imposes conditions to be satisfied before the gift can vest. The most common contingency is to require the beneficiary to reach a certain age, for example, 'I give £10,000 to my grandson, Oliver, provided he reaches the age of 25'. Only if Oliver reaches 25 will he be entitled to the £10,000. If he is under 25 when his grandfather dies the money will be held on trust until he reaches 25. If he were to die under 25 his estate will not be entitled to the cash which will instead pass to the person(s) expressed to be entitled in default or, if none, with the residue of his grandfather's estate.

The testator must decide how he will make the gift and, if contingent, the nature of the contingency. For further discussion of this topic see **12.6**.

Lapse

A beneficiary who predeceases the testator is not able to take a legacy. The legacy will normally fail or 'lapse' and will pass with residue unless the will provides for a substitute beneficiary.

Wills Act 1837, s 33 provides a limited exception to the doctrine of lapse. It provides that where a gift to the testator's child or remoter descendent fails because that person pre-deceases the testator, but leaves issue living at the testator's death then those issue will take the gift.

Examples of effect of Wills Act 1837, s 33

Fred leaves his estate to 'such of my children who survive me'.

Ben and Jill survive Fred. Greg pre-deceases him. If Greg has no issue alive at Fred's death, the estate will be split equally between Ben and Jill. However, if Greg has issue who survive Fred, the one-third share which he would have taken will be divided among his issue.

Nobody can take an interest under s 33 if he has a parent alive.

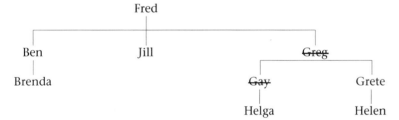

Brenda takes nothing because her father is alive. Greg's one-third share is divided into two. Helga takes the one-sixth her mother, Gay, would have taken. Grete takes the other one-sixth. Helen takes nothing as her mother Grete is still alive.

The section can be excluded by contrary intention expressed in the will. It is usual to include an express substitution provision rather than to rely on the implied provisions.

Burden of tax, etc

It is important to consider where the burden of any tax or other costs associated with the gift may fall. Where the will is silent the statutory order contained in the Administration of Estates Act 1925 (AEA 1925) applies. Usually this means that tax is paid from the residue, and any debts charged on specific assets will be paid from that asset. It is important to expressly vary this if the testator does not want this to happen, and even where he does it is usual to state matters expressly.

The most common concern is usually whether the IHT attributable to the gift should be borne by the residue (in which case the gift should be stated to be 'free of tax') or by the beneficiary of the gift (in which case the gift should be stated to be 'subject to tax'). The testator should be made aware of the consequences of the different wording. In particular, in certain circumstances, it can make a difference to the overall amount of tax payable on the estate. This is the case where a partially exempt transfer occurs (see **11.3**).

11.2.5   Drafting considerations for certain types of beneficiary

11.2.5.1   Gifts to a class of beneficiary

Where the testator does not name his beneficiary but makes a gift to a class which could continue to grow after his death, it is sensible to impose a closing date for entry to the class. For example, a gift of '£20,000 to my nephews and nieces' would include those alive at the death of the testator and those later born, which would make the gift very inconvenient to administer. A sensible closing date would be the death of the testator, for example, 'to my nephews and nieces alive at my death'. However, if the will is silent there are a number of class closing rules which may apply to close the class at an artificially early date. In the example just given, the class closing rules would close the class at death provided there was at least one member; if there was no nephew or niece living at that date, the class would remain open until all possible members were ascertained.

11.2.5.2   Gifts to charitable bodies

It is important to identify accurately the charitable body. To avoid argument later the solicitor should include the address and registered charity number of the body for identification.

A further issue to consider is how the executors will obtain a receipt from the charity for the gift. Without express provision stating otherwise, all members of an unincorporated association would have to sign a receipt. To avoid this, it is normal to authorise the executors to accept the receipt of an authorised officer of the charity. The clause should provide that the receipt of the person who appears to be the treasurer or other proper officer of the organisation will be sufficient. This avoids the need for the executors to check the constitution of the body to establish the identity of the proper officers.

A further problem to consider is that the charitable body may dissolve, amalgamate or change its objects before the date of death. It is useful to state that the gift is to the body 'for its general charitable purposes'. This may help establish that the gift has not failed, because those purposes can continue to be performed by another organisation, or help establish that the testator had general charitable intention and so allow the gift to be applied cy-près to a similar charity. A further option is to provide in the will that the executors may choose a similar charity to pay to, if the original recipient charity has ceased to exist.

11.2.6   The subject matter of the gift

It is essential that the property which is the subject matter of the gift is clearly identified. This is particularly important for non-pecuniary gifts. There are several important drafting considerations for specific gifts.

11.2.6.1 Ademption

A general problem is ademption. This is the failure of the gift because the specific item described no longer exists within the testator's estate at death. A testator should be alerted to the fact that this could happen. For example, a gift of 'my gold and ruby necklace' could fail because during the testator's lifetime the testator gives it to someone else, sells it or loses it in a fire or burglary. This is the case even if the testator has bought another similar necklace to replace it. This is because the 'my' indicates that the testator is referring to the specific item in his possession at the date of the will and not to whatever item matching that description he happens to own at death. If the testator wants the beneficiary to have a substitute benefit if the original gift adeems, the will should provide for a replacement or substitute.

11.2.6.2 Burden of costs

There may be costs associated with the packing or transport of the specific gift. Unless the will provides otherwise the beneficiary will bear these costs. The testator should consider if these costs will be too great for the beneficiary and if so provide that the gift is free of these costs. As a result they will be paid from the residue of the estate.

11.2.6.3 Gift involving selection

The testator may leave a gift to several people inviting them to select an item from the estate. To prevent argument, the testator should indicate the order of choosing or provide for a means of resolving any dispute. It is normal to provide that the decision of the executors will be final. It is also wise to require the selection to be done within a time-limit to avoid delays in the administration.

11.2.6.4 Gifts of specific company shares

These are especially susceptible to ademption, not just because the owner may buy and sell shares on a regular basis, but also because the company may be renamed or taken over, and the will should provide for this. Shares may also be subject to a charge secured on them. To avoid the usual rule that the beneficiary will take subject to this charge, the will should expressly provide otherwise.

11.2.6.5 Gift of specific land

Again this type of gift is susceptible to ademption. A gift of the testator's main residence at death will avoid some problems but will not provide for situations where the testator owns no land at all. A house or flat is also likely to be subject to a mortgage. As with gifts of shares it is necessary to expressly provide for a gift to be free of mortgage if the testator does not want the beneficiary to pay the mortgage, or to leave the benefit of any mortgage insurance policy to the beneficiary too.

11.2.7 Gift of the residue

It is important that the will contains a gift of the residue and that care is taken to ensure that it does not fail, as the result would be a partial intestacy.

11.2.7.1 Is a trust required?

Where the testator wishes to leave the residue on trust of some kind (for example, a life interest trust) then clearly there will be a trust expressly declared in the will. However, a trust may arise in less obvious circumstances. Where any of the beneficiaries is under 18 years at the death of the testator and the testator does not want the minor's parent or guardian to give a receipt on his behalf, there will need to be a trust of that person's entitlement until he reaches 18 and can give a good receipt. Where there is a possibility that this could occur (and even if all the primary beneficiaries are adults there may be a possibility of a substitution being made) it would be preferable to declare a trust expressly in the will and so control the terms and trustees.

It is also desirable to declare a trust where contingent gifts are made, so that property can be properly dealt with until the contingency is satisfied (or fails).

Where the residue is passing outright to adult (or charitable) beneficiaries, there is no need for an express trust. However, it is not unusual to create a trust of the residue in these circumstances.

Whether or not the residue is left on express trust, there should be an express direction for the payment of all debts, expenses and legacies to be made from the residue before it is distributed to the beneficiaries. In the absence of such a direction, the statutory order set out in the AEA 1925 will apply and this can lead to problems.

11.2.7.2 Avoiding partial intestacy

If a gift of residue fails, the property will pass under the intestacy rules. The testator may be happy with this but it is preferable to include substitutional gifts to cover the possibility of the primary gift failing. For example, where the residue is left to the testator's child, there could be an express substitution of grandchildren. It is also worth considering a 'longstop' beneficiary to inherit if all the intended arrangements fail. Although this could be another person, it is also worth considering charitable bodies as there is little possibility of the gift failing. The testator may prefer to benefit a favourite charity in preference to distant relatives or the Crown as *bona vacantia*.

A gift of the residue to more than one person also raises some drafting issues. For example, assume that the testator has three children, A, B and C and wishes to leave them an equal share. He could leave one-third to each named child. This carries risks. He may have more children before he dies who will be excluded. Also any or all of the children may pre-decease him. If this were to happen, Wills Act 1837, s 33 would provide for the failed one-third share to pass to any child of the dead child, but if there were none, the failed one-third share would pass on intestacy.

Therefore, it is wiser to omit names and specific shares in the residue, and refer only to any children the testator may have at the date of death. Using the phrase 'for such of my children as survive me and if more than one in equal shares' will ensure that there will be a partial intestacy only if all children pre-decease the testator. The testator will normally want to provide that the share of a child who pre-deceases should pass to his or her own children, if any.

The testator may desire to establish a trust rather than make an outright gift of the residue. Various types of trust that can be useful in a will are considered in **Chapter 12**.

11.2.8 Directions and declarations

It is common to include declarations of the testator's wishes. Examples of such declarations are set out below.

11.2.8.1 Survivorship

Unless a will states otherwise, a beneficiary only has to be alive at the death of the testator to acquire a vested interest. This may have an unfortunate effect where the beneficiary dies a very short time after the testator. This can happen where, for example, members of the same family are involved in a common accident.

The testator's property will pass in accordance with the will or intestacy provisions of the deceased beneficiary, which may mean passing to a person the testator would not want to inherit.

Example

Thelma leaves property to her married son. She dies and he dies a week after her. He leaves everything to his wife. Thelma might well have preferred her assets to pass to beneficiaries of her own choice rather than to her son's wife.

There will also be the burden and expense of the property being part of the administration of two different estates. Lastly, there may be adverse IHT consequences. To avoid this and give the testator more control over the destination of his property, a survivorship clause may be used. This usually directs that the beneficiary must survive the testator by a minimum period of time. The time usually chosen is about a month, stated either as a calendar month, or a period of 28 or 30 days. Using a longer period may lead to delays in the administration of the estate. The period should not exceed six months or the gift will be treated as creating a settlement without an interest in possession.

The testator may declare that a general survivorship period is to apply to all gifts in the will, or only to certain of the gifts.

11.2.8.2 Directions concerning the body

Some testators wish to include directions concerning how their body is to be disposed of, for example, cremation or donated for medical research. The testator should be aware that such directions are of no legal effect. The testator must ensure that his close family and friends are aware of his wishes, and, where he wishes to donate organs, carry an organ donor card.

11.2.9 Administrative provisions

Personal representatives (PRs) and trustees have a number of statutory administration powers. The AEA 1925 gives certain powers to PRs, and the TA 1925 and TA 2000 give powers to both trustees and PRs. However, it is usual to extend or modify some of these statutory powers where they are not regarded as sufficient. Even where the statutory powers are adequate it is common to put in an express provision on the basis that it makes the will easier to construe.

A will which might give rise to a trust (for example, because there is a substitutional gift to children of a primary beneficiary who predeceases the testator) will benefit from quite extensive express administrative provisions. However, even a simple will leaving everything to adults or to a charity will benefit from some express provisions.

We have divided the administrative provisions below into those that should be considered for inclusion in any will irrespective of whether or not it might give rise to a trust and those which should be considered only if a trust might arise.

11.2.9.1   Administrative provisions to consider in relation to all wills

Power to charge

We have already dealt with this at **11.2.3.6**. If the testator wishes to give the executors (and trustees) power to charge, the power can either be included as part of the appointment clause or with the other administrative provisions. When drafting such a clause it is important to be clear whether a person engaged in any profession or business can charge for time spent on the administration (for example, a brain surgeon) or whether only a person whose profession involves administering estates and trusts can charge (for example, a solicitor or accountant).

Power for trust professional to charge

> Any Trustee who acts in a professional capacity may charge reasonable remuneration for any services provided to the trust.
>
> For this purpose a Trustee acts in a professional capacity if he acts in the course of a profession or business which consists of or includes the provision of services in connection with the administration or management of trusts.

Power for any business person to charge

> Any Trustee who is engaged in a profession or business may charge reasonable remuneration for any services provided to the trust.

Extended power to appropriate assets without consent of legatee

The AEA 1925, s 41 gives PRs the power to appropriate any part of the estate in or towards satisfaction of any legacy or any interest in residue provided that the appropriation does not prejudice any specific beneficiary. Thus, if the will gives a pecuniary legacy to a beneficiary, the PRs may allow that beneficiary to take chattels or other assets in the estate up to the value of his legacy, provided that these assets have not been specifically bequeathed by the will. The section provides that the legatee (or his parent or guardian if he is a minor) must consent to the appropriation.

It is common to remove the need for the legatee's consent.

Express amendment

Specimen clause

> Power to exercise the power of appropriation conferred by s 41 of the Administration of Estates Act 1925 without obtaining any of the consents required by that section.

This provision is commonly included in order to relieve the PRs of the duty to obtain formal consent. Nevertheless, the PRs would informally consult the beneficiaries concerned.

Power to insure assets

The statutory power to insure assets of the estate conferred by TA 1925, s 19 was inadequate and it used to be necessary to extend it. However, TA 2000 substituted a new s 19 which is much more satisfactory. It gives PRs and trustees power to insure assets against all risks, to the full value of the property and to pay premiums out of income or capital.

It is no longer necessary to amend the statutory provision which is now adequate. However, including an express provision makes life easier for lay PRs who will be able to see from the will itself exactly what they can do. The following is a typical provision.

Specimen clause

> Power to insure any asset of my estate on such terms as they think fit and to pay premiums at their discretion out of income or capital and to use any insurance money received either to restore assets or as if it were the proceeds of sale.

Power to accept receipts from or on behalf of minors

Under the general law, an unmarried minor cannot give a good receipt for capital or income. A married minor can give a good receipt for income only (LPA 1925, s 21). Parents and guardians used not to be able to give a good receipt on behalf of minors unless specifically authorised to do so in the will. This meant that without such authority the PRs would have to hold onto a legacy until the minor reached 18 and was able to give a good receipt. The AEA 1925, s 42 gives PRs the power to appoint trustees to hold a legacy for a minor who is absolutely entitled under the will. The receipt of the appointed trustees (who could be the child's parents or guardians) discharges the PRs from further liability. This power does not apply where the child has a contingent interest.

The Children Act 1989 provides that parents with parental responsibility have the same rights as guardians appointed under the Act. These rights are set out at s 3 and include the right to receive or recover money for the benefit of the child. Therefore since the Children Act 1989, parents and guardians have been able to give a good receipt to PRs.

There are often tensions within families and a client may not be happy for a parent or guardian to give a good receipt for a legacy. In such a case, the will should be drafted to leave a legacy to trustees to hold for the benefit of the minor rather than to the child directly. Alternatively, the will may include a clause allowing the PRs to accept the receipt of the child himself if over 16 years old. The provision may be incorporated into the legacy itself or may be included in a list of powers in the will.

Power to continue a sole trader's business

Personal representatives have power only to carry on a business for the purpose of selling it as a going concern. When doing this, they have power to indemnify themselves from the assets of the estate for liabilities they incur.

It is helpful to authorise the PRs to postpone the sale of the business if they so wish and to carry on the business in the meantime. The clause should make clear which assets of the estate can be used in the business. The PRs will be able to indemnify themselves from those assets.

In practice few PRs are going to want to get involved in running a business. Professional trustees will normally refuse to take a grant in such cases. It is preferable to appoint the person(s) taking the business under the will as special executors limited to dealing with the business.

Note: A testator who is a member of a partnership should check that the partnership agreement deals adequately with arrangements for the death of a partner. PRs of a deceased partner have no implied rights to take part in the running of the business.

A testator who runs a business through the medium of a limited company should also consider what will happen after death. The company will continue as a separate legal entity but is there anyone in place who will be able to carry on the business?

Removing need to comply with the Apportionment Act 1870

Section 2 of the Apportionment Act 1870 provides that income such as rent and dividends is to be treated as accruing from day to day and apportioned accordingly. Thus, where assets in the estate produce income (such as bank or building society interest or dividends) which is received after death but which relates to a period partly before and partly after death, the income must be apportioned. The part accruing before death is a capital asset of the estate. The part accruing after death is income relating to the particular asset.

Unless the Act is excluded, s 2 will have to be complied with where a will creates a trust which gives capital to one person and income to another. It also has to be complied with where there is no trust but a will gives an income-producing asset to one person and residue to another. If the apportionment applies, it is necessary to apportion the income between the two beneficiaries.

> **Example: Apportionment Act not excluded**
>
> The testator's will gives 'my ABC Co shares to Fred and my residue to Graham'.
>
> ABC Co declares a dividend of £12,000 three months after the testator's death. The dividend is expressed to cover the previous 12 months.
>
> Three quarters of the dividend relates to the pre-death period and is regarded as capital forming part of the residue of the estate. It will pass to Graham.
>
> One quarter of the dividend relates to the post-death period and is regarded as income passing with the shares to Fred.

This calculation is time consuming and it is common to exclude the need to apportion so that all the income will pass with the income-producing asset.

Specimen clause

> Power to treat as income all the income from any part of my estate whatever the period in respect of which it may accrue and to disregard the Apportionment Act 1870.

> **Example**
>
> If the will in the previous example includes such a clause, the whole of the dividend is treated as relating to the post-death period and will pass with the shares to Fred.

Power to employ agents

The TA 2000, ss 11–15 replace in similar but clearer terms the provisions of TA 1925, s 23(1) by allowing non-charitable trustees to delegate to agents any or all of their 'delegable functions'. Functions personal to the trustees which cannot be delegated include:

(a)   decisions on distributing trust property to beneficiaries;

(b)   allocation of fees or payments to income or capital;

(c)   appointment of trustees;

(d)   appointment of nominees or custodians of trust assets.

Only in the case of delegation of their asset management function is agreement in writing required.

A trustee who satisfies the duty of care in TA 2000, s 1 in relation to the appointment and subsequent review of the appointment of an agent is not liable for the acts and defaults of the appointee. Typically, this power will be used by PRs to employ estate agents, stockbrokers or bankers to carry out executive functions in relation to the administration. For example, PRs may instruct estate agents to sell the deceased's house or stockbrokers to value shares for IHT purposes.

Delegation by power of attorney

The TA 1925, s 25, as substituted by Trustee Delegation Act 1999, s 5, allows trustees and PRs to delegate by power of attorney the exercise of any of the powers and discretions vested in them for a period not exceeding 12 months. However, in this case, the PRs remain liable for the acts of the delegate as if they were their own acts.

This provision is often used by PRs who, having obtained their grant, find that they are unable to be involved personally in the administration for some temporary reason, such as absence abroad on business or on holiday. If, before taking out the grant, a long absence is anticipated, the better course of action would be for the PR to renounce his right to a grant or for others to take a grant reserving power to any absentee executor. It is too late to renounce or reserve power if the grant has already been obtained or if an executor has accepted office by intermeddling in the estate.

11.2.9.2 Administrative provisions to consider in relation to wills which may give rise to a trust

Removing need to comply with the Apportionment Act 1870

We have already seen that a draftsman would consider excluding the Act where an income-producing asset goes to one person and residue to another.

It is normal to exclude the Act where a will creates a life interest trust.

> **Example: Apportionment Act not excluded**
>
> The testator's will gives 'my residue to Larry for life, remainder to Rob'.
>
> ABC Co declares a dividend of £12,000 three months after the testator's death. The dividend is expressed to cover the previous 12 months.
>
> Three quarters of the dividend relates to the pre-death period and is regarded as capital of the estate. It will be held for Larry for life and will eventually pass with the rest of the capital to Rob.
>
> One quarter of the dividend relates to the post-death period and is regarded as income. It will be paid to Larry.

> **Example: Apportionment Act excluded**
>
> The whole of the dividend will be treated as income and paid to Larry.

It is also desirable to exclude the Act where there is a trust with contingent interests. Beneficiaries will fulfil the contingency at different times (or fail to fulfil it) and unless the Act is excluded there will have to be an apportionment of income each time there is a change in beneficial entitlement.

> **Example**
>
> A trust is created for three children contingent on reaching 18.
>
> When the first child reaches 18 any income will have to be apportioned to the pre- and post-birthday period. The first child will be entitled to one third of the post-birthday income but all of the pre-birthday income will be a trust asset.
>
> If the Act is excluded the first child will be entitled to one third of the whole receipt.

Removing need to comply with the equitable rules of apportionment

The equitable apportionment rules apply only where residuary personalty is left to one person for life, remainder to another.

The rules are designed to preserve a fair balance between the competing interests of the life tenant (who wants high income) and the remainderman (who wants capital growth).

Under the rule in *Howe v Dartmouth* (1820) 7 Ves 137, where property is left in this way, trustees are under a duty to sell assets which are either wasting (such as copyrights) or non-income producing (such as reversionary interests) and invest the proceeds in authorised investments.

Where there is a duty to sell and the trustees delay, the trustees must only pay 'a fair yield' to the life tenant and must treat the rest as capital. There is a complicated formula for calculating the fair yield.

Under the rule in *Re Earl of Chesterfield's Trusts* (1883) 23 Ch D 643, where trustees have delayed selling a non-income-producing asset, they must apportion the proceeds of sale and treat some as income and some as capital. Again there is a formula for the calculation.

Under the Rule in *Allhusen v Whittell* (1867) LR 4 Eq 295, debts of the estate must be treated as paid partly with capital and partly with the income that the capital produced. The burden is, therfore, apportioned between tenant for life and remainderman.

The principle behind these rules is admirable. However, the expense involved in making the calculations is rarely justified. It is usual to exclude them when drafting life interest trusts.

Specimen clause

> Power to disregard the rules of equity relating to apportionment including those known as the rules in *Howe v Dartmouth* and *Allhusen v Whittell* in all their branches.

Even where the equitable apportionment rules are excluded, trustees should still strive to achieve fairness between beneficiaries. For example, they must not invest for income at the expense of capital growth (see **14.3.2**).

Power to appropriate assets

Section 41 of AEA 1925 does not apply to trustees. It is necessary to include an express provision, equivalent to s 41, to permit the trustees to appropriate trust property towards beneficial interests arising under the trust.

Specimen clause

> Power to appropriate assets in or towards satisfaction of any beneficial interests arising under the trust without obtaining the consent of any beneficiary.

The power to invest

The TA 2000 contains a new 'general power of investment' giving trustees power to invest as if absolutely entitled to the trust assets (s 3). This general power does not permit investment in land other than by mortgage. However, s 8 allows trustees to acquire land in the UK for investment or occupation by beneficiary or for other reasons, which means that all trustees will now have similar powers to a trustee of land with regard to acquiring land.

Trustees exercising any investment power, whether expressly given or under the TA 2000, must comply with various specific requirements, which include reviewing the investments chosen from time to time (s 4), taking proper advice before investing or reviewing the investments (s 5), and having regard to 'the standard investment criteria' which means considering the suitability to the trust of the investment type chosen and considering the need for diversification in so far as is appropriate to the circumstances of the trust (s 4).

Although an improvement on the previous provisions under the Trustee Investments Act 1961 (TIA 1961), it may still be desirable to expressly state the investment powers and make some modifications and additions to the effect of the TA 2000. For example, the trust instrument should contain express permission to:

(a)   purchase foreign investments including land; and/or

(b)   retain or purchase non income-producing investments, such as insurance policies; and/or

(c)   retain investments originally settled, for example, shares in the settlor's family company; and/or

(d)   pursue an 'ethical' investment policy; and/or

(e)   borrow (and use trust property to be charged) for the purposes of investment; and/or

(f)   exclude the obligation to diversify the trust fund.

It is not possible to exclude s 4 (which requires the trustees to have regard to the need for diversification when investing). However, particularly where the trust contains primarily one type of asset and it is intended that the trustees should not sell this (for example, shares in a private company) it is advisable to state this expressly.

The TA 2000 provides that the management of trust assets can now be delegated (s 15) and that trustees may also appoint certain persons as nominees (s 16). Previously an express power was required for these actions. There are a number of special requirements to be observed if a trustee wishes to delegate asset management and investment decisions, for example, the trustee must create a written policy document to guide the delegates and review this from time to time. It is not clear whether this requirement applies to all trustees, or only to those exercising power under the TA 2000. In practice, though, it is usual for trustees to set out the investment aims of the trust when appointing managers to deal with the investment decisions.

See **14.3** for a further discussion of trustee investments.

Power to purchase land

The TA 2000, s 8 gives trustees power to acquire freehold or leasehold land in the UK for 'investment, for occupation by a beneficiary or for any other reason'. When exercising their power, the trustees are given 'all the powers of an absolute owner in relation to the land'.

Specimen clause

> My Trustees may apply trust money in the purchase or improvement of any freehold or leasehold dwelling-house and may permit any such dwelling-house

> to be used as a residence by any person with an interest in my residuary estate upon such terms and conditions as my Trustees may think fit.

This clause gives trustees an express power to use trust money to buy or improve land for use as a residence by the beneficiaries. It leaves the question of responsibility for the burden of repairs and other outgoings to the discretion of the trustees.

The statutory power does not authorise the purchase of land abroad, nor does it allow trustees to purchase an interest in land with someone else (eg, a beneficiary). An express power will be needed if the trustees are to have such powers.

Power to sell personalty

Trustees holding land in their trust have the power to sell it under their powers of an absolute owner under TA 2000 (see above). However, there is some doubt whether trustees who hold no land and where there is no express trust for sale have power to sell personalty. For this reason, some wills may continue to impose an express trust for sale over residue. The alternative solution is to include power in the will (among the administrative provisions) giving the trustees express power to sell personalty.

Specimen clause

> Power to sell mortgage or charge any asset of my estate as it they were an absolute beneficial owner.

Power to use income for maintenance of beneficiaries

Where trustees are holding a fund for a minor beneficiary, TA 1925, s 31 gives them power to use income they receive for the minor's maintenance education or benefit.

Section 31 (as amended by TA 2000) states (inter alia):

(1)   Where any property is held by trustees in trust for any person for any interest whatsoever, whether vested or contingent, then, subject to any prior interests or charges affecting that property—

(i)   during the infancy of any such person, if his interest so long continues, the trustees may, at their sole discretion, pay to his parent or guardian, if any, or otherwise apply for or towards his maintenance, education, or benefit, the whole or such part, if any, of the income of that property as may, in all the circumstances, be reasonable, whether or not there is—

(a) any other fund applicable to the same purpose; or

(b)   any person bound by law to provide for his maintenance or education; and

(ii)   if such person on attaining the age of eighteen years has not a vested interest in such income, the trustees shall thenceforth pay the income of that property and of any accretion thereto under subsection (2) of this section to him, until he either attains a vested interest therein or dies, or until failure of his interest:

Provided that, in deciding whether the whole or any part of the income of the property is during a minority to be paid or applied for the purposes aforesaid, the trustees shall have regard to the age of the infant and his requirements and generally to the circumstances of the case, and in particular to what other income, if any, is applicable for the same purposes; and where trustees have notice that the income of more than one fund is applicable for those purposes, then, so far as practicable, unless the entire income of the funds is paid or applied as aforesaid or the court otherwise directs, a proportionate part only of the income of each fund shall be so paid or applied.

(2)   During the infancy of any such person, if his interest so long continues, the trustees shall accumulate all the residue of that income by investing it, and any profits from so investing it, from time to time in authorised investments, and shall hold those accumulations ... .

(3)   This section applies in the case of a contingent interest only if the limitation or trust carries the intermediate income of the property ... .

Examples of the application of s 31

Example: Trust 1

The trustees are holding £100,000 for Mary (16) who has a vested interest in the capital. Under s 31(1), the trustees have the power to pay all or part of the income to Mary's parent or guardian or 'otherwise apply' it for Mary's maintenance, education or benefit. This could include paying bills (eg, school fees) directly.

The power is limited to so much of the income as is 'reasonable'. The proviso directs the trustees to take into account various further points such as Mary's age and requirements and whether any other fund is available for her maintenance.

Section 31(2) directs the trustees to accumulate any income not used for maintenance and invest it.

Example: Trust 2

The trustees are holding £100,000 for Dora (14) who has a contingent interest in the capital. They may pay or apply the income for Dora's maintenance, education or benefit in the same way as the trustees of Trust 1.

The trustees are holding £100,000 for Charles (19) who also has a contingent interest in the capital. Section 31(1)(ii) directs them to pay all the income to Charles until his interest vests (ie, until he is 21) when he will receive the capital, or fails (ie, if he dies before he is 21). The same will apply to the income from Dora's share from her 18th birthday onwards.

Example: Trust 3

The trustees are holding £200,000 for Henry for life with remainder to Stephen (10). They have no power to use the income for Stephen's benefit as Henry is entitled to it. If Henry dies while Stephen is still a minor, s 31 will apply to allow the trustees to apply income for Stephen's maintenance etc during the period from Henry's death until Stephen is 18 (when they will transfer the capital to Stephen).

Extending s 31: specimen clause

Section 31 of the Trustee Act 1925 shall apply to the income of my estate as if the words 'as the Trustees shall in their absolute discretion think fit' were substituted for the words 'as in all the circumstances be reasonable' in paragraph (i) of subsection (1) thereof and the proviso to subsection (1) had been omitted and as if the age of 21 years were substituted for all references to the age of 18 wherever they occur in s 31 (references to 'infancy' being construed accordingly).

The clause begins by removing the 'reasonable' limitation in s 31. It gives the trustees complete discretion over whether to pay or apply income for minor beneficiaries and over how much income they pay or apply.

Secondly, it removes the right for a contingent beneficiary to receive all the income from the age of 18. The trustees' discretion under s 31 to pay or apply income for maintenance or to accumulate any surplus will continue until the beneficiary is 21. Thus in Trust 2 the trustees would have a discretion over the payment of income to Charles even though he is over 18.

Power to use capital for advancement of beneficiaries

The TA 1925, s 32 allows trustees in certain circumstances to permit a beneficiary with an interest in capital to have the benefit of part of his capital entitlement sooner than he would receive it under the basic provisions of the trust.

Section 32 states:

(1)   Trustees may at any time or times pay or apply any capital money subject to a trust, for the advancement or benefit, in such manner as they may, in their absolute discretion, think fit, of any person entitled to the capital of the trust property or of any share thereof, whether absolutely or contingently on his attaining any specified age ... and whether in possession or in remainder or reversion ...

Provided that—

(a)   the money so paid or applied for the advancement or benefit of any person shall not exceed altogether in amount one-half of the presumptive or vested share or interest of that person in the trust property; and

(b)   if that person is or becomes absolutely and indefeasibly entitled to a share in the trust property the money so paid or applied shall be brought into account as part of such share; and

(c)   no such payment or application shall be made so as to prejudice any person entitled to any prior life or other interest, whether vested or contingent, in the money paid or applied unless such person is in existence and of full age and consents in writing to such payment or application.

Examples of the application of s 32

Example: Trust 1

Mary has a vested interest in the £100,000 capital. Section 32 allows the trustees to release some of the capital for Mary's benefit. 'Benefit' is widely construed: money could be used to pay educational or living expenses. The amount the trustees may advance is limited to one half of Mary's entitlement, ie, £50,000.

Example: Trust 2

Charles and Dora have contingent interests in the capital, their presumptive shares being £100,000 each. Section 32 applies to allow the trustees to release up to £50,000 for the benefit of either beneficiary. The trustees could give money directly to Charles as he is old enough to give a valid receipt. The power applies even though the interests of Charles and Dora are contingent. If either beneficiary dies before the age of 21 there is no right to recover any advance even though that beneficiary's interest in capital has failed.

Section 32(1)(b) requires advances to be brought into account on final distribution. If the trustees give £50,000 to Charles now, he will receive £50,000 less than Dora when the fund is finally distributed to them.

Example: Trust 3

Henry has only an interest in income and s 32 does not permit the release of capital to him. The section does apply to Stephen's vested interest in remainder, and permits the trustees to apply up to £100,000 (half his interest) for Stephen's benefit.

Such an advance would prejudice Henry since his income would be substantially reduced. Section 32(1)(c) provides that no advance may be made without Henry's written consent.

Extending s 32: specimen clause 1

> Power to apply for the benefit of any Beneficiary as my Trustees think fit the whole or any part of the share of my residuary estate to which that Beneficiary is absolutely or presumptively entitled and I leave it within the discretion of my Trustees whether and to what extent the beneficiary shall bring into account any payments received under this clause.

This clause extends the limit in s 32(1)(a) to the full amount of the beneficiary's share. Up to £100,000 could be advanced for Mary (in Trust 1) or for Charles and Dora (in Trust 2). In Trust 3, the whole fund could be advanced for Stephen provided that Henry consents.

The second part of the clause supersedes s 32(1)(b) and means that, if in Trust 2 £50,000 was advanced to Charles, the trustees could on distribution still divide the remaining fund equally between Charles and Dora.

Extending s 32: specimen clause 2

> Power to pay or apply capital money from my residuary estate to any extent to or for the benefit of my husband.
>
> Power to advance capital money from my residuary estate to my husband by way of loan to any extent upon such terms and conditions as my Trustees may in their absolute discretion think fit.

These provisions would permit the trustees in Trust 3 to give or lend capital from the fund to Henry even though he has only an interest in income, not capital. Such a clause may be included to give more flexibility in case the income proves insufficient for Henry's needs. Henry still remains dependent on the discretion of the trustees.

Note: Section 31 specifically allows trustees to pay income to the parents or guardian of a minor beneficiary or 'otherwise apply it' for the minor's 'maintenance, education or benefit'. Similarly s 32 allows trustees to pay or 'apply' capital for the beneficiary's advancement or benefit. Thus, even before the passing of the Children Act 1989, the trustees could take a good receipt from parents or guardians.

Control of trustees by beneficiaries

Section 19 of TLATA 1996 provides that, where beneficiaries are *sui juris* and together entitled to the whole fund, they may direct the trustees to retire and appoint new trustees of the beneficiaries' choice. This means that in a case where the beneficiaries could by agreement end the trust under the rule in *Saunders v Vautier* (1841) 4 Beav 115, they now have the option of allowing the trust to continue with trustees of their own choice. The provision may be expressly excluded by the testator. If, under the terms of the trust, the position could arise where all the beneficiaries are in existence and aged over 18 but the trust has not ended, the testator may wish to prevent the beneficiaries from choosing their own trustees.

Specimen clause

> The provisions of section 19 of the Trusts of Land and Appointment of Trustees Act 1996 shall not apply to any trust created by this will so that no Beneficiary shall have the right to require the appointment or retirement of any Trustee or Trustees.

Trusts of land

The TLATA 1996 gives special powers (see below) to a beneficiary under a trust of land who has an interest in possession. If, under the terms of the will, a trust with an interest in possession could arise, the will may amend those powers. The Act does not define 'interest in possession', so it presumably has its usual meaning; a beneficiary has an interest in possession if he is entitled to claim the income of the fund as it arises (normally either because he has a life interest, or because he is over 18 and entitled to claim income under TA 1925, s 31).

Duty to consult beneficiaries

Trustees exercising any function relating to the land must consult any beneficiary who is of full age and beneficially entitled to an interest in possession in the land and, so far as consistent with the 'general interest of the trust', give effect to the wishes of any such beneficiary (TLATA 1996, s 11). The duty to consult may be excluded by the will.

Specimen clause

> The provisions of section 11 of the Trusts of Land and Appointment of Trustees Act 1996 shall not apply so that it shall not be necessary for my Trustees to consult any Beneficiaries before carrying out any function relating to land.

Beneficiary's rights of occupation

A beneficiary with a beneficial interest in possession, even if not of full age, has the right to occupy land subject to the trust if the purposes of the trust include making the land available for occupation by him or if the trustees acquired the land in order to make it so available (TLATA 1996, s 12). There is no power to exclude s 12, but a declaration that the purpose of the trust is not for the occupation of land may be included in the will.

Specimen clause

> The purposes of any trust created by this will do not include making land available for occupation of any Beneficiary [although my Trustees have power to do so if they wish].

11.3 Partially exempt transfers

Sometimes only a part of an estate on death is exempt for IHT purposes and the other part is not exempt. Difficulties may arise in determining how much tax is payable. Any tax relating to the non-exempt part of the estate can affect the calculation of the size of the exempt beneficiary's inheritance. Provisions designed to resolve these difficulties are contained in IHTA 1984, s 38. In general, these provisions apply relatively rarely and give rise to complicated calculations. It is, however, important to understand their effect where there are legacies on which tax is chargeable combined with a gift of residue to an exempt beneficiary. This could happen, for example, where the residue passes to a spouse and there are legacies to children.

> Example
>
> In her will, Polly gives £308,000 to her son Mark and the rest of her estate to her husband, Harry. Polly has made no lifetime gifts in the seven years preceding her death. Her estate is worth £400,000. The legacy to Mark exceeds Polly's nil rate band, and there will be tax to pay. Residue is exempt. The amount of tax payable depends on who is liable to pay the tax.

(a)   If Polly's will gives the legacy to Mark 'subject to tax', simply calculate tax on the legacy in the usual way.

Calculate tax on £308,000

		£
	£275,000 @ 0%	Nil
	£33,000 @ 40%	13,200
Distribution:	Tax bill	13,200
	Mark receives legacy (less tax)	294,800
	Harry receives residue	92,000
		400,000

(b)   If Polly's will gives the legacy to Mark 'free of tax', the calculation is more complicated. Section 38(3) of the IHTA 1984 provides that the value transferred is the aggregate of the value of the gift and the 'tax which would be chargeable if the value transferred equalled that aggregate'.

The value transferred is, therefore, made up of the £308,000 which Mark takes (the net sum) PLUS the tax attributable to it.

In order to ascertain the value transferred, it is necessary to calculate what sum would, after deduction of tax at the appropriate rate, leave £308,000: ie, the legacy must be grossed up.

Gross up Mark's legacy:

		£
	£275,000 (grossed up @ 0%)	275,000
	£33,000 (grossed up @ 40%) $33,000 \times \dfrac{100}{60}$	55,000
	Gross gift	330,000

Calculate tax on £330,000

	£275,000 @ 0%	nil
	£55,000 @ 40%	22,000
Distribution:	Mark receives legacy	308,000
	Tax bill	22,000
	Residue to Harry (after payment of tax)	70,000
		400,000

It is particularly important to be aware of these provisions when drafting a will. If a legacy is given 'free of tax', the tax bill may be considerably higher than if the legacy were given 'subject to tax'. Compare the tax paid in the example above. The alternatives should be explained to the testator so that clear instructions can be taken and express provision included as to whether the legacy is to be free of tax or subject to tax.

A will may direct that residue is to be divided between an exempt and a non-exempt beneficiary. The share of the non-exempt beneficiary attracts tax whereas the share of the exempt beneficiary does not. The IHTA 1984, s 41 provides that an exempt share of residue shall not bear any part of the tax attributable to the non-exempt share of residue even if the will directs otherwise. The non-exempt share of residue must bear its own tax and the non-exempt beneficiary will receive less benefit from the gift than will the exempt beneficiary.

Example

Douglas (who has exhausted his nil rate band) leaves the residue of his estate after payment of debts, expenses and tax to be divided equally between his wife and his son, Henry.

After paying debts, expenses and tax attributable to non-residuary gifts, the residue is £600,000. His wife will receive £300,000. Henry will receive £300,000 less 40% tax ie, £180,000. Tax of £120,000 is paid on Henry's share of residue.

In this example, Douglas may object that he does not want his son to receive less than his wife. He may ask if the tax can be paid first and then what is left be divided into two equal shares. This is not possible because s 41 provides that a chargeable share of residue must bear its own tax and any provision to the contrary in a will is void.

However, he could direct that the residue be divided unequally between his wife and son in such proportions that after the payment of tax attributable to his son's share they each end up with the same amount.

Chapter 12

Will Trusts

12.1 Introduction

Apart from the formal aspects and the administrative powers given to executors and trustees, the main contents of a will are the dispositive provisions, ie, the clauses which actually leave property to the beneficiaries.

The purpose of this chapter is to consider in more detail the different ways in which a testator may leave his property.

12.2 Flexible provision by will

If the testator is uncertain about the precise nature of the beneficial gifts, he may wish to draft his will in a form which, in effect, delays the decision as to who shall benefit on death until a later date. Often this can be achieved by authorising the trustees, or others, to determine the matter after death. To achieve this position the will should be drafted in flexible form containing trusts. These trusts may relate to non-residuary gifts and/or the gift of the residue.

There are a number of possibilities for the testator to consider when planning a will which delay the ultimate choice of beneficiary until after his death. A trust is usually involved and in each case the succession and taxation implications must be balanced carefully. This chapter discusses each of these matters as well as the drafting considerations which arise.

12.3 Precatory trusts

12.3.1 Misnomer

To create a binding trust, there must be certainty of words, ie, words of an imperative nature such as 'on trust', of subject matter and of objects, ie, the beneficiaries. No binding trust is intended by the testator where he uses 'precatory words' in his will. The testator will intend an absolute gift of property, often of jewellery or other personal chattels, to a beneficiary but will couple this with an expression of wish that the property be distributed by the beneficiary in a given way. The absence of imperative words sufficient to create a trust combined with the precatory words, show that the phrase 'precatory trust' is a contradiction in terms.

12.3.2   Using the clause

Precatory trusts are normally used by testators when disposing of personal chattels, and in particular their jewellery. They are useful where the testator is undecided who should benefit from what on his death, especially in respect of property which may change in extent between the date of the will and the subsequent death. The clause introduces a degree of flexibility giving the testator the opportunity to change his mind as to his wishes but without needing to change the will by codicil or, possibly, by executing a new will.

12.3.3   Drafting the clause

Sample clause

> I give and bequeath all my personal chattels as defined by section 55(1)(x) of the Administration of Estates Act 1925 to [my wife] for [her] own absolute use and benefit and I express the wish (but without imposing any legal obligation on [her]) that [she] should distribute such assets in accordance with any instructions I communicate to [her] whether orally or in writing at any time and from time to time.

12.3.3.1   Definition of personal chattels

Although it is convenient to adopt the definition used in the AEA 1925 for personal chattels, thought should be given as to whether it is appropriate. For example, if a testatrix wishes to make a gift of jewellery only, the clause should be modified by inserting an appropriate description of the gift in place of the words 'personal chattels as defined by section 55(1)(x) of the Administration of Estates Act 1925'.

12.3.3.2   The nature of the gifts

There is an absolute gift to the testator's wife. She could retain all the personal chattels but the testator hopes that through the use of the precatory words she will retain only certain chattels and will distribute the rest. Flexibility is achieved since the instruction to the testator's wife can be changed as often as the testator pleases by giving further non-testamentary instruction.

12.3.4   Taxation implications of the precatory trust

12.3.4.1   Inheritance tax (IHTA 1984, s 143)

The gift takes effect as an absolute gift to the beneficiary named in the clause. Inheritance tax is initially calculated on this basis. Thus, as in the sample clause, no IHT will become payable because of the spouse exemption. If no exemption is available, IHT may be payable immediately on the testator's death.

Section 143 provides that where the named beneficiary transfers property in compliance with the testator's wish within two years after the death of the testator 'this Act shall have effect as if the property transferred had been bequeathed by the will to the transferee'. Section 17(b) supports this by stating 'the transfer (by the named beneficiary) shall not be a transfer of value'. The benefit of s 143 is given automatically and does not need to be specifically claimed. Thus the distribution of the property by the named beneficiary in accordance with the 'precatory words' is not a PET by the beneficiary and so will not attract IHT if the named beneficiary dies within seven years of the distribution.

Example

Martha by will leaves her jewellery to her daughter Emma coupled with the wish that Emma shall distribute it to persons named in a letter handed to her before Martha's death. Emma distributes half of the jewellery to members of the family named in the letter and keeps the remainder.

No IHT exemption is available so that on Martha's death tax is payable on the value of the jewellery. No adjustment of the position will be needed when Emma distributes one half of the jewellery. Whether the property passes to Emma or, following the distribution, to others the IHT position is unchanged. Emma makes no transfer of value provided she re-distributes the jewellery within two years of her mother's death.

12.3.4.2 Capital gains tax

There are no CGT provisions equivalent to s 143 of IHTA 1984. The named beneficiary will make a disposal of assets each time property is transferred in accordance with the precatory trust. However, CGT will be payable only if there is a gain on disposal (after allowing for indexation) which is beyond any available exemption or relief. In view of the timescale between the death and the later transfer of the property, it is unlikely that any taxable gain will arise.

12.4 Wills containing discretionary trusts

12.4.1 Using the discretionary will

Being unable to anticipate accurately the circumstances prevailing at his death, whether in relation to the extent of his property or his family, the testator may decide his will should be drafted in 'flexible' form. This can be achieved by giving a legacy or the residue (or part of residue) to the executors and trustees on discretionary trusts together with wide powers of appointment over the capital and income. If the powers of appointment are not exercised by the trustees, the property will pass 'in default of appointment' to beneficiaries chosen by the testator and named in the will.

A will of this type enables the trustees to take into account the circumstances prevailing at the death of the testator and use the trust property as best suits those circumstances. For example, a testator's spouse may be financially well provided for and so not require the provision under the testator's will. If so, the trustees could exercise their powers over the income and capital in favour of the testator's children. If the circumstances were different and the spouse was in need of the testator's estate, the whole of it could be made available by exercise of the trustee's power of appointment in favour of the spouse.

12.4.2 Planning the discretionary will

Instructions will be required from the testator on various matters before the will can be drafted.

12.4.2.1 Legacy or residue on discretionary trusts?

A 'settled legacy', ie, a legacy of property to be held on discretionary trusts, is often incorporated into a will which then leaves the residuary estate to other beneficiaries absolutely.

Sample clause – settled legacy

(1) I give to my Trustees free of all taxes the sum of [ ] thousand pounds (which said sum and all investments and property for the time being representing the

same is hereinafter referred to as 'the Settled Legacy') upon the trusts and with and subject to the powers discretions and provisions contained in the succeeding paragraphs of this Clause

(2) For so long during the period of eighty years from my death (the perpetuity period applicable hereto) as any of the persons hereinafter mentioned is living my Trustees shall have power at any time and from time to time if and whenever they shall in their absolute discretion think fit to pay or apply the whole or any part or parts of the income or of the capital or of the income and the capital of the Settled Legacy to or for the benefit of all or any one or more exclusively of the others or other of the following persons that is to say my [spouse and issue] and with power during the period of twenty-one years after my death to accumulate any income of the Settled Legacy not so paid or applied and to add any such accumulations to the capital thereof

(3) Subject to the foregoing provisions of this Clause and to any and every exercise of the powers and discretions hereinbefore conferred upon them my Trustees shall hold the Settled Legacy upon trust for such of my [children and grandchildren] ...

If there is no settled legacy, the will may provide absolute legacies, for example, to the testator's children and then leave the residuary estate on discretionary trusts for a class of beneficiaries possibly including the testator's spouse and issue.

If a will contains a settled legacy to be held on discretionary trusts, it is generally inadvisable for the will to contain another such trust (eg, residue should not be given on discretionary trusts as well). The IHTA 1984, s 62 provides that if two settlements are made on the same day by the same person (the testator on the day he dies), they are 'related settlements'. The implications of s 62 are that the IHT benefits which are hoped for by using the settled legacy may be lost if two or more discretionary trusts are included in the will. The IHTA 1984, s 80 provides that a life interest in favour of a surviving spouse will not be a related settlement so that there is no harm if residue is left on interest in possession trusts for the testator's spouse.

12.4.2.2   Duration of the discretionary trust

The discretionary trust, whether as a settled legacy or of residue, may be drafted so as to be capable of lasting for a full perpetuity period of up to 80 years. Even if it is drafted in this way, it is unlikely that it will in fact last so long. Trustees will normally exercise their powers of appointment over capital far earlier.

It is more common to limit the duration of a discretionary trust of residue to a maximum period of two years. A two-year discretionary trust takes advantage of the IHT reliefs afforded by IHTA 1984, s 144 (see **12.4.3.1**).

12.4.2.3   Extent of the property within the discretionary trust

Where the discretionary trust is a settled legacy, it may be limited to property to the value of the available nil rate band for IHT at the testator's death. Such 'nil rate band discretionary trusts' have the advantage that no IHT is payable from them when the trustees exercise their discretionary powers (see further **12.4.3.1**). If the testator does not wish to restrict the discretionary trust to the nil rate band or instead prefers to impose such a trust over his residuary estate, there is no limit otherwise restricting the extent of the property which may become subject to the trusts.

12.4.3 Taxation implications of discretionary trusts in wills

12.4.3.1 Inheritance tax

Section 144 relief

Whether or not a discretionary trust of the residue is drafted as a two-year discretionary trust, consideration must be given to the relief provided by s 144 of IHTA 1984. This section is specifically designed to permit distribution of property from a discretionary trust within two years of the testator's death, without liability to IHT. The section will not apply if the distribution is made within three months of death (see below).

The section applies where property is settled by a will if two conditions are satisfied:

(a)   no interest in possession subsists in the settled property, ie, the property is held by the trustees on discretionary trusts; and

(b)   an event occurs in relation to the settled property within the period of two years after the death of the testator which would otherwise be chargeable to tax, for example, the distribution of trust property by the trustees to a beneficiary.

If the conditions are met there are two consequences:

(a)   the discretionary will trust is taken outside the normal charging regime for discretionary trusts (see further **10.2**). Thus, the charge to IHT which would normally arise where property ceases to be comprised in a settlement will not apply to the distribution by the trustees; and

(b)   the event, ie, the distribution by the trustees, is taxed as if the will had provided that on the testator's death property should be held as it is held after the distribution. A 'writing back' effect is, therefore, achieved in a manner similar to a post-death variation when an election is made (see **13.2.1.1**).

Example

Mary by her will creates a discretionary trust of her residuary estate of £525,000. The beneficiaries are her husband Henry and their children and grandchildren. She dies in March 2006, having made no lifetime transfers.

Death of Mary: £100,000 IHT is payable (£525,000 – £275,000 = £250,000 @ 40%). The spouse exemption is not available.

Distribution by Mary's trustees in October 2006 (within two years of Mary's death but after three months (see below)) as follows:

£275,000 to trustees on A & M trusts for the grandchildren: within nil rate band.

The rest to Henry absolutely: spouse exemption

No IHT is now payable on Mary's death as the trustees' distributions are 'read back' into Mary's will.

This writing back effect is automatic; no election is required. The IHT paid by the PRs to obtain the grant of probate will be repaid (with interest) by the Revenue. Where (as is often the case) the PRs apply for the grant before making an appointment, they will have to pay IHT on the basis of there being no spouse exemption. When they make the appointment to the spouse, they will obtain a refund of IHT paid with interest.

Section 144 works to provide the writing back effect only where a charge to IHT would otherwise have arisen on the distribution by the discretionary trustees. No exit charge arises within the first three months of any discretionary settlement; there must be at least one complete quarter (see **10.2.3**). Any appointment within three months of Mary's death would not be read back into her will. Spouse relief would not be available and, using the figures from the previous example, £100,000 IHT would remain payable (see further *Frankland v IRC* [1996] STC 735).

Distributions after two years from death

If the discretionary trust of the residuary estate is not limited to the two-year period following the testator's death, s 144 relief may only be claimed for distributions made within the two-year period. Later distributions will be taxable in accordance with normal principles which apply to trusts where there is no interest in possession (see **10.2**).

Nil rate band discretionary trusts

Nil rate band discretionary trusts (a settled legacy, see **12.4.2**) are designed to provide flexibility of testamentary provision while at the same time using the testator's nil rate band for IHT, or as much of it as is available on death. However, to be fully effective, it is important that in addition:

(a)   the residuary estate is given by the will to an exempt beneficiary, for example, the testator's spouse (or, less usually, a charity); and

(b)   the will does not contain any related settlement (see **12.4.2**).

Nil rate band discretionary trusts rely on the usual discretionary trust charging regime for their effectiveness (see **10.2.4**). The advantage is that distributions made by the trustees before the first 10-year anniversary will not attract IHT liability.

Example

Raymond had made PETs of £75,000 which became chargeable on his death last year. By his will he creates a discretionary trust of the balance of his nil rate band of £200,000 and leaves the residue of his estate to his wife Wendy. The beneficiaries of the trust are Wendy, his children and grandchildren.

(a)   Calculate the IHT on Raymond's death

No IHT is payable because:

(i)   the funds in the nil rate band discretionary trust are taxed at 0% because the balance of Raymond's nil rate band is available (£275,000 – £75,000 = £200,000);

(ii)   the residuary estate has the benefit of the spouse exemption.

(b)   Distribution by the trustees

Three years after Raymond's death, Wendy tells the trustees that she can manage without relying on the nil rate band discretionary trust fund and she asks if they will distribute it to the children. The trustees agree to do so. No IHT is payable by the trustees from the discretionary trust. The settlement rate will be nil.

Using the method illustrated in **10.2.4** (exit charge before the first 10-year anniversary), the calculation is:

Step 1:	Hypothetical chargeable transfer (value of funds settled by will)		£200,000
Step 2:	Ascertain tax payable		
	Raymond's cumulative total	£75,000	
	Nil rate band (balance)		£200,000
Step 3:	Ascertain settlement rate		nil

Note: the settlement rate will always be nil within the first 10 years so long as a testator has no cumulative total of chargeable transfers and the funds entering the discretionary settlement at death are limited to the nil rate band:

Step 1:	Value of funds	£275,000
Step 2:	Available nil rate band	£275,000
Step 3:	Ascertain settlement rate	nil

12.4.3.2 Capital gains tax

No special rules exist for CGT where distributions are made from discretionary trusts created by a will. In particular, there is no writing back effect for CGT. Thus, ordinary principles must be applied to calculate any liability (see further **10.2.7**). However, in outline the following is the position.

When a beneficiary becomes 'absolutely entitled' to trust property as against the trustees, the trustees are 'deemed to dispose' of the property at its market value and to re-acquire it at the same value as bare trustees, ie, it remains in the names of the former trustees but is now the absolute property of the beneficiary.

Example 1: nil rate band discretionary trust

A testator's will creates a nil rate band discretionary trust. Three years after death the trustees appoint the trust property to the testator's spouse who thereby becomes absolutely entitled to it. Although the property will remain in the trustees' names (until it is actually transferred to the spouse), they now hold it as 'bare trustees' for the testator's spouse. Hold-over relief is usually available whenever property leaves the discretionary trust so that no CGT liability will actually arise for the trustees provided the appropriate election is made by the trustees and beneficiary (IHTA 1984, s 260 – see **4.4.5.2**).

Example 2: two-year discretionary trust

A testator's will creates a two-year discretionary trust. The trustees exercise the power of appointment which is read back into the testator's will. As there is no chargeable transfer by the trustees, ie, IHTA 1984, s 144 applies, hold-over relief will not be available under TCGA 1992, s 260. If the trust property is 'business assets', hold-over relief under TCGA 1992, s 165 may be available.

12.4.3.3 Income tax

Once the discretionary trust is set up following the death, income over £500 from the settled property received by the trustees will attract tax at the rate of 40% (the rate applicable to trusts). This, and the position of the beneficiaries, is considered in **Chapter 14**.

Distributions by trustees from discretionary trusts created by a will do not create settlements which fall within the income tax anti-avoidance provisions discussed at **4.6.2** and **4.6.4**.

Example

David appoints his wife, Sheena, as his executor and trustee. His will bequeaths her a substantial legacy and leaves his residuary estate on a two-year discretionary trust for Sheena and their children. David dies leaving two young children.

Within two years of David's death, Sheena distributes the residuary estate onto new A & M trusts for their infant children. Even though the children's trust was created by appointment by their mother, the appointment onto the new trusts is not a 'settlement' by a parent on her child within the income tax anti-avoidance provisions. Sheena creates the new settlement in her capacity as trustee of David's will, not as a parent.

However, compare the position in relation to post-death variations (see **13.4.2** where the anti-avoidance legislation can apply).

12.5 Drafting discretionary trusts of residue

The clauses which follow should be inserted into the will after the clauses directing the payment of the testator's debts, legacies, funeral and testamentary expenses and hence establishing the residuary fund to be 'the Trust Fund'. Many of the provisions used to create a discretionary trust by will are similar to those used to establish a discretionary trust by lifetime settlements. The comments on the clauses which follow are confined to those relevant only to will trusts.

12.5.1 Trust definitions

Sample clause

In my Will where the context so admits

(1)   'the Trust Fund' shall mean

    (a)   my Estate after the payment of my debts funeral and testamentary expenses and legacies and

    (b)   all money investments or other property accepted by the Trustees as additions and

    (c)   all accumulations (if any) of income directed to be held as an accretion to capital and

    (d)   the money investments and property from time to time representing the above

(2)   'the Trustees' shall mean my Executors or other of the trustees for the time being of the Trust Fund

(3)   'the Trust Period' shall mean the period ending on the earlier of

    (a)   the last day of the period of eighty years from the date of my death which period (and no other) shall be the applicable perpetuity period or

    (b)   such date as the Trustees shall by deed at any time or times specify (not being a date earlier than the date of execution of any such deed or later than a date previously specified)

(4)   'the Discretionary Beneficiaries' shall mean

    (a)   [my wife] [my husband]

    (b)   my children and remoter issue (whether living at my death or born thereafter)

    (c)   the husbands wives widowers and widows of my children and remoter issue

    (d)   any company trust or other body regarded as charitable under the law of England and Wales

(5)   'the Discretionary Period' shall mean [the period of two years (less one day) from the date of my death] [the Trust Period]

(6)   'the Accumulation Period' shall mean the period of twenty-one years from the date of my death which shall be the applicable accumulation period for all purposes

Clause (5) contains alternatives. If the period of 'two years (less one day) from the date of death' is selected the trust will comply with the provisions of s 144 of IHTA 1984, ie a two-year discretionary trust will have been established. By limiting the trustees to a period of two years less one day, it is intended to remove uncertainty as to whether the distributions in fact occurred within two years of the testator's death. Difficulties can arise if an exact period of two years is used instead.

12.5.1.1   Nil rate band discretionary trust

The clauses set out above may be used to establish a discretionary trust which is not limited to the nil rate band available at the testator's death. If a nil rate band discretionary trust is to be created, these clauses can be used but the definition of the trust fund must be altered to limit its extent.

Sample clause

> 'the Trust Fund' shall mean
>
> (1)   the greatest value (if any) which such Trust Fund can have within the nil rate band of inheritance tax applicable at the date of my death which does not cause inheritance tax to be charged (other than at the said nil rate) in respect of my estate as a consequence of my death
>
> (2)   (a)–(d) [as for (1) in the previous clause]

12.5.2   Residuary gift: discretionary trusts

Sample clause

> (1)   The Trustees shall hold the capital and income of the Trust Fund upon such trusts in favour or for the benefit of all or such one or more of the Discretionary Beneficiaries exclusive of the other or others of them in such shares or proportions if more than one and with and subject to such powers and provisions for their respective maintenance education or other benefit or for the accumulation of income for any period expiring before the end of the Accumulation Period (including administrative powers and provisions and discretionary trusts and powers to be executed or exercised by any person or persons whether or not being or including the Trustees or any of them) and so that the exercise of this power of appointment may be delegated to any extent and in such manner generally as the Trustees (subject to the application (if any) of the rule against perpetuities) by any deed or deeds revocable during the Discretionary Period or irrevocable and executed during the Discretionary Period shall appoint provided always that no exercise of this power shall invalidate any prior payment or application of all or any part or parts of the capital or income of the Trust Fund made under any other power or powers conferred by my Will or by law and provided further that this power may be exercised whether or not the administration of my Estate has been completed and whether or not a transfer of the Trust Fund has been effected by my Executors under Clause [   ]

All powers and provisions established by the clause are exercisable by the trustees. It is arguable that these powers are not exercisable until the end of the administration period, ie, when the trust is fully established by the executors transferring the assets remaining in the estate to the trustees. In addition, it is sometimes argued that the powers cannot be exercised by the trustees before the grant of probate has been obtained. The proviso at the end of this clause is designed to overcome these arguments by expressly authorising the trustees to exercise the powers in the way set out in the clause.

Sample clause (continued)

(2)   Until and subject to and in default of any appointment under sub-clause (1) the following provisions of this sub-clause shall apply to the Trust Fund during the Discretionary Period

(a)   the Trustees shall pay or apply the income of the Trust Fund to or for the benefit of all or such one or more of the Discretionary Beneficiaries exclusive of the other or others of them as shall for the time being be in existence and in such shares if more than one and in such manner generally as the Trustees shall in their absolute discretion from time to time think fit

(b)   notwithstanding the provisions of sub-clause (2)(a) the Trustees may in their absolute discretion instead of applying all or any part or parts of the income accumulate the same in the way of compound interest by investing or otherwise applying it and its resulting income from time to time in any applications or investments authorised by my Will or by law and subject to sub-clause (2)(c) below shall hold such accumulations as an accretion to capital

(c)   the Trustees may apply the whole or any part or parts of the income accumulated under sub-clause (2)(b) as if it were income arising in the then current year

(d)   notwithstanding the trusts powers and provisions declared and contained in this sub-clause the Trustees may

(i)   at any time or times pay or apply the whole or any part or parts of the capital of the Trust Fund to or for the benefit of all or such one or more of the Discretionary Beneficiaries exclusive of the other or others of them in such shares if more than one and in such manner generally as the Trustees shall in their absolute discretion think fit

(ii)   (subject to the application (if any) of the rules against perpetuities) pay or transfer any income or capital of the Trust Fund to the Trustees of any other trust wherever established or existing under which all or any one or more of the Discretionary Beneficiaries is or are interested (whether or not all or such one or more of the Discretionary Beneficiaries is or are the only objects or persons interested or capable of benefiting under such other trust) if the Trustees shall in their absolute discretion consider such payment or transfer to be for the benefit of all or such one or more of the Discretionary Beneficiaries

(3)   At the end of the Discretionary Period and subject to and in default of any appointment under sub-clause (1) the Trustees shall hold the Trust Fund upon trust for ...

If this clause is used to create a nil rate band settled legacy, the ultimate default trusts in clause (3) would generally provide that the property in the settled legacy should pass to the residuary beneficiary under the will of the testator.

12.6   Gifts by will for the testator's minor children

A testator has a choice when considering gifts for his minor children. The choice is between vested and contingent gifts for the testator's children as minor beneficiaries. This calls for a consideration of the succession and taxation consequences of each.

12.6.1 Vested gifts

12.6.1.1 Succession

A vested gift by will to an adult beneficiary takes effect in possession on the testator's death. This is the usual situation where the will leaves a beneficiary a legacy or an interest in the residuary estate. If the gift is of land, it cannot take effect in possession because a minor is unable to hold land. A receipt clause in the will may permit the minor, if aged (say) 16 years, to give a valid receipt for the assets other than land. In such cases, the property may be transferred to the beneficiary by the executors.

In other cases, the minor's parent or guardian will give a good receipt for the asset under the Children Act 1989 unless the will has provided that trustees are to hold the asset on a bare trust for the minor.

Minors with vested interests own the assets even if someone else is holding them. The death of the minor beneficiary, who will inevitably be intestate, will cause the property to pass under the intestacy law to his surviving parent or remoter relative. If this is considered undesirable, the gift to the minor beneficiary should be made contingent on attaining a given age (see **12.6.2**).

12.6.1.2 Taxation

Vested gifts are not treated as gifts into a settlement for any of the three principal taxes. The tax position is the same as in the case of any other property owned absolutely by a tax payer.

Inheritance tax

On the death of the minor beneficiary, his 'estate' includes the vested gift. Inheritance tax will be payable on its value to the extent the nil rate band on death is exceeded. In view of the age of the beneficiary, and his probable financial circumstances, it is unlikely that a liability will arise.

Capital gains tax

Disposals of the property during the minor beneficiary's lifetime will occur if the trustees holding the property sell it, for example, shares into which the gift has been invested are sold following advice of stockbrokers. Gains (or losses) are determined on normal principles working on the basis that the property belongs to the minor beneficiary. Thus, after the indexation allowance, reliefs and exemptions available to the minor beneficiary may be claimed. The higher £8,500 annual exemption will be available; not the trustees' lower £4,250 exemption. Any gain (after applying taper relief) will be taxed at rates equivalent to the minor beneficiary's income tax rates.

Income tax

Income produced by the property will be taxed as part of the beneficiary's income at his marginal rates, for example, dividends on shares bequeathed to the minor beneficiary. Often in these circumstances the minor beneficiary has a gross income which is less than his personal allowance. However, dividends carry an irrecoverable 10% tax credit which satisfies the beneficiary's basic rate liability. If he is not liable at that rate, he cannot recover the credit from the Revenue. The higher rate of tax on dividends (32.5%) is payable if the minor beneficiary pays tax above basic rate.

12.6.2 Contingent gifts

12.6.2.1 Succession

A gift which vests at a particular age or other future event requires trustees to hold the property until then. If the beneficiary dies after the testator but before the contingency is satisfied, the property will not pass under the beneficiary's intestacy. Instead, it will devolve on the beneficiary next entitled under the original trusts. Such a beneficiary may either be named expressly as being entitled 'in default', ie, the person to inherit if the contingent gift fails; alternatively, he may be the beneficiary who inherits the residuary estate under the testator's will, ie, the gift is declared on failure of the principal trusts to 'fall into and form part of my residuary estate'.

A testator may wish to leave property, particularly a gift of his residuary estate, to trustees upon express trust for minor beneficiaries with provision that the gift vests in possession when the beneficiary attains a stated age, for example, when a beneficiary is 21 or 25 years old. In such cases, the testator should be advised to establish a class gift for 'such of my children as shall attain the age of 21 or 25 years' and will provide for gifts over for his grandchildren. A gift of this type permits the testator to achieve a certain degree of flexibility in the terms of the trusts and in particular through the powers given to the trustees.

12.6.2.2 Taxation

Contingent gifts are gifts into settlement for each of the three principal taxes. It is, therefore, necessary to consider the taxation position of the trustees and of the minor beneficiary separately. It is also advisable to contrast the taxation position of contingent gifts generally with the position relating to vested gifts. A particularly unfavourable taxation position might significantly influence a testator in his choice of gift. However, as always, the taxation position needs careful balancing against the succession consequences.

Inheritance tax

On the death of a minor beneficiary before the contingency is satisfied, the gift fails. The property is not in the minor beneficiary's 'estate', ie, he does not have an interest in possession in it, so that IHT will not be payable on the value of the property.

If the beneficiary dies after attaining the age of 18 but before the contingency is satisfied, for example, he becomes entitled to the property at 21, IHT may be payable. In these circumstances, s 31 of TA 1925 gives the beneficiary a right to the income produced by the property held in trust for him once he reaches 18, ie, the beneficiary now has an interest in possession in the settled property. If a beneficiary with an interest in possession dies, IHT is payable on the value of the settled property as part of his 'estate' for IHT, even if he dies before the contingency has occurred.

> Example
>
> Simon by will leaves his residuary estate on trust for his only child Cathy contingent on reaching 21. Cathy is 15 when her father dies. Section 31 of TA 1925 applies to Simon's will.

(a)   Cathy dies aged 17. No IHT is payable on Simon's will trust as a result of Cathy's death as it does not form part of her estate.

(b)   Cathy dies aged 19. She obtained an interest in possession in the income of Simon's will trust at 18. Inheritance tax is payable by the trustees of the trust fund (calculated by adding the value of the trust fund to Cathy's free estate and apportioning the IHT between it and the trust fund).

A contingent gift by will to a minor beneficiary will normally qualify as an A & M settlement as discussed in **Chapter 8**. As a consequence, the settlement will benefit from the favourable provisions introduced by s 71 of IHTA 1984 to exclude A & M settlements from the main charging provisions applying to settlements with no interest in possession (IHTA 1984, s 71(4) – see **10.3.2.1**). The ability to rely on these provisions makes the contingent gift by will to minor beneficiaries particularly attractive to testators, although the capital gains tax and income tax position should not be overlooked. For IHT, there are two advantages in using an A & M settlement. There is no liability to tax when the beneficiary attains an interest in possession, normally on his 18th birthday (unless s 31 of TA 1925 is modified); nor is there liability when the trustees vest the property in the beneficiary when he satisfies the contingency.

Example

Samantha by will settles her residuary estate on trust for her only child Charles at 25. Charles is 16 when Samantha dies. Section 31 of TA 1925 applies to Samantha's will.

(a)   Charles becomes 18. No IHT is payable on Charles attaining an interest in possession (under TA 1925, s 31).

(b)   Charles becomes 25. No IHT is payable when the contingency occurs and the trustees transfer the property to him (he is already deemed 'beneficially entitled' to the entire settled property).

However, liability may arise if the beneficiary dies after attaining an interest in possession but before satisfying the contingency (as Cathy did in the previous example).

Capital gains tax

Any sales of the trust property by the trustees before the beneficiary satisfies the contingency will be a disposal by the trustees for CGT. The trustees' liability will be determined by applying normal principles. If a gain is made (after allowing for indexation), the trustees deduct their exemptions and reliefs, for example, the annual exemption of £4,250 (not the higher exemption available to individuals). Any tax, calculated by charging the net gain (after applying taper relief) at 40%, will be paid by the trustees from the settled property.

Example: actual disposal (sale)

Property is held by the trustees of a will trust for Angela at 25, and s 31 of TA 1925 applies. She is 10 when the testator dies but is 16 when the trustees sell an investment for £20,000.

	£
Disposal consideration	20,000
Less: Acquisition cost (probate value at the testator's death)	5,000
	15,000
Less: Indexation allowance (say)	1,750
	13,250
Less: Annual exemption	4,250

Chargeable gain (subject to taper relief based on the trustees' period of ownership which is applied before deducting the annual exemption)	9,000
Tax @ 40%	£3,600

When the beneficiary satisfies the contingency, he becomes absolutely entitled to the settled property as against the trustees. They are 'deemed' to dispose (see **10.2.7.1**) of each item of the settled property at its market value at the time and to re-acquire it at the same value as bare trustees, ie it is now the property of the beneficiary although it remains in the names of the bare trustees until they transfer it to the beneficiary.

Example: deemed disposal

The facts are the same as in the previous example. Angela attains 25 and becomes entitled to the settled property.

	£
Disposal consideration (market value of the asset at Angela's 25th birthday)	55,000
Less: Acquisition cost (say)	25,000
	30,000
Less: Indexation allowance (say)	8,750
	21,250
Less: Annual exemption	4,250
Chargeable gain (subject to taper relief)	17,000
Tax @ 40%	£6,800

The gain on the deemed disposal by the trustees when the property leaves the settlement on Angela's 25th birthday will only attract hold-over relief if the assets are relevant business assets under TCGA 1992, s 165 (see further **10.3.2.2**). However, the relief will be available automatically if the settlement qualifies as an A & M settlement when the contingency is satisfied. This will be achieved only if the absolute entitlement occurs at the same time as the interest in possession arises. The nature of the assets within the settlement will not affect this position. If hold-over relief is available, taper relief and the annual exemption are not applied.

Examples: hold-over relief

(a)   A will leaves property for Alec at 18. Section 31 of TA 1925 applies. Hold-over relief will be available when Alec reaches 18 and becomes entitled to the settled property. A & M status is satisfied.

(b)   A will leaves property for Brenda at 21. Section 31 of TA 1925 applies. Hold-over relief will not be available. The settlement lost A & M status when Brenda became 18.

(c)   A will leaves property for Carol at 21. Section 31 of TA 1925 is varied so that an interest in possession arises at the age of 21. Hold-over relief will be available when Carol reaches 21 and becomes entitled to the settled property. Again, A & M status is satisfied.

If the settlement fails to qualify for hold-over relief based on its A & M status, hold-over relief will only be available if the settled property is 'business assets'.

Income tax

Income produced by the settled property will initially be taxed as income of the trustees. The rate of tax depends on the nature of the beneficial interests in the trust (see further **Chapter 14**). If no beneficiary has a vested interest in the income, ie there is no interest in possession, the trustees pay at 40% (32.5% on dividends) on income in excess of £500. (Income tax is charged on the first £500 of income at 22%, 20% or 10%, depending on the type of income.) Section 31 of TA 1925 will normally ensure the beneficiary attains a vested interest in income at the age of 18. Once an interest in possession arises, the trustees pay at basic rate (22%). Tax at this rate is deemed satisfied by the 20% tax deducted at source from interest payments and by the 10% tax credit carried by dividends.

Example

Roy by will leaves his residuary estate on trust for Sulima at 25. Section 31 of TA 1925 applies. Sulima is aged 16 when Roy dies.

(a)   Until Sulima becomes 18: trustees pay income tax on income in excess of £500 at 32.5% on dividends and at 40% on other income. (The trustees will pay at 22%, 20% or 10% on the first £500 income.)

(b)   After Sulima's 18th birthday: trustees pay income tax at 22% (s 31 of the TA 1925 gave Sulima a vested entitlement to the income).

The income tax position of the beneficiary depends also on the nature of his interest in the income of the settled property.

Example

The facts are as in the previous example.

(a)   Until Sulima becomes 18, she is liable to pay income tax only on the income applied by the trustees for her maintenance, education or benefit under TA 1925, s 31. The trustees must ensure they have paid tax at the 'rate applicable to trusts' (40%) on all income applied for Sulima. As they have paid tax at only 32.5% on dividends and at 22%, 20% or 10% on the first £500 income, they will be assessed for the extra tax due (and must ensure they reserve sufficient funds for the purpose). If Sulima's own rate of income tax is less than the 40% paid by the trustees, she may reclaim the difference between her own rate of income tax and the tax paid by the trustees from the Revenue. For Sulima, the source of her income is the trustees, not the dividends. This means that the irrecoverable 10% credit on dividends will not apply to her. If appropriate to her, she may reclaim all tax paid by the trustees.

Assume trust dividend income of £1,000 – £400 (40%) = £600 net. The trustees apply all the net income in payment of Sulima's school fees. She has no other income and so is not a taxpayer. She will be entitled to a repayment of £400 from the Revenue since her gross income is less than her personal allowance of £4,895.

Any income retained by the trustees, ie, income not used for Sulima's benefit, is accumulated after relevant tax has been paid. As this tax is lost to the Revenue once it has been accumulated, the trustees should consider applying the income where possible.

(b)   After Sulima's 18th birthday, she has a vested entitlement to the settlement income. She is liable to pay tax on all income at her marginal rate. In line with the general rule, she will not be able to reclaim the irrecoverable 10% tax credit on dividends.

Assume trust dividend income of £900 (credit £100) = £1,000 gross. The credit satisfies her liability at basic rate. The trustees will pay the income to Sulima as she is entitled to it. If she is a higher rate tax payer, she pays at 32.5% (the Sch F higher rate) on £1,000, but may deduct the £100 credit from the liability. If she has no other income, she will not be entitled to a repayment from the Revenue since the 10% credit is irrecoverable.

12.7 Wills containing a terminable life interest

12.7.1 Form of the will

Many testators wish to provide adequately for their surviving spouse and yet wish to incorporate into their wills flexibility whereby other members of the family may benefit should the surviving spouse not require the provision when the testator dies. Although a will containing discretionary trusts (see **12.4**) may be used to achieve the testator's wishes, the testator may prefer a will which gives his surviving spouse a direct benefit in the form of a life interest (coupled with powers of advancement in her favour over the capital) with flexibility provided by 'an overriding power of appointment'. This power, exercisable by the trustees after the testator's death, would enable the trustees to divest the surviving spouse of entitlement should this course of action prove desirable and to 'redirect' the property among a class of beneficiaries identified by the will.

12.7.2 Drafting life interest trusts subject to an overriding power of appointment

After the usual provisions dealing with payment of debts, legacies, testamentary expenses etc and after the residuary fund defined as 'my Trust Fund' has been established, the clauses creating the beneficial trusts should be set out. Extracts of the principal clauses are set out below in the order they usually appear, ie, the life interest for the surviving spouse follows the overriding power for the trustees.

Sample clause

> My Trustees shall hold the capital and income of the Trust Fund upon such trusts in favour or for the benefit of all or such one or more of the Beneficiaries exclusive of the other or others of them in such shares or proportions if more than one and with and subject to such powers and provisions for their respective maintenance education or other benefit or for the accumulation of income ... as my Trustees (subject to the application (if any) of the rule against perpetuities) by any deed or deeds ... shall appoint ...

This clause subjects the whole of the trust fund to a wide power of appointment. It may be exercised by the trustees to create absolute interests or interests under trusts in favour of the beneficiaries who will have been identified earlier in the will in a clause setting out various definitions (see **6.2.4**). Normally, the beneficiaries would include the testator's spouse, children and remoter issue and their respective spouses. The testator's intention would be that the trustees exercise this power only after consulting the surviving spouse (although there is no express provision requiring the consent of the spouse) and after they have taken into account all the circumstances existing at the testator's death. In such circumstances, it would not be unusual for the testator to appoint the surviving spouse as a trustee. The effect of exercising the power is to bring to an end the surviving spouse's life interest (see the following clause) in the whole or part of the trust fund although if included in the class of beneficiaries, the trustees may appoint capital to the former life tenant.

Sample clause

> Until and subject to and in default of an appointment under clause [   ]
>
> (a)   My Trustees shall pay the income of the Trust Fund to the Life Tenant for life [or until remarriage] [if the Life Tenant shall survive me by [   ] days]
>
> (b)   (i)   My Trustees may at any time or times during the Trust Period as to the whole or any part of the Trust Fund in which the Life Tenant has

for the time being an interest in possession transfer or raise and pay the same to or for the absolute use or benefit of the Life Tenant or raise and pay or apply the same for the advancement or otherwise for the benefit of the Life Tenant in such manner as my Trustees shall in their absolute discretion think fit

(ii) In this clause 'interest in possession' shall have the same meaning it has for the purpose of the Inheritance Tax Act 1984 and any statutory modification or re-enactment of such Act

(c) ...

(d) ...

This clause gives the trustees express power to advance capital to the life tenant (who would also be identified in the definition clause in the will) should his circumstances so require. Sub-clauses (c) and (d) would set out the further trusts in the event of the trustees not exercising their overriding power of appointment.

12.7.3 Taxation implications of an overriding power

12.7.3.1 Inheritance tax

Death of the testator

No IHT is payable on the death of the testator since the spouse exemption is available as a result of the interest in possession given to the surviving spouse. Thus, a grant of probate can be obtained without the need to negotiate a loan to pay any IHT. This is an advantage which may not be available where the will contains a discretionary trust (see **12.4.3.1**).

Exercise of the overriding power

If the trustees contemplate exercising the power, they should first consider the taxation consequences. Any appointment of capital by the trustees will bring about the 'ending of an interest in possession', ie, the life interest will be wholly or partly terminated. In so far as capital is appointed to the life tenant, no IHT will arise. If the power is exercised in favour of the other beneficiaries, the ending of the interest in possession is a transfer of value which may be a PET (depending on who benefits from the appointment and on what terms) by the life tenant so that IHT is payable only if death occurs within seven years (IHTA 1984, s 52). Thus, in both cases the IHT position is similar to that discussed at **10.1.4.1** in relation to partitioning trust funds.

12.7.3.2 Capital gains tax

If the exercise of the power results in someone becoming 'absolutely entitled' to the settled property against the trustees, there is a deemed disposal by the trustees. Absolute entitlement can occur where property leaves the trust following an outright appointment in favour of a beneficiary or where the trustees appoint property to trustees to hold on new trusts (see further **10.4**). Either of these methods is possible under the power of appointment set out at **12.7.2**.

The calculation of the trustees' liability, the exemptions, reliefs and rates of tax is also similar to that for lifetime trusts (see **10.1.4.2**).

12.7.4 Drafting the deed of appointment

The drafting of the deed, and its contents, will follow closely the drafting of the deed of appointment discussed at **10.2.8**.

Chapter 13

Post-death Arrangements

13.1 Types of arrangement

13.1.1 Introduction

Beneficiaries and trustees may wish to rearrange dispositions of property in an estate following a death. Reasons for rearrangements include:

(a) a beneficiary's wish to redirect benefits to other members of the family who are less well provided for, either as a result of the death or generally; and

(b) the saving of tax, usually IHT, particularly where the disposition of the estate does not fully utilise the deceased's nil rate band.

There are many ways of redirecting assets. Most methods take advantage of specific statutory provision while others use taxation exemptions and reliefs. The following are among the more usual.

13.1.1.1 A lifetime gift by the beneficiary of an inheritance under a will or under an intestacy

This may be an outright gift by the beneficiary. If so, it will constitute a PET for IHT and a disposal for CGT by the beneficiary. If instead the beneficiary transfers the property to trustees to hold on trust, it will be a PET or lifetime chargeable transfer depending upon which type of trust is selected. For CGT, a gift to trustees will be a disposal whichever type of trust is selected. Creation of trusts by lifetime gift is considered in **Chapter 5**.

13.1.1.2 'Precatory trusts' and wills creating two-year discretionary trusts

These are flexible dispositions created by the testator. The exact testamentary effect of the will is, effectively, determined after death by the act of the personal representatives (and in some cases, the beneficiaries), and not by the testator at the time of making the will. Wills containing this type of provision were considered in **Chapter 12**.

13.1.1.3 Orders made under the Inheritance (Provision for Family and Dependants) Act 1975 and the capitalisation of a life interest on an intestacy

Both of these amount to rearrangements of the disposition of an estate on death. In either case, the estate is treated as if left in accordance with the terms of the rearrangement. This 'writing back' effect will affect the extent of the liability to IHT on the estate on death. (See further LPC Guide, *Pervasive and Core Topics*.)

13.1.1.4   Post-death variations of the dispositions of the deceased's estate

If the variation is made in the appropriate form, the effect is to write the provisions of the variation back into the terms of the deceased's will or the intestacy law for tax purposes. The estate on death is then charged to IHT on the basis of the amended provisions but the beneficiary suffers no adverse tax consequences. If the writing back effect is not obtained, the beneficiary is left in the position of making lifetime gifts as discussed above. Variations are discussed further at **13.2**.

13.1.1.5   Disclaimer of benefit

A disclaimer may not achieve the objectives of the beneficiary wishing to make the post-death rearrangement. Disclaimers amount to a rejection of the benefit of the gift under the will or the intestacy law. They will be appropriate for use only if, following the rejection, the property passes to the person who the original beneficiary intends to benefit. However, despite this limitation on their use, in some cases disclaimers offer advantages not available in the case of variations.

13.1.2   Variation or disclaimer?

These provisions permit the redirection of property after a death by a beneficiary whether the deceased died testate or intestate. They offer estate planning opportunities for the beneficiary who can afford 'not to receive' property for whatever reason.

It is very important to think through the effect of a disclaimer carefully, especially where the statutory trusts on intestacy are involved. *In re DWS (Deceased); In re EHS (Deceased); TWGS (A Minor) v G and Others* [2000] 3 WLR 1910 illustrates this. A child of the deceased was unable to take on intestacy (his interest was forfeited because he had killed his parents). The child's own children could not replace him because issue are entitled under the statutory trusts only where a child predeceases the intestate. Section 47(2) provides that unless issue take an 'absolute vested interest', the intestate is to be treated as having left no issue and those next entitled on intestacy will take. Thus, the deceased's grandchildren took nothing and the property went to the relatives next in line. The principle will apply just as much to disclaimer as to forfeiture.

Post-death variations and disclaimers are both used to redistribute property among members of the family following a death, but variations offer wider possibilities. A variation permits the beneficiary positively to redirect the devolution of the property whereas a disclaimer is merely 'negative' in its operation, ie, the beneficiary rejects the gift. As the variation permits redirection by the original beneficiary, it is possible to introduce 'new beneficiaries' into the terms of the deceased's will or the provisions of the intestacy law. If not used to redirect the property among the family, a variation will often be used to provide charitable payments by will attracting the IHT exemption.

A beneficiary can control the devolution of the property by using a variation but not by using a disclaimer. Thus, if the disclaimed property would pass to the 'wrong beneficiary', a variation will be required to redirect its devolution as appropriate. Although a variation will enable the desired rearrangement to be achieved, the lack of 'writing back' provisions for income tax can cause difficulties where the original beneficiary wants to vary in favour of his/her own minor children. These income tax difficulties are considered at **13.4.2**. The advantage of redirecting property by disclaimer is that there is no equivalent income tax disadvantage. Thus, where possible, a disclaimer by a parent is the favourable method of effecting a post-death rearrangement in favour of minor children.

13.2 Post-death variations

13.2.1 The conditions (IHTA 1984, s 142 (as amended by FA 2002, s 117); TCGA 1992, s 62 (as amended by FA 2002, s 51))

13.2.1.1 Inheritance tax

To achieve the desired writing back effect, the beneficiary must enter into the variation, in writing, within two years of the deceased's death. For variations made on or after 1 August 2002 there must be a statement in the instrument of variation, by the persons making it, that IHTA 1984, s 142(1) is to apply to the variation. If the variation will result in additional IHT being payable on the estate of the deceased, the personal representatives must also join in this statement, and they can only refuse to do so if they do not hold sufficient assets to meet the additional tax liability.

Provided the beneficiary complies with these conditions, the variation is not a transfer of value by him and so no IHT will be payable (IHTA 1984, s 17(a)).

13.2.1.2 Capital gains tax

The conditions for CGT are similar to those for IHT: the variation must be in writing and made within two years of the deceased's death. For variations made on or after 1 August 2002 there must be a statement in the instrument of variation, by the persons making it, that TCGA 1992, s 62(6) is to apply to the variation. No CGT is payable on the deceased's death in any event so that the substitution of new beneficiaries will not affect the CGT position on the death. However, electing for writing back means that the beneficiary making the variation does not make a disposal.

(For both taxes for variations made before 1 August 2002, there was no requirement for a statement in the variation, but instead it was necessary to make an election that the relevant subsections were to apply. This could be done in the variation or separately. It was also necessary to give written notice of this election to the Revenue within six months of making it.)

13.2.2 Whether or not to choose the writing back effect

The original beneficiary is the person who decides whether to make use of the writing back effect for either or both taxes.

13.2.2.1 If the original beneficiary makes no statement that IHTA 1984, s 142(1) is to apply to the variation

For IHT purposes the property is treated as passing to the original beneficiary. He is then treated as making a PET to the new beneficiary. If he survives for seven years, the transfer will become fully exempt but if he dies within seven years, it will become chargeable.

13.2.2.2 If the original beneficiary states that IHTA 1984, s 142(1) is to apply to the variation

There will be no possibility of a charge to IHT so far as the original beneficiary is concerned. He is not treated as having made a transfer for IHT purposes. The property is treated as passing from the deceased to the new beneficiary direct.

The effect on the IHT liability of the deceased's estate will depend on several factors, for example, whether the original or new beneficiaries are exempt. There may be no change, there may be a reduction in IHT or there may be an increase in IHT. If there would be an increase this should be weighed against the benefit to the original beneficiary of avoiding making a PET.

13.2.2.3   If the original beneficiary makes no statement that TCGA 1992, s 62(6) is to apply to the variation

The original beneficiary will make a disposal for CGT to the new beneficiary. There may be a gain or a loss if the asset has increased or decreased in value since the date of death. The new beneficiary will be treated as acquiring the asset at market value at the date of the disposal. If the gain is small it may be covered by the original beneficiary's annual exemption. If the original beneficiary has losses available, these will offset the gain. In neither case will any CGT be paid.

13.2.2.4   If the original beneficiary states that TCGA 1992, s 62(6) is to apply to the variation

There will be no disposal by the original beneficiary and, therefore, no question of any liability to CGT. The asset will be treated as passing from the estate of the deceased to the new beneficiary direct. The new beneficiary will be treated as acquiring it at market value at the date of death.

13.2.3   Capacity to make a variation

An original beneficiary under a will or an intestacy can make a variation in relation to his interest provided he has attained 18 years of age and has mental capacity. The beneficiary with an absolute interest may settle it on trusts for the benefit of others or make an outright gift.

Example

David by will leaves £300,000 to John, who wishes to provide for his own child Carol now aged 19 years. By post-death variation, David's will is varied leaving £100,000 in trust for Carol contingently on her attaining 25 and the residue of £200,000 for John.

13.2.3.1   Consent of the court

In some cases, the consent of the court will be needed before a variation can be made. Under the Variation of Trusts Act (VTA) 1958, the court has power to consent on behalf of beneficiaries who are (inter alia) minors or mentally handicapped. The court's powers are wide enough to permit the variation of beneficial interests whether they are vested, contingent or discretionary but it will only exercise the powers where the proposed arrangement is for the benefit of the beneficiary.

However, VTA 1958 applications to the court are expensive and time-consuming so that, to be justified, the tax saving to be achieved by estate planning should be substantial. The Capital Taxes Advanced Instruction Manual for Inspectors says that they may accept deeds unapproved by the court provided, of course, that they are beneficial to the minor or leave the minor's interest substantially unaffected.

Problems of lack of capacity to consent generally do not arise in the context of 'flexible' wills containing discretionary trusts or an overriding power of appointment. In these cases, any rearrangement of the deceased's estate after death occurs as a result of the decision of the trustees acting under the terms of the will. The lack of ability of a beneficiary to consent is not crucial to making the proposed arrangement. This feature of flexible wills tends to make them attractive in practice (see **12.4**).

13.2.3.2 Can the estate of a deceased beneficiary be varied?

Example

Veronica dies leaving the whole of her estate valued at £278,000 to her husband Arthur. He dies soon after his wife leaving his estate of £553,000 (£275,000 of his own plus £278,000 inherited from Veronica) to their child, Damon. Arthur's PRs can make a variation to redirect Veronica's estate to Damon to use up her nil rate band.

Step 1: IHT on Veronica's death

£278,000 subject to spouse exemption = Nil

Step 2: IHT on Arthur's death

£275,000 @ 0% = Nil

£278,000 @ 40% = £111,200

Damon receives £441,800 as a result of his parents' deaths.

Step 3: PRs make a variation of Veronica's estate to pass all her assets to Damon.

(a) Recalculate IHT on Veronica's estate of £278,000

£275,000 @ 0% = Nil

£3,000 @ 40% = £1,200

(b) Recalculate IHT on Arthur's estate of £275,000

£275,000 @ 0% = Nil

As a result of the variation, Damon's total entitlement from his parents' estates is £551,800.

The Revenue accepts that a variation by the PRs of the deceased beneficiary is permitted. Provided the PRs comply with the conditions, the variation will be written back into the will of the first testator to die for IHT purposes.

13.3 The scope of the statutory provisions for variations and disclaimers

It is possible to vary or disclaim 'any of the dispositions (whether effected by will, under the law relating to intestacy or otherwise) of the property comprised in the estate immediately before his death ...' (IHTA 1984, s 142).

In the application of this provision the following points should be noted.

13.3.1 Interests in joint property

An interest in property held as joint tenants is an asset of the 'estate' of a deceased person for IHT. Although an interest in property held in joint tenancy passes on death by survivorship to the surviving joint tenant, it is nevertheless within the IHT (and CGT) provisions permitting variations and disclaimers following a death. This is because these provisions apply where a disposition on death is effected 'or otherwise', ie, by survivorship.

Example

Alice and Bill inherited Rose Cottage as joint tenants many years ago. Since then they and their respective families have used the cottage for holidays.

Alice has just died leaving her estate by will to her only child, Clara, but her share of the cottage passes to Bill by survivorship. Bill feels Clara should have inherited her mother's interest in the cottage.

Bill can effect a variation so that Alice's estate is taxed as if her will had left her half of the cottage to Clara. This will be effective for tax purposes provided Bill makes the elections. To complete the gift Bill must convey the legal estate to himself and Clara by a separate deed.

13.3.2   Interests in property not capable of variation

The 'estate' of a deceased person includes, inter alia:

(a)   the property in which the deceased had an interest in possession immediately before death, for example, a life tenant under an existing will trust; and

(b)   the property to which the deceased is treated as entitled by application of the 'reservation of benefit' rules (Finance Act 1986, s 102 and see **4.6.5**).

Although both of these interests may attract IHT on death as part of the deceased's estate, it is not possible for either to be the subject of a variation (or disclaimer) for taxation purposes. This is because the definition of 'estate' within the meaning of s 142 of IHTA 1984 specifically excludes each of these interests. Any estate planning following the death must, therefore, proceed on the basis of excluding these interests from any calculations.

13.3.3   Do the reservation of benefit rules apply to variations?

Do the reservation of benefit rules apply if a beneficiary (the donor) makes a post-death variation but still continues to enjoy the property? If so, any advantage intended through the post-death variation would be lost.

The IHTA 1984 applies 'as if the variation had been effected by the deceased or, as the case may be, the disclaimed benefit never conferred'.

Thus, the effect for IHT purposes of making use of the writing back effect is that the deceased is to be taken as making the variation and, therefore, is the donor of the gift. The original beneficiary under the will or the intestacy is not the donor. As a consequence, any benefit which is reserved by the variation to the beneficiary who made it cannot come within these provisions.

Example 1

Ellen died leaving a will containing a gift of her house to Rex. Rex occupies the house but subsequently redirects this gift by post-death variation to his only child Paula. The variation contains the relevant statement and Rex remains in occupation. This will not result in a reservation of benefit to him since the gift of the house is taken to be by Ellen for IHT purposes. Rex's estate on his death will be taxed on this basis.

Example 2

Roger dies leaving a substantial cash legacy to Julian absolutely. Julian redirects this property into a discretionary trust by means of a variation containing the relevant statement. Julian is named as one of the beneficiaries of the discretionary trust. No reservation of benefit for IHT will result as the discretionary trust is taken to be made by Roger. However, there may be income tax consequences as there are no writing back provisions for income tax equivalent to those for IHT and CGT. Julian, not Roger, will be treated as the settlor making the discretionary settlement for the purposes of the income tax avoidance rules (see **6.2.11.1**).

13.3.4   More than one variation?

Sometimes beneficiaries may want to make a number of variations in relation to the same will or intestacy. No difficulty will arise provided each variation deals with a separate part of the estate. Clearly, property given by a legacy in a will and the property in the residuary gift are separate parts each capable of being the subject of a variation. It is also accepted that two or more variations, each relating to separate items of property in residue, can be effective. For example, a residuary beneficiary can validly redirect by variation one half of the residuary property to new beneficiary A and the other half to new beneficiary B and in each case achieve the writing back effect for IHT purposes (provided the variations contain the relevant statements).

However, the Revenue has stated (inter alia) that in its view 'an instrument will not fall within s 142 of IHTA 1984 if it further redirects any item or any part of an item that has already been redirected under an earlier instrument'. A second variation in relation *to the same property* will, therefore, not be effective for tax purposes.

13.3.5   Beneficiaries other than members of the family

Normally, the rearrangement will involve redistribution of the deceased's property among members of the family. However, there is no restriction in the legislation, whether for IHT or CGT, which restricts the introduction of a new beneficiary who is not a member of the family. This opens up the possibility of introducing as a beneficiary the following:

(a)   A claimant under the Inheritance (Provision for Family and Dependants) Act 1975. For example, a claim by a person 'maintained by the deceased' under s 1(1)(e) of the Act for reasonable financial provision may be compromised within two years of the death. If the conditions are satisfied, this may take the form of a variation which, provided it contains the relevant statement, will achieve the writing back effect of any other post-death variation and will be effective for both IHT and CGT.

(b)   A charity. A charitable donation, within the IHT exemption, can be made from the deceased's estate by introducing a charity as a legatee. If the conditions are satisfied, the terms of the will or of the intestacy law will then be read as if the deceased had made the donation himself to the named charity.

13.4   Income tax and post-death arrangements

13.4.1   Income before a variation or disclaimer is made

There are no specific income tax provisions equivalent to the IHT and CGT provisions where a variation or disclaimer has been made. Thus, income received before the variation or disclaimer from the property concerned will be taxed as the income of the original beneficiary. This will apply even if the beneficiary has specifically given up all income from the property since the date of death. For example, if the original beneficiary by variation redirects a specific legacy of shares, he remains liable to pay any income tax on dividends paid before the variation.

13.4.2   Income after a variation or disclaimer is made

In most cases, once the rearrangement has been made, the original beneficiary ceases to be liable to pay income tax on income produced after the variation or disclaimer. The new beneficiary becomes liable for income tax on income produced by the property concerned. However, the position will be different where the new beneficiary is the minor child of the original beneficiary. In such cases the parent will remain liable for income tax on the income even though he does not enjoy it or own the property which produces it. The reason is the income tax anti-avoidance provisions discussed at **4.6.2** and **4.6.4**. These are of general application and can apply to pre- and to post-death arrangements.

13.4.2.1   How do the income tax avoidance rules apply to variations?

If the variation creates a settlement for income tax purposes from which the original beneficiary may continue to benefit, he will still be liable to pay income tax on all the settlement income (see **6.2.11.1**). To avoid this, the variation must be drafted so as to exclude the settlor and spouse from all enjoyment from the property which has been redirected, and from its income.

However, the original beneficiary may nevertheless be caught by the anti-avoidance rules and so still be liable to income tax on the income of the property subject to the variation. This will be the case if his minor unmarried children are constituted the new beneficiaries as a result of the variation and the income is paid for the benefit of those beneficiaries and not accumulated. The same result will occur whether the variation gives the children absolute interests or an interest in new trusts which are created by the variation.

If the anti-avoidance provisions apply, they will cease to do so once the children have reached their majority or have married; from then onwards their parents will no longer be taxed on the settlement income.

Example 1

A variation by Hannah (to use up the nil rate band of her recently deceased husband) redirects £275,000 absolutely to her adult children. The children will pay income tax on the income of the property.

Example 2

A similar post-death variation is made by Ania but her children (the new beneficiaries) are minors. Even though the children have an absolute (vested) entitlement to the £275,000, the income of the property is deemed to be Ania's for tax purposes.

13.4.2.2   Disclaimers distinguished

A variation is the positive redirection of benefit by the original beneficiary whereas a disclaimer is merely the rejection of a benefit. The Revenue does not consider a disclaimer to be a 'settlement' and so to come within the income tax anti-avoidance provisions. The consequence is that income of property which is disclaimed by a parent is not taxed as though it is still his, even if his minor unmarried child inherits the property as a result of the disclaimer. Thus, parents who are considering post-death rearrangements for the benefit of their children should, where possible, use a disclaimer instead of a variation which might fall within the provisions.

13.5   Drafting a post-death variation and the election

13.5.1   Is a deed required?

Both IHTA 1984, s 142 and TCGA 1992, s 62 require only an instrument in writing, but as a post-death variation is a gratuitous promise to transfer property, it should be by deed to be enforceable. Further, unless it is by deed the deceased's personal representatives may not be prepared to act in accordance with its terms.

13.5.2 The date and opening words

Sample clause

> This deed of variation is made the [   ] day of [   ]
> Two thousand and …

13.5.3 Parties

Both IHTA 1984, s 142 and TCGA 1992, s 62 require only 'the persons who benefit or would benefit under the disposition … to make the written instrument'. However, often there will be three parties:

(a)   the original beneficiaries (who give up the benefit);

(b)   the new beneficiaries (who receive the property and thus will include trustees if the variation creates a trust); and

(c)   the personal representatives of the deceased's estate (who must also join in any statement that s 142(1) IHT is to apply if additional IHT is payable as a result of the variation).

Sample clause

> BETWEEN
> (1)   [name and address] ('the Original Beneficiary')
> (2)   [name and address] ('the New Beneficiary')
> (3)   [name and address] ('the Executors')

Personal representatives should be made parties for their own protection when they distribute property in accordance with the post-death variation rather than the will in its original form. It is not essential to join the new beneficiaries in receipt of property as parties but many practitioners prefer to do so.

13.5.4 Supplemental to the will or intestacy

The deed of variation is made to relate expressly to the deceased's death.

Sample clause

> Supplemental to the will [with … codicil(s)] ('the Will') of [name] ('the Deceased') and to the other documents and events specified in the Schedule

The Schedule will contain details of the will, date of death, grant of probate, etc.

13.5.5 Recitals

Recitals will always be used in the deed to explain the circumstances giving rise to the variation. Usually the recitals are restricted to statements relating to:

(a)   the entitlement of the original beneficiary under the will or the intestacy of the deceased; and

(b)   the wish of the original beneficiary to vary the provisions of the will or the intestacy in the manner stated in the operative part of the variation.

Sample clause

> WHEREAS
> (A) Under the Will the Original Beneficiary was given [   ] interest ('the Interest') in [all of the] [x% of the] residuary estate of the Deceased

(B) The Original Beneficiary wishes to vary the dispositions effected by the Will in relation to the Interest in the following manner

The interest will be an 'absolute' interest or a 'life interest' and the clause should be completed accordingly, showing whether it relates to the whole or part of the residuary estate.

13.5.6   The operative part

It is often convenient when drafting the operative part of a post-death variation to consider how the will, or a codicil to it, might have been drafted for the testator before his death. This can often give valuable guidance on drafting the post-death variation. For example, in the context of a variation to create a nil rate band legacy for a child, only a short provision is required.

Sample clause

> Now this deed irrevocably witnesses as follows:
>
> By way of variation of the disposition made by the Will the Original Beneficiary declares that the Will shall have effect as if it contained a pecuniary legacy to the New Beneficiary of an amount on which no IHT is chargeable other than at the nil rate on the death of the Deceased such legacy to be discharged from the Interest.

If a legacy is being introduced into the will by the post-death variation, it should be considered whether it is to be a legacy 'subject to' or 'free of' IHT. In the former case, any IHT which does become payable is paid by the legatee. The payment of the legacy will be directed to be made from a particular part of the estate which normally will be the residue.

If trusts, rather than outright gifts, are to be created by the variation, these may either be set out in a schedule to the deed or it may refer to trusts created by a separate instrument. For example, the original beneficiary may wish to direct that his interest be transferred to the trustees of an A & M settlement created by the deceased during his lifetime for his grandchildren.

13.5.7   Achieving the writing back effect

To achieve the writing back effect for tax purposes there must be a statement in the written variation by the beneficiaries making the variation that it is intended that IHTA 1984, s 142(1) and/or TCGA 1992, s 62(6) shall apply to the variation.

If the variation causes additional IHT to become payable, for example, where a spouse gives up a benefit and the spouse exemption is lost, the PRs must join in the statement. Only if the PRs have no funds available to them for payment of any extra IHT may they refuse to join in the statement. This protects PRs who have already distributed the estate before they become liable to pay the extra IHT resulting from the written variation.

If there will be additional IHT payable as a result of a variation made on or after 1 August 2002, the persons making the variation and the PRs must supply a copy of the variation to the Revenue within six months of the variation being made (IHTA 1984, s 218A (inserted by FA 2002)) or be liable for a fine (IHTA 1984, s 245A (inserted by FA 2002)).

Sample clause

> The Parties hereto hereby declare pursuant to section 142(2) of the Inheritance
> Tax Act 1984 and section 62(7) of the Taxation of Chargeable Gains Act 1992
> that section 142(1) of the Inheritance Tax Act 1984 and section 62(6) of the
> Taxation of Chargeable Gains Act 1992 shall apply to the variation made by this
> deed

13.5.8 Stamp duty

The Stamp Duty (Exempt Instruments) Regulations 1987 (SI 1987/516) list categories for exemptions relevant to post-death variations (see **4.9**). Those variations which are outright gifts (the majority) qualify as voluntary dispositions under category L. Where the variation is an exchange of interests it qualifies under category M, provided there is no external consideration.

Where, as a result of a post-death variation, there is a transfer of assets on which stamp duty would otherwise be payable, an appropriate certificate should be included in the document that makes the transfer. Most commonly this will mean shares, and therefore the appropriate certificate should be included on the stock transfer form used to make the transfer.

Chapter 14

Trust Administration

14.1 Introduction

Many aspects of trust administration have been considered in the earlier chapters in this book. Most of these matters have related to the dispositive provisions of the trust instrument, ie, the provisions dealing with the beneficiaries and beneficial entitlement and include the following:

(a) TA 1925, ss 31 and 32 in **Chapters 5** and **10**;

(b) the powers of trustees in **Chapter 11**;

(c) advances and appointments by trustees in favour of beneficiaries in **Chapters 9** and **10**;

(d) capital tax implications of changes in beneficial entitlement arising from (a) and (b).

There are many other matters relevant to the proper administration of a trust the more important of which are discussed in this chapter. These include:

(a) trustee investments;

(b) the appointment of trustees;

(c) vesting trust property in trustees and in beneficiaries;

(d) taxation liability arising during the trust period, including CGT on sales by trustees on rearrangements of the investment portfolio and the income tax liabilities of the trustees and beneficiaries; and

(e) accounting for the trust assets and income.

14.2 Management powers of trustees

When creating a settlement, particularly a discretionary settlement, the settlor will wish to incorporate wide-ranging powers for his trustees covering all aspects of the trust fund and its administration. He must bear in mind the present and future trust property, the wide-ranging nature of the trusts, and the wide class of beneficiaries. The trust may continue for many years so it is necessary to consider all the provisions which may be of assistance to the trustees in the future. The modern policy is to incorporate these wide powers by inserting them in a schedule to the trust instrument.

14.2.1 Other matters relating to the trustees

Apart from the appointment and retirement of the trustees referred to in **14.4**, express provision in relation to the following will normally be made.

14.2.1.1   Self-dealing

The fiduciary position of the trustees prevents them from purchasing the trust property or entering into any other transaction affecting the trust property where the trustees' duties and personal self-interest are in conflict. Express provision may permit self-dealing by the trustees.

14.2.1.2   Losses

To protect an honest trustee, the trust instrument will often contain a general indemnity against loss to the trust fund caused by the trustee or an agent (other than where there is wilful fraud or dishonesty of the trustee).

14.2.1.3   Delegation of powers

The TA 2000 allows trustees to delegate 'delegable functions' to an agent, who can be anyone except a beneficiary. Delegable functions do not include decisions on distributing trust property to beneficiaries, paying fees and appointing trustees. Having made the appointment, the trustee must continue to review it from time to time. It may be desirable to expressly exclude the limitation on a beneficiary being an agent. Section 25 of TA 1925 (as substituted by the Trustee Delegation Act 1999) permits the trustees to delegate by power of attorney any of their powers and discretions for up to 12 months. In addition, s 9 of TLATA 1996 permits trustees of land to delegate by power of attorney their functions in relation to the land, for example their power of sale, to beneficiaries of full age who are beneficially entitled to an interest in possession in the land.

14.3   Trustee investments

14.3.1   Retention of the original trust fund

For a settlement to be effective, it needs property to be subject to the trusts. When a settlement is created the initial trust fund may consist of cash, or assets (eg, shares or land), or a combination of cash and assets. The trustees must decide whether they are permitted to keep the initial trust fund as it is and, if so, whether in fact they should do so.

Most lifetime settlements and will trusts are drafted by professionals who will ensure that the settlement gives the trustees the widest possible powers of investment and enables them to keep any assets transferred to them by the settlor or from the estate.

The TA 2000 implies similar powers into trusts where there are no express powers, for example, where a statutory trust arises under the AEA 1925 on the death of someone intestate.

14.3.2   Suitable investments

In deciding whether to retain permitted assets, the trustees must consider the suitability of the assets for the aims of the settlement. This is also a governing factor when deciding how to invest any cash that may have been settled.

Example 1

A settlement is created for Donna for life with remainder to Nigel. The trustees are faced with competing needs: Donna requires an income from the trust fund whilst Nigel needs the real value of the capital to improve. As a general rule, assets producing a good income return, for example, a building society account, offer little or no capital growth, and vice versa.

The trustees need to invest the trust fund in a range of investments which provide overall income and capital growth; perhaps gilts and a National Savings Income Bond for income and quoted shares or unit trusts for growth.

Example 2

An A & M settlement is created for Adam and Belinda, 6-year-old twins contingent as to both capital and income on their attaining 25 years of age. They are unlikely to need any income for at least the first five years of the settlement and any income accumulated in the settlement will suffer 40% income tax (see **14.5.2**).

As there is no need for income, the trustees can concentrate on improving the capital value of the trust fund, perhaps by investing in quoted shares.

Note: There may be circumstances where the settlor does not want the trustees to hold a balance. For example, a testator may leave his property to his elderly wife for life and the remainder to charity. His major concern may be that his wife should be well provided for and he may not be very concerned as to the amount the charity eventually takes. He can leave a statement of wishes but the trustees will be at risk of an action for breach of trust from the remainderman. To protect them, he should include a direction in the trust stating that the trustees are not to be required to invest impartially.

14.3.3 Subsequent changes to the trust fund

Although with an express power of investment the bulk of the fund is likely to be invested in land and/or securities, most trustees should consider retaining a degree of liquidity by holding a small amount of cash in an interest-bearing instant access bank or building society account. This will provide the trustees with cash to meet expenses, such as solicitors' or accountants' fees, and their own out-of-pocket expenses. It will also provide them with the ability to make a new purchase for the trust fund if an opportunity suddenly arises. On occasion, they may also use such an account to retain the proceeds of sale of an investment where there is not to be an immediate reinvestment of the realised fund.

Once a settlement has been created, trustees need to review the trust fund regularly. Trustees can make many of the investments which an individual concerned with his personal estate planning might make (see **Appendix 2**). How often trustees review their investments depends on a number of factors but should not be less than once a year and may be more frequently. This is to ensure that the fund continues to provide for the aims of the settlement; to minimise the liability to CGT; and to protect the fund against economic forces.

Regular review is particularly important now that the TA 2000 has imposed a duty to review on trustees. Trustees should ensure that there are minutes of trustees' meetings confirming that review took place.

14.3.3.1 Changes to reflect the aims of the settlement

Settlements are designed to last for many years. An investment strategy that was appropriate at the outset may not be appropriate 10 years later; in particular, the beneficiaries needs may have changed or there may be about to be a change in the beneficial interests in the settlement. Trustees may need to alter the investments in the trust fund to reflect these changes.

Example

Twelve years ago, Damien settled £100,000 cash on discretionary trusts for his three grandchildren then aged 5, 4 and 2 years. The children had no immediate need for income and, as all income accumulated within the trust suffers income tax which is non-recoverable, the trustees invested the majority of the trust fund in low income, high growth shares and unit trusts. The trust fund is now worth £180,000 and produces £3,500 per annum income. The eldest beneficiary intends to start medical school in three months' time and the trustees have decided to exercise their discretion and pay her £5,000 per annum income from the trust fund.

The trustees must, therefore, sell some of their investments and reinvest the proceeds to increase the income generated by the trust fund. As a known amount of income is required, the trustees might consider achieving this by investing in gilts or a guaranteed rate building society account.

14.3.3.2   Minimising CGT

A large proportion of a trust fund is likely to be invested in assets such as quoted shares which attract a charge to CGT on their disposal. As trustees have only an annual exemption of £4,250 and gains are charged at 40% in all settlements, it is sensible (where possible) to manage the fund to minimise the liability. For example, trustees may invest in land to be occupied by a beneficiary under a trust as his residence. If so, any gain on sale by the trustees would qualify for the principal private residence exemption. If such investment and occupation occur under the terms of a discretionary trust, this (at least in the view of the Revenue) may amount to giving the beneficiary an interest in possession in the part of the settled property represented by the private residence (see **4.7.3**).

A charge to CGT will arise on two occasions: on a deemed disposal when a beneficiary becomes absolutely entitled to trust property; and on an actual disposal when trust property is sold as a result of investment changes (see **14.5**). Trustees should always aim to utilise their annual exemption as it cannot be carried forward to future tax years or transferred to beneficiaries.

In a year in which a deemed disposal will occur, trustees should consider carefully whether any investment changes need to be made or whether they can leave the changes to the next tax year so keeping their annual exemption available to set against the charge on the deemed disposal.

14.3.3.3   General reviews

Most investors who invest in the stock market, whether through the direct purchase of shares or via unit trusts, do so to make money rather than as a desire to be part of a particular company. The stock market is divided into sectors with companies predominantly involved in particular activities being grouped together, for example, both WH Smith plc and Marks & Spencer plc are in the 'Retailers General' sector whilst Lloyds TSB plc and Bradford & Bingley plc are both 'Banks'. Trustees, like most individual investors, are looking for a spread of investments, investing in companies from a number of sectors rather than concentrating on companies in one sector. This is because sectors of the economy perform differently depending on different economic factors and, if one sector is suffering, the value of the shares in the majority of companies in that sector is likely to fall. It is unusual, however, for all sectors to be depressed at the same time and the theory of investing in a number of sectors is that the gains and losses should be evened out.

Trustees may be advised to sell their shares in companies in a particular sector and invest the proceeds in a different sector for a while, or to change companies within a sector.

Example

The trustees of an A & M settlement have invested one quarter of the trust fund in gilts and the remainder equally between A plc (an insurance company), B plc (a food manufacturer) and C plc (an oil company). Their stockbrokers advise that the insurance market is depressed and that the value of their shareholding is falling but that companies in the 'Water' sector look set to make large profits. The trustees decide to sell their shares in A plc and use the proceeds to buy shares in D plc, a water company.

14.4 Appointment of trustees

14.4.1 The original trustees

14.4.1.1 Choice of trustees

The choice of the original trustees of the settlement is made by the settlor at the time he makes a settlement. Their appointment as trustees takes effect immediately the trust instrument is executed. Once appointed, they are in a fiduciary position and so must act with good faith. Their duty is to administer the trust for the benefit of its beneficiaries.

14.4.1.2 Number of trustees

Although every trust must have at least one trustee, it is usual for the settlor to appoint between two and four individuals to act as trustees of his settlement. A maximum of four trustees can be appointed for trusts of land but at least two trustees (or a trust corporation) are required to give a buyer a valid receipt for the proceeds of sale of land held in a settlement. There is no limit to the number of trustees who can be appointed for trusts of personalty but the appointment of more than four can cause the trust administration to be unnecessarily cumbersome.

14.4.1.3 Selection of trustees

The settlor should take great care in choosing the original trustees. It is possible to appoint a trust corporation to act as trustee but most settlors prefer to appoint individuals because of the personal involvement this will bring to the administration of the trusts. The settlor should consider the following.

A professional trustee

It is of advantage if a solicitor or other professional person is appointed to be a trustee (often together with member(s) of the settlor's own family). Where a professional is appointed, the administrative provisions of the trust should include a charging clause. Even if a professional is not appointed at the outset, it is a good idea to include a charging clause in case a professional is appointed as a trustee in the future (see **14.2.3**).

The settlor as trustee

The settlor may appoint himself to be the sole trustee or one of several trustees of his settlement. This allows him to retain an involvement in the settlement and have some influence over how it is administered, for example, he will have a say in whether the trustees should exercise their discretion in favour of a particular beneficiary under a discretionary settlement. If he is appointed a trustee, the settlor must not allow his personal wishes to overshadow his duties as trustee.

Instead of being appointed a trustee, the settlor may prefer to exercise some influence over the trustees through the use of a 'letter of wishes' (or a side letter) addressed to the trustees. Clearly, such a letter will have no binding effect on the trustees but, by setting out how he hopes the settlement will be administered in the future, the settlor hopes the trustees will have some regard to his intentions.

A beneficiary as trustee

The settlor may appoint one or more of the beneficiaries to be a trustee of the settlement but this may cause difficulty, for example, a conflict of interest may arise between the individual's position as trustee on the one hand and as beneficiary on the other. In view of this, a beneficiary should not be a sole trustee. Two or more trustees provide safeguards in that they must supervise one another, must be unanimous in the exercise of their powers (an important protection for the beneficiaries) and their appointment will ensure a continuing trustee if one were to die or to retire from the trusts.

14.4.2 Subsequent trustees

14.4.2.1 Appointment by the settlor

Once the original trustees have been appointed the settlor has no further power to appoint trustees. If a settlor (who is not also a trustee) wishes to control the selection of trustees during his lifetime, he can only do so if the trust instrument gives him the express power to appoint new trustees.

Sample clause

> During the lifetime of the Settlor the power of appointing new trustees shall be vested in the Settlor.

14.4.2.2 The statutory power of appointing new or additional trustees

If there is no person nominated in the trust instrument (eg, the settlor), s 36 of TA 1925 provides wide statutory powers for the appointment of new trustees.

Replacement trustees (TA 1925, s 36(1))

The appointment of a new trustee must be made in writing (but will normally be by deed, see **14.4.4**) by:

(a)   the surviving or continuing trustees, including any retiring or disclaiming trustee if he wishes to join in the appointment; or

(b)   the personal representatives of the last surviving trustee.

A new trustee can be appointed under s 36(1) to replace, inter alia, a trustee who has died, is incapable of acting, or who retires.

Additional trustees (TA 1925, s 36(6))

The appointment of additional trustees must be made in writing by the continuing trustee(s). The number of trustees after the new appointment is made must not exceed four.

Directions as to trustees (TLATA 1996, s 19)

If there is no person still alive nominated in the trust instrument to appoint new trustees, the beneficiaries of full age and capacity who together are entitled to the trust property can give written directions to the trustees for the retirement and appointment of a trustee. As it is possible for the trust instrument to exclude s 19, settlors should be invited to consider whether they prefer future control over the appointment and retirement of trustees to remain with the existing trustees or to pass instead to the beneficiaries.

14.4.3 Vesting the trust property in the trustees

14.4.3.1 On creation of the settlement

Once the original trustees have been appointed, the settlor must transfer to them the 'settled property', ie, the assets mentioned in the trust instrument as being subject to the trusts of the settlement. It is a duty of the trustees to bring all the trust property under their control.

The settlor will transfer the settled property to the trustees by whatever means of transfer is appropriate to that property. For example, stock transfer forms will be used to transfer shares; a deed will be used to transfer the legal estate in land.

14.4.3.2 On the appointment of replacement or additional trustees

Following a change in the trustees, the trust property must be vested in the new trustee(s). If the appointment of the new trustee(s) is by deed, s 40(1) of TA 1925 provides that the vesting of the trust property will occur automatically. There are, however, circumstances where s 40(1) does not apply so that formal transfer of the trust property to the new trustee(s) will be required. In particular, there is no automatic vesting of stocks and shares. In these cases, a stock transfer form transferring the shares into the names of all the trustees must be signed by the 'old trustees' and registered with the company. Although the shares are held by the trustees as trust property, there is no reference to this on the company's membership register. Shares are shown as registered in the individual names of the trustees without reference to their capacity as trustees.

14.4.4 Drafting a deed of appointment of new trustees

Heading and date

Sample clause

> DEED OF APPOINTMENT AND RETIREMENT
> DATE: [   ]

Parties

Who the parties are will depend on the circumstances giving rise to the appointment of new trustees. The person(s) with the power to appoint will always be parties; so too will the new trustee(s) and any retiring trustee.

Sample clause

> BETWEEN
> (1)   [name and address] ('the Continuing Trustees')
> (2)   [name and address] ('the New Trustee')
> (3)   [name and address] ('the Retiring Trustee')

Recitals

Normally, there will be three or four separate provisions detailing the circumstances giving rise to the change of the trustees.

Sample clause

> RECITALS
> (A)   This Deed is supplemental to the settlement ('the Settlement') [and to the other documents and events] specified in the [First] Schedule.

(B)   The statutory power of appointment applies to the Settlement and is exercisable by the Continuing Trustees and the Retiring Trustee.

(C)   The Continuing Trustees and the Retiring Trustee are the present trustees of the Settlement.

(D)   The Continuing Trustees and the Retiring Trustee wish to appoint the New Trustee to act as a trustee of the Settlement in place of the Retiring Trustee.

(E)   It is intended that the property now in the Settlement [, details of which are set out in the Second Schedule,] shall be transferred to, or under the control of, the Continuing Trustees and the New Trustee

Such clauses allow for the retirement of the trustee. If no trustee is retiring, all references to 'the Retiring Trustee' should be deleted from the clauses as well as from 'the parties'.

Clause (E) is intended to enable the trust property to be detailed in the schedule to the deed of appointment. It is not an express declaration vesting property in the new trustee.

The operative part

By this clause, those with the power to do so make the appointment of the new trustee. If power to appoint new trustees has been retained by the settlor (see **14.4.2**), the settlor, defined as 'the Appointor', would be added as a 'party' and would make the appointment in the operative part. If the present trustees are to exercise the statutory power to appoint the new trustees, they will do so in this part of the deed.

If a trustee is retiring, it is usual to include a statement in the deed confirming that there is no intention for the residence status of the trust to change. Where a trust 'emigrates' (see **Chapter 15**) there is a CGT charge, and this can result in anyone who has been a trustee within the 12 months prior to the emigration of the trust being liable. The statement will help prevent a retired trustee being liable.

Sample clauses

Appointment of New Trustee in place of Retiring Trustee

In exercise of the power of appointment conferred by the Trustee Act 1925 and of all other powers (if any), the Continuing Trustees and the Retiring Trustee hereby appoint the New Trustee as a trustee of the Settlement to act jointly with the Continuing Trustees in place of the Retiring Trustee who hereby retires and is discharged from the trusts of the Settlement.

Declaration as to residence

It is hereby declared that, at the date hereof, there is no proposal that the Trustees of the Settlement might become neither resident nor ordinarily resident in the United Kingdom.

Again, if no trustee is to retire, the references to 'the Retiring Trustee' should be deleted and there is no need to refer to the residence of the trust. The appointment is then made by 'the Continuing Trustees', ie, they do so in exercise of the statutory power.

Schedules

It is usual to include in the schedules particulars of the settlement to which the deed of appointment is supplemental as well as details of the trust property currently held by the trustees. This list of trust property is useful for the new trustee who must now exercise his duties as trustee in relation to it.

14.5 Taxation during the administration of a settlement

The settlor's liability to IHT and CGT on the creation of the settlement is considered in **Chapter 5**, and liability to the same taxes which arises on trust advances and appointments is considered in **Chapter 10**. Broadly, these earlier chapters covered the capital tax position on creation and termination of the settlement. The liability to CGT and income tax arising on the trust capital and its income during the administration of a settlement are considered below; any relevant IHT liabilities during the trust's existence are considered in the chapters referred to above.

14.5.1 Actual disposals: CGT

If the trustees of the settlement rearrange their portfolio of investments, CGT liability may arise on any sales. If so, the trustees are liable to pay the tax and will do so from the settled funds. Sales by the trustees are 'actual disposals' giving rise to CGT liability in a manner similar to disposals by an individual.

Example

Trustees are holding 5,000 XYZ plc shares as part of a trust fund. These shares are sold for £30,000 having been worth only £5,000 when they were acquired by the trustees. There is an indexation allowance of £1,000.

			£
Disposal consideration			30,000
Less:			
	(a)	Acquisition cost, ie, the value of the shares when they were acquired by the trustees	5,000
			25,000
	(b)	Indexation allowance	1,000
Chargeable gain (subject to taper relief for non-business assets, depending on the trustees' period of ownership)			24,000

The calculation is the same as any CGT calculation. It is based on the trustees' disposal consideration and their acquisition cost, ie, the value of the shares when transferred to them by the settlor at the time the settlement was created. The indexation allowance and taper relief are applied in the normal way.

14.5.1.1 Reliefs, exemption and rates of tax

Rates of CGT

Trustees of discretionary settlements, accumulation and maintenance settlements and interest in possession settlements all pay CGT at the uniform rate of 40%.

If the settlor has 'an interest in his settlement', for example, he is a beneficiary of a discretionary settlement which he created, under TCGA 1992, ss 77 and 78, discussed at **6.2.11**, all gains are deemed made by the settlor and not by the trustees. The settlor, and not the trustees, must therefore pay tax on the settlement gains at the rate appropriate to the settlor, ie, 20% or 40% depending on his income tax position. The exclusion of the settlor from benefiting from his own settlement is also discussed at **6.2.11**.

Exemptions

Trustees of any settlement are entitled to an annual exemption of £4,250, ie, one half of the exemption for individuals. If the settlor has created a number of settlements, the exemption is divided between them with a minimum of £850 in each case.

Reliefs

Hold-over relief is not available to the trustees (it is available only on deemed disposals by trustees). They must pay tax, after claiming the annual exemption, at 40%. Taper relief may be available.

Assuming the trustees reinvest the proceeds of sale after paying any tax, the purchase price of the new investments is their acquisition cost for CGT purposes, ie, on any future sale this price will be deducted when calculating any gain (or loss).

14.5.1.2   Losses

Example

Trustees of an A & M settlement sell the trust's holding of shares in A plc which are now worth £10,000 having been purchased three years ago for £25,000.

	£
Disposal consideration	10,000
Less: Acquisition cost	25,000
	Loss (15,000)

As this loss is incurred by the trustees they are entitled to claim loss relief. They do so by setting the loss against gains they make on other sales in the same tax year. If there are none, or if there are insufficient gains to absorb the loss, the trustees may carry the loss forward to set against gains made in future years.

14.5.2   Income tax

It is necessary to distinguish the liability of the settlement trustees from the beneficiary's liability.

14.5.2.1   Trustees' liability

The trustees must pay tax on all income produced by the trust assets. In many cases, the trustees will receive savings income after tax has been paid or credited as paid. The 10% credit attributable to dividends and the 20% deduction at source on interest will satisfy their liability to pay at basic rate. On any untaxed income, the trustees pay at 22%. Whether the trustees have any further income tax liability depends on the type of settlement since the nature of the beneficial interests in the settlement governs the rate of tax for which the trustees are liable. Generally, the existence or not of an interest in possession in settled property will determine the appropriate tax rate.

Interest in possession trusts

The rate of tax is 22%. This is satisfied by:

(a)   the 10% credit on dividends; and

(b)   the 20% deduction at source on interest payments.

As, in the majority of cases, the trustees will receive 'net' income, no further liability to income will arise. Any 'gross' income receipt will be taxed in their hands at 22%.

Example

Trustees of an interest in possession trust receive the following income in the tax year 2005/06:

£4,500 dividends (net)   (£5,000 gross)

£1,600 interest (net)   (£2,000 gross)

The trustees have no further income tax to pay as their liability has been satisfied by the 10% tax credit on the dividends and the 20% tax deducted from the interest. If they had also received £10,000 rent (gross) in that tax year, the trustees would be liable for tax at 22% on this, and would have to pay £2,200.

No interest in possession trusts

Trustees of discretionary and accumulation trusts must pay 'the rate applicable to trusts' on income which is to be accumulated or which is payable at their discretion (ICTA 1988, s 688(1A)). It is not charged on income which is properly used to pay management expenses (ICTA 1988, s 686(2)(d)). Since 6 April 2004 the rate of 40% applies as follows:

Income	Credit		Charge		Rate
interest	20	+	20%	=	40%
other income (net)	22%	+	18%	=	40%
other income (gross)	–		40%	=	40%

In the case of dividends, the rate is reduced to 32.5% as follows:

Dividends	10% (irrecoverable)	+	22.5%	=	32.5%

However, since 6 April 2005 for non-interest in possession trusts a basic rate band applies. It will apply to the first £500 of income as follows:

(a)   non-dividend income within this level that would have been charged at the trusts rate of 40% will instead be charged at 20% (if savings income), or at 22% (for other non-dividend income).

(b)   dividend income that would have been charged at 32.5% will instead be charged at 10%.

This change means that around one-third of trusts previously liable to the trusts rate will no longer pay the trusts rate of tax on any of their income because their total income falls below the £500 threshold.

Example 1

Trustees of a discretionary trust receive the following income in the tax year 2005/06:

(a)   £150 rent income (gross);

(b)   £80 interest (net) (gross £100);

(c)   £90 dividends (net) (gross £100).

All the gross income falls within the £500 band so:

(a)   The gross rent (£150) is charged at 22% = £33.

(b)   The gross interest (£100) is charged at 20% = £20.

(c)   The gross dividend income (£100) is charged at 10% = £10.

Total tax is £63.

There is a credit of £20 on the interest and £10 on the dividends, leaving £33 to pay.

Where the trustees have annual income above £500, the excess will be chargeable at the trusts rate, but the basic rate band will still apply to the first £500 slice of income.

Example 2

Trustees of a discretionary trust receive the following income in the tax year 2005/06:

(a)   £150 rent income (gross);

(b)   £200 interest (net) (gross £250);

(c)   £450 dividends (net) (gross £500).

The gross income is £900. That part of the gross income that falls within the £500 band escapes the trusts rate (40%) or dividend trusts rate (32.5%) so:

(a)   The gross rent (£150) is charged at 22% = £33,

(b)   The gross interest (£250) is charged at 20% = £50,
        (£400)

This leaves only £100 of the basic rate band, so:

(a)   £100 of the gross dividend income is charged at 10% = £10.

(b)   The remaining gross dividend income (£400) is charged at 32.5% = £130.

(c)   Total tax is £223.

There is a credit of £50 on the interest and £50 on the dividends, leaving £123 to pay.

For those trusts that consistently have income below £500 per annum, a self assessment tax return would be issued only periodically; the current proposal is once every five years. Trustees would still be under an obligation to notify the Revenue where they had a liability to tax, whether on income or chargeable gains.

14.5.2.2   The beneficiary's liability

It is convenient to distinguish the position of a beneficiary who has a right to the income of the settled property, ie, the beneficiary with an interest in possession, from other beneficiaries, for example, beneficiaries of a discretionary settlement.

Interest in possession

The beneficiary with a vested entitlement to the settlement income will receive dividends and interest from the trustees after tax at 22% has been paid (or credited as paid) on it. The beneficiary is liable to tax on this income in the same way as he pays tax on any other income he may have. As the trustees have paid tax at 22%, the beneficiary's liability (if any) is confined to tax at 32.5% on dividends and 40% on interest. To justify their payment of tax, the trustees provide the beneficiary with a tax deduction certificate in Form R185 which he will pass on to the Revenue.

Example 1

Trustees are holding a trust fund for 'Tony for life, with remainder to June'. Tony, the life tenant, has an interest in possession. The trustees' gross dividend income is £1,000 (£900 net). They pay £900 to Tony to whom they give Form R185 justifying the payment of tax at basic rate. Tony's gross income from the trust is £1,000, ie, £900 + £100.

Tony's tax position depends on the amount of his other income:

(a)   If he is a higher rate tax payer

gross trust dividend income £1,000 × 32.5% =	£325
Less tax @ 10% credited as paid by the trustees	£100
tax due	£225

(b)   If he is not a tax payer, he will not be able to reclaim the £100 tax credit.

(c)   If he pays tax at basic rate (22%), he has no further tax to pay.

Example 2

Trustees hold property on A & M trusts for Eva on attaining the age of 25. Eva is now aged 21. The TA 1925, s 31 gave Eva the right to the income of the trust property from the age of 18, ie, she now has an interest in possession. The trustees receive a dividend of £900 which they pay to Eva, together with Form R185. Eva's position is the same as Tony's position in the previous example.

No interest in possession

Where no beneficiary has the right to receive the income of the trust property, the trustees may exercise their discretion to pay it to a beneficiary, or they may accumulate the income. If they do pay out income to a beneficiary, they must provide the beneficiary with a Form R185. This states the amount of tax paid on the income by the trustees. The beneficiary will pass it on to the Revenue and will receive a tax credit for the tax paid by the trustees. All income received by the beneficiary is treated as income received net of 40% tax.

Example 1: income accumulated

The trustees of a discretionary settlement receive, after deduction of 20% tax at source, bank interest of £800. This £1,000 gross income is taxed as follows:

The first £500 is taxed at 20% = £100, and the remaining £500 is taxed at 40% = £200. There is a total tax liability of £300, of which £200 has already been deducted at source, leaving the trustees to pay an additional £100.

They have no expenses. None of the income is paid to beneficiaries. The trustees accumulate the remaining £700 by adding it to the capital of the trust. The £300 tax paid on the gross income of £1,000, ie, £200 (credit) plus the £100 additional tax, cannot be recovered from the Revenue.

Had the income come from dividends, the trustees would have received £900 net of 10% tax (£1,000 gross). They would have paid an additional 22.5% on the gross income above the first £500 income (ie, £112.50). As in the previous example, the tax paid would not have been recoverable from the Revenue.

Example 2: income applied

The facts are the same as in Example 1 but the trustees pay £300 of the remaining income to a discretionary beneficiary, Abdul. His income from the trustees is treated as the net amount from which 40% tax (the trusts rate) has been deducted. Therefore the gross value of this £300 received by Abdul is £500.

Abdul's tax position depends on the amount of his other income:

(a)   If he is a higher rate tax payer

		£
gross trust income £500 × 40% =		200
Less tax treated as paid by the trustees at 40%		200
	no further tax due	0

(b)   If he is a basic rate tax payer

	£
tax treated as paid by the trustees at 40%	200
tax at basic rate £500 × 22%	110
refunded by the Revenue	90

(c)   If he is not a tax payer (ie, he has no other income)

	£
net income	300
tax treated as paid by the trustees at 40% (refunded by the Revenue)	200
gross income	500

Where beneficiaries are not taxpayers or are basic rate taxpayers, the trustees should exercise their discretion over the income and pay it for the maintenance, education or benefit of the beneficiaries rather than accumulating it. The tax paid by the trustees can then be repaid to the beneficiaries (see Example 2). If the income is accumulated as in Example 1, the tax cannot be reclaimed.

Trustees of discretionary settlements who pay income to a beneficiary provide the beneficiary with a new source of income for his own tax purposes. The source of the income is the trustees, not the underlying companies which pay dividends or banks which pay interest to the trustees. This creates a difficulty for trustees. Any shortfall between tax due at the rate of 40% and the rate at which it is actually paid (22%, 20% or 10% for the first £500 income and 32.5% in the case of any other dividend income) will be assessed on the trustees (ICTA 1988, s 687). Trustees should ensure they retain sufficient income to meet this extra liability unless they are willing to have recourse to capital to cover the additional tax due. (For further discussion of this see, for example, *Revenue Law: Principles and Practice*, 22nd edn (LexisNexis, 2004).)

14.6   Distributing the trust funds

14.6.1   Accounting to the beneficiaries

Trustees must prepare capital and income accounts when changes in the beneficial interests under the settlement occur. The most likely occasions of this happening are:

(a)   when a beneficiary becomes entitled to receive settled property from the trustees, for example, following the exercise of a power of advancement under s 32 of TA 1925; or

(b)   when the trustees exercise a power of appointment, for example, when they appoint property to or for a beneficiary.

The accounts will show the investments and any cash in the trust fund together with any income which the trustees hold in their income account. From these accounts the beneficiary can ascertain precisely what his entitlement amounts to. The task of producing these accounts will be considerably eased if the trustees have kept full and accurate records of all transactions affecting the trust during the period of its administration. These will include records of sales and purchases of investments, advances made to the beneficiaries and any tax liabilities discharged.

14.6.2   Form and content of accounts

There is no prescribed form for trust accounts. The aim is to present clear and concise accounts which can easily be understood by the beneficiaries. Normally, trust accounts are produced in a vertical format showing the trust fund, payments made from it, for example, IHT and solicitors' costs and a balance for the beneficiary. A separate income account will reveal the income available for distribution, less any expenses payable from it, for example, any income tax due to the Revenue. The form of trust account shown in **Appendix 7** adopts this more usual vertical format.

14.6.3   Vesting the trust property in beneficiaries

Once the trustees have paid any tax liabilities and have prepared their accounts, the trust fund (or the appropriate part of it) must be transferred to the beneficiary. The means of vesting property in the beneficiary will depend on the nature of the property. The legal estate in land can be vested in the beneficiary by means of a deed; a stock transfer form will be required to transfer shares. Chattels (if any) pass to the beneficiary by delivery and any remaining cash will be transferred by cheque drawn on the trustee's bank account.

Chapter 15

The Overseas Dimension

15.1 The foreign element

The previous chapters in this book assume that private clients are UK resident and are domiciled in the UK. It has also been assumed that the property owned by these private clients is situated in the UK. However, the affairs of many private clients have an overseas dimension, for example:

(a) a UK resident and domiciled client may be leaving the UK to work abroad, or may be leaving the UK to emigrate; or

(b) an individual, while remaining a UK resident, is buying property overseas; or

(c) a foreign national is proposing to come to the UK on a temporary or long-term basis, or intends to invest in the UK.

15.1.1 The issues involved

There are many practical and legal issues where a client's affairs take on an overseas dimension.

15.1.1.1 Practical issues

The solicitor in the private client department tends not to be involved with the many practical issues when a client intends to leave or come to the UK. These matters include visa applications, work permits and accommodation. Clearly, in these areas there are legal issues involved about which the solicitor may be asked to advise but generally the client will be able to handle practical matters for himself.

15.1.1.2 Legal issues

The solicitor should be asked to advise and become involved as early as possible where legal issues arise. Two particular aspects may call for early consideration.

Ownership and devolution of property

The UK client may need advice in relation to a property he is proposing to buy in a foreign country. If, for example, he is purchasing a holiday cottage in France, he will need advice as to French succession law and the extent to which he can leave that property by a will made in England or in France.

As a minimum this advice should be given by a lawyer from, or specialising in the law of, the jurisdiction in which the property is situated, but ideally the lawyer should also be qualified in the law of England and Wales. Not only may the laws of the foreign country differ from those of the UK, but the law may vary from state to state within that country.

Taxation, and in particular the concepts of residence, ordinary residence and domicile

These concepts affect such matters as the basis of assessment, territorial scope and reliefs in relation to UK taxes. The private client will need to know the extent to which he becomes or remains liable to income tax, CGT and IHT following immigration to or emigration from the UK.

15.1.2 Scope of this chapter

Where a foreign element is involved, there are always many complex issues to be considered. Essentially, a solicitor is required to plan the client's affairs in relation to the international dimension to achieve the most favourable tax position for his client. There is often a considerable degree of urgency so that appropriate advice must be given quickly before the client changes his residential or domiciliary status. The remainder of this chapter is limited to introducing some basic tax concepts as a basis for further study.

15.2 Residence and domicile

Whether a client is an immigrant or an emigrant or whether he intends to invest in the UK or overseas, the rules of income tax, CGT and IHT can apply to him but frequently in a modified form depending on his particular circumstances. The keys to an understanding of a client's tax position are the concepts of residence and domicile.

15.2.1 Residence

In view of the importance of residence within the UK tax system, it is surprising that there is no statutory definition. There are three statutory provisions in ICTA 1988, Pt VII, Ch V entitled 'Residence of Individuals'. These provisions merely adapt the concepts of residence and ordinary residence as developed by the courts in a series of cases over many years. The decisions have developed the criteria against which residence is assessed. In order to give practical guidance, the Revenue has produced a set of rules in its booklet IR20 (1999) *Residents and non-residents – liability to tax in the UK*. Although without statutory authority, and therefore capable of challenge, this booklet is generally accepted by practitioners as a basis from which to provide advice to immigrant and emigrant clients.

Residence as a concept is concerned with physical presence in the UK. If an individual is physically present in the UK at some time in a tax year, it is a question of fact whether he is resident for tax purposes for that year. The fact that an individual is in the UK involuntarily is not generally relevant to this question. Basically, an individual will be considered resident in the UK if, for the time he is in the UK, it can be said to be his 'home'. It is not necessary that he owns a property in the UK; he may be resident even if he is living in hotel accommodation.

Any of the following tests may determine whether an individual will be treated as resident in the UK.

15.2.1.1 183 days in the UK: temporary residence

An individual will generally be treated as resident if he is present for, in aggregate, six months or more in the year of assessment. Six months is taken as 183 days but days of arrival and departure are ignored. In the Revenue's view 'there are no exceptions to this (rule)' (IR20 (1999) para 1.2), even in cases of hardship, for example, where an individual's presence continues through ill-health.

Visits to the UK for some temporary purpose only (eg a holiday), and which are for less than six months, will not usually give rise to tax. In determining whether the visit is for a 'temporary purpose', any available accommodation in the UK is disregarded.

15.2.1.2 Regular visits (IR20 (1999) para 3.3)

An individual will be treated as UK resident if he makes 'habitual and substantial' visits to the UK. The Revenue regards visits averaging three months per annum over four years as both 'habitual' and 'substantial'. If the average is met, he is treated as resident for tax purposes from the fifth year. Generally, days spent in the UK because of exceptional circumstances beyond the individual's control are ignored, for example, an extended stay in the UK because of ill-health.

15.2.1.3 Available accommodation in the UK

Until 6 April 1993, one of the most important factors in determining whether an individual was UK resident was the availability of accommodation in the UK for his use. The Revenue's view was that if he had available accommodation any visit, however short, would cause the individual to be treated as UK resident. Property could be available even if not owned by the individual, for example, if it was owned by the individual's employer or a relative who kept it for the individual's use. In certain circumstances UK accommodation was ignored, for example, property which an individual owned but which was let on lease while the owner was abroad.

However, since 5 April 1993, available accommodation in the UK is no longer a factor when determining whether a 'person is in the UK for some temporary purpose only and not with the intention of establishing his residence there' (ICTA 1988, s 336(3)).

15.2.2 Ordinary residence

The phrase 'ordinary residence' is often used in the legislation, particularly in relation to CGT, but nowhere is it defined. The concept of ordinary residence is used to prevent an individual from avoiding liability to tax simply by ceasing to be resident in the UK.

The courts have considered the phrase on a number of occasions. It is best described in the following extract from the judgment in *Lysaght v Commissioners of the Inland Revenue* [1928] AC 234:

> ordinarily means ... established custom or practice or a matter of regular practice or occurrence ... to be contrasted with casual or occasional.

The Revenue has given its view as to the meaning of ordinary residence in the booklet IR20 (1999) para 1.3 as follows:

> If you are resident in the UK year after year, you are treated as *ordinarily resident* here. You may be resident but not ordinarily resident in the UK for the tax year if, for example, you normally live outside the UK but are in this country for 183 days or more in the year [see **15.2.1.1**]. Or you may be ordinarily resident but not resident for a tax year if, for example, you usually live in the UK but have gone abroad for a long holiday and do not set foot in the UK during that year.

15.2.2.1 Domicile

Unlike residence and ordinary residence, an individual's domicile is not confined to determining liability to taxation. It is relevant to many other matters, for example, when determining in private international law which system of law governs succession to property owned in a foreign jurisdiction. Like residence and ordinary residence, domicile is not defined in statute but its meaning has been established by the courts in a number of decisions. An individual can only be domiciled in a country which has its own system of law, for example, England and Wales. The Revenue in its booklet IR20 (1999) at para 4.2 states:

> Broadly speaking you are domiciled in the country where you have your permanent home. Domicile is distinct from nationality or residence. You can only have one domicile at any given time.

An individual is usually domiciled in the country which he considers as 'home'. Thus, an individual who emigrates to the USA where he lives for 20 or 30 years will not necessarily cease to be domiciled in some part of the UK.

15.2.2.2 Domicile of origin

Every individual must have a domicile. Normally, a domicile of origin will be determined at birth, ie, a child acquires as his domicile of origin his father's domicile at the date of his birth. This may not be the country in which the child is actually born; nor need it be a country which the child has visited.

15.2.2.3 Domicile of dependency

A child under 16 who derived his domicile of origin from his father will acquire a new domicile, ie, a domicile of dependency in place of his domicile of origin if his father acquires a new domicile (see below).

15.2.2.4 Domicile of choice

Domicile can change where an individual voluntarily acquires a new domicile, ie, a domicile of choice. There is a heavy burden of proof before an individual can show that a domicile of choice has been acquired. Domicile is a matter of intent but a mere intention to change domicile is insufficient. Many factors are relevant including abandoning an existing domicile. Unless all connections with the previous domicile are broken, it may be difficult (if not impossible) to show the acquisition of a domicile of choice.

A client who, at the time of emigrating from the UK, is considering acquiring a new domicile of choice should compile all available evidence of intention. Inter alia, the following should be considered:

(a)   he should take up residence in the country involved, preferably acquiring property in that country and selling all property in the UK; and

(b)   he must have a permanent intention to remain indefinitely in the new country in order to show a change in domicile. This requirement as to intention is often the most difficult obstacle for a client to overcome when endeavouring to change domicile. Ideally, he should make a written statement, or statutory declaration, before leaving the UK, setting out all personal circumstances giving rise to the decision to change domicile. Such a statement is not conclusive but will always be of assistance when attempting to convince third parties, particularly the Inland Revenue, of the change of domicile; and

(c)   in addition to purchasing a residence in the new country, he should forge as many associations with that country as possible while at the same time ending associations with the old country. He should consider a new business or employment, make a will valid under local law, open a new bank account, sell investments and reinvest in the new country, etc.

15.2.3 United Kingdom

The UK consists of England and Wales, Scotland and Northern Ireland. It does not include the Channel Islands or the Isle of Man which, because of their relatively lower tax rates, are often termed 'tax havens'.

It is incorrect to link the concept of domicile with the UK. An individual has a domicile in a territory or a state which has its own legal system. Thus, an individual may be domiciled in Scotland or in England and Wales.

15.3 Taxation of the individual and the foreign element

The effect of the rules as to residence and domicile on an individual's liability to tax depends upon the tax involved. Spouses are independent persons for tax purposes. Their residence and ordinary residence status, and their domicile, are determined by reference to their individual circumstances and so may not coincide with the status of their spouse.

Transfers of property between spouses both of whom are domiciled in the UK are free of IHT by virtue of the spouse exemption. However, transfers by a UK domiciled spouse to a non-UK domiciled spouse are exempt up to a cumulative limit of £55,000 (IHTA 1984, s 18(2)).

15.3.1 Income tax and CGT

15.3.1.1 Income tax

An individual who is UK resident is liable to income tax on his worldwide income, ie, he must pay income tax on all income whether its source is within the UK or elsewhere.

A non-UK resident is only liable to income tax on income arising from a source within the UK. The rules to determine whether a person is resident in the UK are considered at **15.2**.

Whether a source of income is within the UK depends on the type of income. For example, income from employment within the UK, rent from land within the UK and dividends from companies whose membership register is kept within the UK are all sources of income within the UK. If the duties of the employment, the situation of the land or the membership register are outside the UK, the income will have a non-UK source.

15.3.1.2 Capital gains tax

An individual who is UK resident is liable to pay CGT on gains made on disposals of assets wherever they are situated. A non-resident individual will not necessarily avoid liability to CGT since liability is extended to cover gains made by someone who is 'ordinarily resident' in the UK, for example, a person whose residence is within the UK but who is temporarily overseas.

If an individual is neither resident nor ordinarily resident in the UK, he is not normally liable to CGT whether the gains arise on disposals of assets in the UK or elsewhere.

15.3.2 Effect of ceasing to be resident and ordinarily resident for income tax and CGT

If an individual is resident in the UK for part of a tax year and absent for the remainder of it, the general rule is that income tax and CGT is charged for the whole tax year. By concession, the Revenue may split the tax year so that an individual is treated as resident in the UK for only part of the year. For example, where an individual leaves to live permanently outside the UK, the Revenue treats him as non-resident from the date of departure (IR20 (1999), para 1.5).

Tax planning by emigrating from the UK is perhaps the ultimate form of tax avoidance. To be successful, the individual will need to convince the Revenue that he is no longer resident or ordinarily resident in the UK on the date on which the liability to tax arose.

The operative date will depend on the tax in question. For CGT purposes, liability arises on the date of disposal of the asset in question. This is generally the date on which a binding contract is made (and not the date of later completion). If an individual is still a UK resident when the terms of the contract were substantially agreed, the Revenue may argue that this should be taken as the date of disposal, even though a formal contract had not yet been made. For effective tax planning, therefore, a client may be best advised to become non-resident well before negotiations are concluded.

If emigration is for a relatively short period, even though technically it may meet the non-residence test, the Revenue may argue that absence from the UK was always intended as temporary and, therefore, the individual was never truly non-resident. Although there is nothing to stop an emigrant from subsequently returning to the UK and resuming resident status, it is usually advisable for the period of emigration to be for at least one tax year if non-residency is to be achieved.

15.3.2.1 Temporary non-residence – CGT

To prevent abuse by UK resident individuals leaving the UK on or after 17 March 1998, Finance Act 1998, s 127 has introduced a new anti-avoidance measure into TCGA 1992, s 10A. No longer can the individual, who is about to realise a large capital gain, avoid CGT by the simple expedient of making the relevant disposal in a tax year when he is neither resident nor ordinarily resident in the UK. To avoid CGT on such a gain, the individual must now ensure non-UK residence or ordinary residence for a five-year period before returning to the UK. If return occurs within the five-year period, gains will be charged in the tax year of the return to the UK.

15.3.2.2 Employment overseas

Although an employee going overseas to work full time on a contract of employment may not consider he is emigrating, he is effectively doing so for income tax and CGT purposes. The employee will be treated as non-resident and not ordinarily resident from the day after leaving the UK to the day before returning if all the following conditions are satisfied (IR 20 (1999) para 2.2):

> If you leave the UK to work full time abroad under a contract of employment, you are treated as not resident and not ordinarily resident if you meet all the following conditions:
>
> (i)   your absence from the UK and your employment abroad both last for at least a whole tax year; and

    (ii)   during your absence any visits you make to the UK:

        (1)   total less than 183 days in any tax year; and

        (2)   average less than 91 days a tax year (the average is taken over the period of absence up to a maximum of 4 years; any days spent in the UK because of exceptional circumstances beyond your control, for example, the illness of yourself or a member of your immediate family, are not normally counted for this purpose).

Once in the overseas employment, the employee can dispose of assets within the UK without liability to CGT on gains realised. To achieve this, he should be advised to enter into contracts disposing of assets likely to realise substantial gains only after he has gone overseas and achieved non-resident status (see above).

Any income which the employee may have from sources within the UK remains subject to income tax.

15.3.2.3 Longer-term emigrants

Emigrants in circumstances where an overseas employment is not intended will need to convince the Revenue of change in their residential status. Normally, this would entail selling a UK house before departure and purchasing a house in the new country. Return visits should be avoided in the tax year of departure and limited in the immediately following years. The individual may be treated as UK resident subsequently, if he falls foul of the tests set out at **15.2.1**.

Emigration of itself does not give rise to a disposal of assets for CGT purposes so that assets showing large in-built gains should be sold after the individual is no longer ordinarily resident in the UK.

Emigration within six years of a gift

Hold-over relief on the disposal of assets by way of gift has been discussed at **4.4.5.2**. The relief is available only if an election is made by the donor and donee and if the donee was resident or ordinarily resident in the UK at the time. If the donee emigrates within six years of the gift, an emigration charge arises whereby the heldover gain becomes immediately chargeable. Tax is payable by the donee but the Revenue can recover it from the donor if it remains unpaid 12 months after the due date. The charge does not apply if the donee is an employee who leaves to work abroad under a full-time contract of employment.

Example

In 1992, Dana gave her son her shareholding in ABC Ltd. The gain of £10,000 was held over. In 1995, her son emigrated from the UK and took up residence in France. The £10,000 is immediately chargeable, ie, at the rates of tax relevant in 1995. The actual value of the shareholding in 1995 is irrelevant.

15.3.2.4 Long-term immigrants – remittance basis

Foreign nationals who retain their original domicile but who work in or are based in the UK for a certain length of time may, under the rules considered above, become 'resident' or 'ordinarily resident'. They will thus, in principle, become liable to UK taxation on all their income and gains, wherever arising. However, if such individuals still retain their foreign domicile, the rules are relaxed. Broadly, their foreign income suffers UK tax only to the extent that it is remitted to the UK. Furthermore, their overseas gains become chargeable only if remitted (in any form) to the UK.

15.3.3 Double taxation treaties

An individual may be liable to tax in the UK and in a foreign country at the same time. The client may be 'dual resident' because the residence criteria in the two countries where he has lived treat him as resident in each country. If there is a double taxation agreement between the countries, this will provide relief from double taxation of income and gains. If no double taxation agreement exists, unilateral relief may be granted by one of the countries. There are no special EU tax rules and the rules of individual Member States have not yet been harmonised, but there are various double taxation provisions and reliefs between EU countries.

15.3.4 Inheritance tax

Residence (or ordinary residence) is not relevant as a concept to determine liability to IHT. Instead, an individual's domicile governs liability to IHT.

An individual who is domiciled in (some part of) the UK is liable to IHT on a transfer of value of assets whether the assets are in the UK or elsewhere. If an individual is not domiciled in the UK, liability arises only on the transfer of value of property situated in the UK, although there are some exceptions to this rule, for example, exempt gilts (government stock).

15.3.4.1 Deemed domicile for IHT (IHTA 1984, s 267)

Section 267 of IHTA 1984 contains provisions extending the meaning of domicile. An individual not domiciled in the UK under the principles discussed at **15.2.3** may nevertheless be deemed to be domiciled in the UK for IHT. This can happen in one of two circumstances.

The domicile test

An individual actually domiciled in the UK within the three years immediately preceding a transfer of value will be deemed domiciled there at the time of the transfer. The aim of this provision is to stop an individual transferring his property from the UK and then emigrating in the hope of avoiding IHT on future transfers of his property.

> Example
>
> Alexis acquired a domicile of choice in California in January 2002 when she emigrated there from England. She died two years later. As Alexis had given up her UK domicile within three years of her death (the transfer of value), her entire estate is chargeable to IHT.

The residence test

An individual who was resident in the UK for income tax purposes in not less than 17 of the 20 years of assessment ending with the year in which the transfer of value occurs is deemed to be domiciled in the UK. In determining whether an individual is resident in any year, the income tax tests discussed at **15.2** are used (ignoring from 6 April 1993 onwards any available accommodation in the UK).

This provision is intended to bring long-term residents who have not become UK domiciliaries into the charge to IHT.

> Example
>
> Alexandra's employment in the UK since July 1980 has just ended following the failure of her employer's business. As a result, she plans to return home to Greece as soon as possible. Last year, she gave some land she owned outside Athens to her daughter. In view of Alexandra's residence in the UK for over 20 years, she will be

deemed domiciled in the UK so that her death within seven years of the gift of the land would cause the gift to become subject to IHT.

15.3.4.2 Death of a UK domiciliary with foreign property

Succession

If the testator left two wills, one dealing with his foreign property, and an English will dealing with his other assets, a foreign lawyer should be instructed to prove the foreign will and to administer the foreign property in accordance with its terms.

If the testator left only an English will, this should be proved in the usual way and then a foreign lawyer instructed either to reseal the English grant in the foreign jurisdiction or to extract the appropriate grant in that jurisdiction using sealed and certified copies of the English grant and will. As a grant obtained in the UK contains a 'notation of domicile', ie, the deceased's domicile at death is stated on the grant, the grant will be recognised in other parts of the UK without further formality Administration of Estates Act 1971 (AEA 1971). Thus, the English executors of a deceased client can prove title to property in Scotland or Northern Ireland without resealing their grant in either jurisdiction (and vice versa).

Devolution of foreign property, particularly land, is often subject to local succession taxes (or equivalent) and to local laws of entitlement which may override (to a given extent) the terms of an English will. For example, in Scotland, Spain and France a stated proportion of the testator's estate passes automatically (and not by will) to certain relatives; in the USA and Scandinavian countries there is 'community of property' provision for spouses. In view of these local succession laws, it is usually appropriate for the clients to be advised to make a will in the particular jurisdiction taking local law into account; any English will should in terms exclude the property in the foreign jurisdiction.

Inheritance tax

Worldwide assets are part of the estate of a client domiciled in the UK for IHT purposes (under either of the tests discussed above) and should be disclosed in Inland Revenue Account IHT 200. Subject to any relief under a double taxation agreement or convention, the English PRs are liable to pay any IHT which is due although their liability is limited to the extent of assets received or which might have been received but for their neglect or default (IHTA 1984, s 204). Unless the testator's will provides otherwise, the beneficiaries of the foreign property bear the burden of the IHT which that property attracts (IHTA 1984, s 211). Thus, the UK PRs, having paid the IHT to the Revenue will need to recover an equivalent amount from the beneficiary of the property.

15.3.4.3 Death of a non-UK domiciliary with UK property

Succession

Foreign PRs may obtain title to the property in the UK by resealing their foreign grant in the appropriate court in the UK. Except in Scotland (where local laws apply), succession to the property is generally in accordance with the terms of the deceased's will.

Inheritance tax

Certain government stock and other property is exempt from IHT, even though situated in the UK, if owned by an individual who is neither domiciled nor ordinarily resident in the UK. Otherwise, property physically situated in the UK is subject to IHT. All such property should be disclosed in Inland Revenue Account IHT 201.

15.4 Trustees and the foreign element

The residence and ordinary residence of trustees is generally determined separately from the status of the settlor or the beneficiaries and without regard to the location of the trust assets.

15.4.1 Income tax

For income tax purposes, the residence of trustees is governed by Finance Act 1989, s 110. If there is one trustee who is a UK resident and others who are not, all the trustees will be regarded by the Revenue as UK resident. This means that the trustees are subject to UK income tax on all trust income, whether from a UK or an overseas source. All tax (including on the overseas source income) can be assessed on the UK resident trustee.

15.4.1.1 Overseas settlors

The rule mentioned above does not apply if the settlor was neither domiciled, resident nor ordinarily resident in the UK when he created the settlement. If all the trustees of such a settlement are non-UK residents, the trust is liable only to UK tax on UK source income. For this purpose, if at least one of the trustees is resident in the UK and the others are not, the UK trustee(s) will be regarded by the Revenue as resident outside the UK. If, however, all of the trustees become UK resident, then all trust income, whatever the source, is subject to UK tax.

Non-resident trustees are not liable to UK income tax other than on income arising in the UK (see above). In such cases, basic or lower rate tax (22 or 20%) is generally deducted at source so that the trustees receive income net of tax. Trustees of A & M settlements and discretionary settlements are liable to tax at the 'rate applicable to the trust', ie, to an extra 18% or 20% (see **14.5.2**); in practice, the Revenue often cannot collect this extra tax from the non-resident trustees because there is no means of withholding it at source, nor can it enforce the liability in the overseas jurisdiction.

15.4.2 Capital gains tax

Trustees are treated as 'a single continuing body of persons distinct from the persons who may from time to time be the trustees' (TCGA 1992, s 69). Thus, normally, if one trustee is replaced by another there is no disposal for CGT purposes.

The general rule is that trustees are not treated as UK resident and ordinarily resident if the general administration of the trust is carried on outside the UK and the trustees (or a majority of them) are not resident or ordinarily resident in the UK. If these conditions are satisfied, the trustees are treated as non-resident and are, therefore, outside the UK CGT net so that disposals by them do not attract CGT. It is this exemption from CGT which has in the past made non-resident settlements attractive to UK taxpayers.

15.5 Non-resident settlements

15.5.1 What is a non-resident settlement?

Because the trustees of a settlement are treated as a single and continuing body of persons, a settlement is a separate entity for CGT purposes no matter what type of settlement it may be, and whether or not it is resident in the UK. The only exceptions to this general rule are where the trustees are either nominees or bare trustees when the trust property is treated as belonging to the beneficiary. If such property is sold, any gain (subject to any relevant relief or exemption) is the beneficiary's gain, and taxed accordingly.

A settlement, and its trustees, is treated as being non-UK resident if:

(a) all or a majority of its trustees are neither resident nor ordinarily resident in the UK; and

(b) the general administration of the trust is ordinarily carried on outside the UK. This includes such matters as trust administration, investment management decisions and trust banking and accounting. Although not entirely free from doubt, trustees' decisions, for example, as to the exercise of a fiduciary power can probably be made within the UK without denying the trust its non-resident status.

A trustee resident in the UK is none the less treated as non-resident if:

(a) his business includes trust management;

(b) he is acting in the trust in the course of his business; and

(c) the settlement was created by an individual who was at the time not resident, ordinarily resident or domiciled in the UK.

This rule permits professional trust companies in the UK to carry on the administration of a non-resident trust without prejudicing its non-resident status. Some solicitors' firms have their own trust company (a company whose objects include trust administration and whose shares are owned by partners) to run and manage non-resident trusts in this way.

15.5.1.1 Sheltering trustees' gains

Non-resident settlements have been popular with clients and estate planners as providing a ready method of sheltering the trust's gains from CGT. Non-resident trustees are in the same position as individuals who are not resident in the UK. Thus they are not liable to pay CGT on their chargeable gains on disposal of trust assets, provided the settlement is a non-resident settlement for the entire tax year in question. If the trustees become non-resident part way through the year, the Revenue will not split the year for assessment purposes so allowing avoidance of CGT for the period when the trust is non-resident. Ideally a client should be advised to set up his non-resident trust, or export his existing trust (see below), well before 6 April in the relevant year.

15.5.2 Anti-avoidance legislation

Ever since the introduction of CGT in 1965, estate planners have advised clients to use non-resident settlements (normally discretionary settlements) to shelter the trustees' gains from CGT. Over the same period, various legislative attempts have been made to counter loss of revenue through use of these settlements but only recently has the large-scale use of non-resident settlements been substantially halted. Even now some opportunities remain for use of such settlements.

On the whole, clients were less concerned with avoidance of inheritance tax (or its predecessor capital transfer tax) or income tax in relation to their non-resident settlement, although sometimes this was the result even if not the overriding intention. Often clients wished for some continuing enjoyment from the settled property or its income. The real objective, therefore, was sheltering the non-resident gains from CGT while, so far as the legislation permitted, continuing to enjoy the property.

Anti-avoidance legislation is always complex even if the objective is reasonably certain. Whether the objective is achieved, is, of course, another matter. Apart from 1965 (with the introduction of CGT), there have been two principal occasions when anti-avoidance legislation has been introduced: the first by Finance Act 1981, s 80, and the second 10 years later by Finance Act 1991, Sch 16. Neither of these was entirely successful in that estate planners continued to find ways round the provisions and so defeat the intention of the legislation. Each of these provisions has been retained, and strengthened, and appear now as ss 86 and 87 of TCGA 1992. A further provision, TCGA 1992 s 80, has introduced an export charge. Section 80 is discussed below. Sections 86 and 87 are beyond the scope of this book and will not be considered further. However, for anyone involved in advising settlor clients seeking to avoid CGT, they must be fully understood.

15.5.3   Anti-avoidance legislation – the position now

The current position in relation to anti-avoidance legislation is set out below.

15.5.3.1   Migrant settlements – export charge (TCGA 1992, s 80(2))

Consider the following example.

Example

Derek Godfrey formed his electrical engineering company. He settled the shares on UK resident trustees to hold on family discretionary trusts. He continued to draw director's fees. Expecting imminent growth in value of the shares due to the success of the company, the UK trustees retired in favour of non-resident trustees. The company prospered. The non-resident trustees sold the shares realising a substantial capital profit.

Derek Godfrey's tax position:

(a)   deemed disposal on transfer of shares to the UK trustees: no significant capital gains realised and so covered by the indexation allowance and the annual exemption;

(b)   appointment of non-resident trustees: no disposal, the trustees are a single continuing body of persons (TCGA 1992, s 69, see **15.4.2**).

The consequence of these transactions (before 1981) was that any increase in value of the shares by the time the appointment of the new trustees was not charged to capital gains tax. The gain (often large) was free of CGT. To counter this, an 'export charge' was introduced to tax gains which had accrued but which had not been realised to the date of the appointment of the non-resident trustees by Finance Act 1981, s 83 (now TCGA 1992, s 80).

Advice to clients contemplating the 'export' of their settlement covers two main aspects; legal and taxation issues.

Legal issues

What is at issue is the export of a UK trust to avoid CGT. Export of the trust is simply achieved by appointing persons who are resident abroad as trustees and ensuring that the administration of the trust is carried on outside the UK (see **15.5.1**). But what considerations should the present trustees have in mind when faced with a proposal that the trust be exported? First, there is no absolute bar in English law preventing the appointment of non-resident trustees of a UK trust and, secondly, such an appointment should be made only in 'appropriate circumstances' because the result is to remove the trust from control by the English courts. The following extract is from the judgment of Pennycuick V-C in *Re Whitehead's Will Trusts; Burke v Burke and Others* [1971] 1 WLR 833:

> The law has been quite well established for upwards of a century that there is no absolute bar to the appointment of persons resident abroad as trustees of an English trust. I say 'no absolute bar', in the sense that such an appointment would be prohibited by law and would consequently be invalid. On the other hand, apart from exceptional circumstances, it is not proper to make such an appointment, that is to say, the court would not apart from exceptional circumstances, make such an appointment; nor would it be right for the donees of the power to make such an appointment out of court. If they did, presumably the court would be likely to interfere at the instance of the beneficiaries. There do, however, exist exceptional circumstances in which such an appointment can properly be made. The most obvious exceptional circumstances are those in which the beneficiaries have settled permanently in some country outside the United Kingdom and what is proposed to be done is to appoint new trustees in that country.

Clearly, if the court would appoint non-resident trustees, it will be proper for the trustees themselves to do so, for example, where all the beneficiaries are resident in the country where the trust is to become resident following the appointment. If the trustees made an appointment where the court might not, there is unlikely to be any real concern if all the beneficiaries have approved the non-resident appointment. This will require all beneficiaries to be ascertained and to be *sui juris*. If the trustees are in doubt about a proposed appointment, it would be sensible to apply to the court first (as in *Re Whitehead*).

In many cases, there will be appropriate express provision in the trust instrument for the trustees to retire in favour of non-resident trustees. Such a power can be exercised without further consideration by the trustees, provided its exercise is in the best interests of the beneficiaries.

The choice of overseas jurisdiction requires some thought by the trustees. It is prudent to appoint the non-resident trustees in a jurisdiction which will, if necessary, enforce the trustees' duties; the concept of a trust and the division of legal and beneficial ownership is not known in many civil law jurisdictions. Care should also be taken to choose a country where tax laws are less stringent than the UK since, otherwise, the trustees may be taxed as heavily, if not more so, than in the UK. It is also sensible to choose a jurisdiction which is likely to be stable – the Channel Islands or the Isle of Man – and to select reputable trustees, for example, a well-known trust company or a firm of lawyers practising within the jurisdiction.

Taxation issues

The export charge is levied under TCGA 1992, s 80 in a manner familiar to the CGT legislation. When the trustees become neither resident nor ordinarily resident in the UK, they are deemed to have disposed of the trust assets at market value and to have re-acquired them at the same value. The retiring trustees are primarily responsible for the tax due on the chargeable gain; if it is not paid by them within six months of the due date, the Revenue can recover the tax from any person who was a trustee in the 12 months before the export of the trust (unless, broadly, when he ceased to be a trustee there was then no proposal to export the trust). Because of their personal liability for the tax, the retiring trustees should retain sufficient assets under their control so that they can pay the tax due.

Tax is charged at the rate appropriate to the trustees. As the settlement is likely to be a discretionary settlement, the rate will be 40%. If the settlor has 'an interest in his (UK) settlement', for example, the settlor or his spouse can benefit from the settled property or its income, the gains deemed made by the trustees will be assessable on the settlor (TCGA 1992, ss 77–79).

This export charge may not necessarily deter the use of a non-resident settlement by a settlor, particularly where the growth in the settled assets is expected to occur after the export rather than before it.

The charge is suspended in cases where an 'inadvertent' change in the residence status of the settlement occurs provided the UK resident status is resumed within six months. For example, the death of the only UK resident trustee leaving two non-resident trustees, would cause the settlement to become non-resident. If the trustee is replaced by another UK trustee within six months no charge is made under s 80.

None of the three final anti-avoidance provisions is considered further here:

(a)   non-resident settlements – attribution of gains to settlors (TCGA 1992, s 86 and Sch 5);

(b)   non-resident settlements – attribution of gains to beneficiaries (TCGA 1992, s 87);

(c)   non-resident settlements – the supplementary charge (TCGA 1992, ss 91–95).

APPENDICES

Appendix 1 – Income Tax Rates and Allowances

Rates		2005/06	2004/05
Starting rate	10%	£1–£2,090	£1–£1,020
Basic rate	22%	£2,091–£32,400	£2,021–£31,400
Higher rate	40%	Over £32,400	Over £31,400
Savings income			
under starting rate limit		10%	10%
under basic rate limit		20%	20%
above basic rate limit		40%	40%
Dividend savings income			
under the basic rate limit		10%	10%
above the basic rate limit		32.5%	32.5%

			Reduction in tax	
Allowance	2005/06	2004/05	2005/06	2004/05
			10%	10%
	£	£	£	£
Personal	4,895	4,745		
aged 65–74	7,090	6,830		
aged 75 and over	7,220	6,950		
Married couple				
aged 65–74	5,905	5,725	590.50	572.50
aged 74 and over	5,975	5,795	597.50	579.50
Blind person	1,610	1,560		
Income for age-related allowances	19,500	18,900		

Note:

(a) The 'Reduction in tax' columns show the amount of tax credit available where relief is restricted to 10%. It is given by reducing the individual's total liablity by the amount of the credit.

(b) Age-related allowances:

income limit:	£19,500/£18,900.
income below limit:	allowance in full.
income exceeds limit:	allowance reduced by 50% of the excess.

Appendix 2 – Investment and Financial Products

The purpose of this Appendix is to provide a brief introduction to some of the more popular types of investment and financial products currently available to individuals and trustees. It is not intended to be a definitive list. Suggestions are made as to the type of client for whom the investment might be suitable but many factors will determine the actual choice of investment for a particular client. The tax rules are those for the client and not for the product. Where appropriate, for each investment there is a brief summary indicating risk and showing income and capital growth potential.

The investments listed are:

(1) Bank accounts

The two most common accounts are the current account and the deposit account.

Current account

The current account is one where the saver's money is immediately available to him and he may have a cheque book and a cash card to enable him to spend the money in or withdraw the money from the account at any time. Because the money is always available the bank is unlikely to pay interest to the saver on the amount in the account, and where it does, the interest rate will be very low.

Deposit account

A deposit account is an account which pays interest to the saver. The saver can withdraw money from the account on demand but will lose interest equivalent to that which would have been earned during the notice period. The bank will require notice (generally of seven days) of an intended withdrawal to release funds from the account. Amounts in accounts and transactions are shown by the bank on regular statements which are sent to the saver.

Tax

All interest paid by a bank on these accounts will be paid net of lower rate tax. If the saver is a non-tax payer, he may sign a declaration to this effect and hand it to the bank so enabling it to pay the interest gross. A tax repayment claim by the client can thus be avoided in appropriate cases.

Suitability

The majority of a solicitor's clients both individuals and trustees will have at least a current account in which a sufficient balance is maintained to enable regular expenditure such as utility bills to be met.

However, because of the lack of interest or comparatively poor interest rates it is inadvisable for the majority of a client's savings to remain in such an account.

Banks and building societies encourage people to place their savings with them by offering interest on the money deposited. The bank or building society then uses this money to fund loans and mortgages to borrowers. The borrowers pay back not only the amount borrowed but also interest on the loan. This rate of interest is higher than that paid to the people saving with the bank or society. The difference covers the institution's running costs and provides a profit for the bank or society.

Example

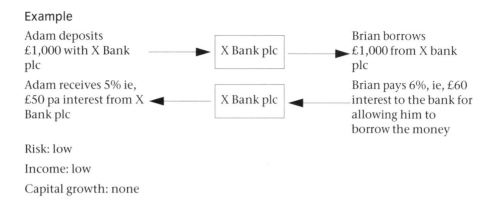

Adam deposits £1,000 with X Bank plc → X Bank plc → Brian borrows £1,000 from X bank plc

Adam receives 5% ie, £50 pa interest from X Bank plc ← X Bank plc ← Brian pays 6%, ie, £60 interest to the bank for allowing him to borrow the money

Risk: low

Income: low

Capital growth: none

(2) Building society accounts

Building societies offer deposit accounts and an array of share accounts. Ownership of an account is evidenced by a passbook held by the account holder in which the building society records all payments to and withdrawals from the account. Interest rates vary from time to time.

Deposit accounts

Money is repayable on demand and interest calculated on a daily basis is paid on the amount in the account. In the event of the building society ceasing to exist, deposit account holders will receive back their money in priority to all other savers. Hence, this is the safest type of building society account and, therefore, pays a lower rate of interest than a share account.

Share accounts

There are a wide variety of accounts offered by the various societies. For small sums or as an alternative to a current bank account, an ordinary share account offers a higher rate of interest than a deposit account and access to all money in the account on demand. Where immediate access is not required, higher rates of interest are paid on 'notice' accounts, for example, 28-day access account. The saver has to give the society a specified length of notice of his intention to withdraw his money. The longer the notice period, the higher the rate of interest paid on the account.

These accounts often also have a tiered interest system so that interest is paid at different rates on the amount in the account.

Example

Charly has £30,000 in a 60-day notice account. She is paid interest on:

(a)   the first £10,000 @ X% pa;

(b)   the next £15,000 @ X + ½% pa;

(c)   the balance @ X + ¾% pa.

The best rates for both bank and building society accounts are now paid on accounts which have internet-only access.

Tax

The tax treatment of building society accounts is exactly the same as for bank accounts.

Suitability

Building societies offer a relatively safe investment with a reasonably good rate of return. Most clients concerned with financial planning should consider holding at least one share account as they offer liquidity and interest. However, if the interest is required to supplement income, the underlying value of the capital will be eroded by inflation.

Trustees with wide express investment powers can invest in all types of building society account.

Risk: low.

Income: low.

Capital growth: none.

(3) TESSAs

Since their introduction by the Government in January 1991, Tax Exempt Special Savings Accounts (TESSAs) were offered by most banks and building societies enabling savers to receive tax-free income on investments up to £9,000. A TESSA must run for five years. Single capital payments are made into the account each year. In the first year the maximum amount is £3,000 with a maximum of £1,800 pa over the next few years (subject to the overall £9,000 maximum).

'Follow-up' TESSAs

The first TESSAs matured in January 1996 and the interest earned on the account thereafter is taxable. However, investors who held their first TESSA for the full five years and invested £3,000 or more could reinvest the capital (not the interest) up to £9,000 in the first year of a new TESSA – a follow-up TESSA.

If capital of more than £3,000 but less than £9,000 is reinvested in the follow-up TESSA, investment up to the overall maximum of £9,000 can then be made subject to the maximum of £1,800 pa and the usual five-year period.

An individual may own only one TESSA.

New TESSAs cannot be started after 5 April 1999 when Individual Savings Accounts (ISAs) became available (see **(21)** below). Existing TESSAs may run their course and can then be transferred into an ISA when the TESSA matures. A TESSA-only ISA can be held in addition to other ISAs.

Tax

Interest is credited to the TESSA account annually. That interest, after deduction of lower rate tax, can be withdrawn by the saver or it can be left in the account and reinvested.

If the capital remains in the account for the full five years, the tax payer receives a refund of the tax deducted from the interest and after five years can withdraw the capital and interest tax free.

It is possible for the capital to be withdrawn within the five years but the saver then loses the right to recover the income tax.

Suitability

TESSAs were popular with small savers who could afford to tie up a small amount of capital for five years and with higher-rate taxpayers because of the tax-free income. For a wealthy individual the £9,000 ceiling means that a TESSA is only a small part of his overall financial planning strategy.

Risk: low.

Income: medium.

Capital growth: low.

(4) National Savings

National Savings are schemes offered by the Government which guarantee the security of the money invested with it. There are a number of National Savings products and some of the most common are identified below.

National Savings Bank accounts

This bank offers an investment account which is operated with a passbook through the saver's local post office, and from 1 August 2004, an easy access savings account which is operated via phone, post or post office.

Interest is paid annually on both accounts, but is higher on the deposit account. The interest rate may change from time to time.

Easy access savings

The minimum amount for each payment into the account is £100 and the maximum holding in an individual account is £2 million.

Tax

The interest is taxable but is paid gross.

Suitability

It may be particularly useful for non-tax payers such as children and the elderly providing easy and convenient access and a small amount of tax-free income. By receiving the income gross, non-tax payers do not have to worry about tax reclaims or filing tax returns. The low rate of interest is unlikely to make it an attractive account for others. The once a year interest payment makes it unattractive for those needing a regular income.

Risk, income and capital growth: low.

Investment account

The minimum investment at any time is £20 and the maximum that can be held in the account is £100,000. The rate of interest is competitive with banks and building societies but one month's notice must be given before any withdrawal can be made.

Tax

All the interest is taxable but is paid gross.

Suitability

The convenience of withdrawing money at the post office and the receipt of gross interest appeal to the elderly. The notice period and annual interest payment can be deterrents for those needing regular income or access to capital.

Income bonds

Income bonds provide a regular monthly income. Ownership is evidenced by a bond or certificate. The minimum purchase is £500 and the maximum holding £1 million. Income is paid monthly to the investor. The interest rate may vary from time to time. Three months' notice is required to cash in all or part of the bond.

Tax

All the interest is taxable but paid gross.

Suitability

The bond provides an attractive rate of interest for non-tax payers and a regular income. It is, therefore, particularly suitable for elderly clients with limited savings. The main disadvantages are the need for tax payers to account for income tax on income received each year and the lack of protection of the capital against inflation.

Risk, income and capital growth: low.

National Savings Certificates

National Savings Certificates can be purchased from the Post Office and offer tax-free interest. In return for the purchase of Certificates the interest rate is guaranteed. The rate of interest increases each year the Certificates are held over a two-year or five-year period but averaged over the two years or five years is equivalent to the guaranteed annual rate. For example, a guaranteed average rate of 2.9% pa over five years will be achieved by paying 2% in year 1 increasing to 3.5% in year 5. The interest is added to the capital each year and only paid out when the Certificates are cashed. To achieve the maximum interest the Certificates must be held for the full five years. The minimum purchase is £100 and generally the maximum holding in any issue is £15,000.

Certificates should normally be cashed in after the two-year or five-year period as thereafter the annual rate of interest paid drops significantly.

Certificates can be repaid early but this is penalised by interest being calculated at a lower rate for the period of ownership.

Tax

There is no income tax or CGT to pay.

Suitability

Because of their favourable tax treatment, National Savings Certificates offer an attractive investment to higher-rate tax payers. They are also suitable for parents or trustees wishing to invest money for minor children.

Because the interest is compounded and only paid out when the Certificates are redeemed, this is not a suitable investment for anybody requiring a regular income.

Risk and income: low.

Capital growth: medium (interest is added to the capital).

Pensioners Guaranteed Income Bonds

In 1994, Pensioners Guaranteed Income Bonds ('granny bonds') were introduced for people aged 65 (reduced to 60 for 1996/97) or over. The minimum investment is £500; the maximum investment is £1 million. Income rates can be guaranteed for five years. Alternatively, a one- or two-year period can be chosen. After five years the money may be withdrawn without any penalty.

Tax

Income is taxable but is paid gross.

Suitability

These bonds are suitable for elderly people with modest amounts of cash to invest. There is little risk and no capital growth. Income rates should be compared to rates available from an equivalent investment elsewhere, for example, in a building society.

Premium bonds

Premium bonds can be purchased from the Post Office. Bond holders are automatically entered for regular prize draws. Bonds are divided into £1 units and each unit has a separate chance in the draws, ie, a £100-bond has 100 chances of winning a prize in every draw. Prizes range from £50 to £1 million. Bond holders can reclaim their money from the bonds at any time. The minimum holding is £100; the maximum holding is £30,000.

Tax

All prizes are totally tax free.

Suitability

Statistics suggest that holders of bonds to the maximum limit are likely to receive sufficient prizes to represent an acceptable return on the amount of prizes each year making it a worthwhile purchase for wealthy higher-rate tax payers. For lower holdings, there is no income and no capital growth, merely the gamble that a bond will win one of the larger prizes.

Trustees whose investment powers come from TA 2000 cannot purchase premium bonds as they involve no income or capital growth, and they are unlikely to be suitable for most trusts.

Risk, income and capital growth: low.

(5) Local authority bonds

These bonds are a way of investing in local authorities. When a local authority needs to raise money, it may encourage investors to deposit money with them in return for a competitive rate of interest. The minimum investment is usually £1,000 with no maximum. The bond will last for between one and four years and must be held to maturity. The local authority guarantees the rate of interest to be paid throughout the period.

Tax

There is no CGT on these bonds. The interest is paid net of lower rate tax.

Suitability

The guaranteed interest rate may be attractive at a time of falling interest rates and is usually competitive when compared to other forms of interest-only savings. The safety of the money invested depends upon the standing of the local authority. Because it is a fixed-term investment, these bonds are not suitable for people needing immediate access to their capital. The bonds may be suitable investments for some trustees.

Risk, income and capital growth: low.

(6) Gilts

'Gilts' is the popular name for government stocks otherwise known as 'gilt-edged' securities. They are issued by the UK government as a way of raising money and are a secure form of investment as interest and repayment are guaranteed by the Government.

The majority of gilts pay a fixed rate of interest ('the coupon') over the life of the stock and guarantee repayment of the nominal value of the stock (known as par value) on a given date (known as the redemption date). Interest is usually paid half yearly in two equal amounts.

Example

John purchases £100 nominal of 10% Treasury Stock 2008. He will receive an annual guaranteed income of £10 (10%) gross until 2008 when he will be paid £100.

Normally, when the Government issues the gilt, it does so at a discount to its par (nominal) value.

Example

Assume that in 1998 the Government issued 10% Treasury Stock 2007 at 94p. This means that for every 94p invested with it in 1998, the Government guarantees to pay £1 on redemption in 2007.

So when John purchased £100 nominal in 1998, it actually cost him £94. If he holds the stock until the Government redeems it at par, he will receive £100, ie, a profit of £6.

Once a person has purchased a gilt, he does not have to continue holding it until its redemption date. He can sell his holding to another investor via the stock market. The stock market determines how much a stock is worth on any given day prior to its redemption date. The seller pays commission to the stockbroker for arranging the sale.

Example

Having bought £100 nominal 10% Treasury Stock 2007 in 1998, John needed some money to pay for his holiday in 2004. He therefore decided to sell his stock. The market price on the day of sale is 96p. John will receive £96 less commission.

Tax

The profit made from selling or redeeming a gilt is exempt from CGT. All interest payments are liable to income tax.

Gilts can be bought and sold through a stockbroker. Interest on all gilts is paid net of lower rate tax meaning that non-tax payers have to reclaim the tax deducted.

Suitability

Higher-rate tax payers appreciate the CGT exemption but capital gains tend to be moderate and sales (as opposed to redemption) are subject to commission charges. A fixed rate of interest can be advantageous at times of falling interest rates but, conversely, unattractive if interest rates rise during the period of ownership for people on a limited income. A guaranteed rate of return can help budgeting. Gilts are often suitable investments for trustees where a beneficiary requires income.

Risk: low.

Income: medium/high.

Capital growth: if held to redemption, depends on whether bought for a premium or at a discount; otherwise prices vary according to the coupon and prevailing interest rates.

(7) Quoted shares

An investor may wish to invest money in a company listed (quoted) on the Stock Exchange. The aim is to receive an income and also real (net of inflation) capital growth from the investment. Income is received in the form of dividends paid by the company. The size of a dividend is decided by the company and is normally paid in two, not necessarily equal, instalments. The dividend can vary from year to year.

The capital value of the shares is determined by the market and is based on a number of factors including past and projected profits and takeover rumours.

Shares are, therefore, a speculative investment which may increase or decrease (sometimes spectacularly) in value, and whose value can change daily.

Example 1

In 2003, Taj bought 1,000 shares in A plc at £1 each (cost £1,000). In 2002 he received a dividend of £70 and in 2003 a dividend of £83 as the company made good profits, had good industrial relations and a secure market for its products.

Early in 2005, shares were listed as being worth £1.20 each. Taj sold his 1,000 shares for £1,200 less commission.

Example 2

In 2003, Victor bought 1,000 shares in B plc for £1 each (cost £1,000 plus commission and stamp duty). Soon afterwards the company suffered a strike by its workforce and introduced a new product which incorporated a faulty design and had to be withdrawn and compensation paid to people who had already bought the product. In 2005 the company borrowed money to enable it to pay shareholders a dividend. Victor received £50. Shortly afterwards the company went into liquidation. Victor's 1,000 shares are now worth £20.

Tax

All profits on the disposal of shares are liable to CGT. Any losses made on disposal can be set against gains in the same tax year and any excess carried forward to set against gains in future years.

Dividends are treated as if income tax at 10% has been paid. This credit is irrecoverable. No further liability arises if the recipient is a basic rate tax payer, but higher-rate tax payers will have additional tax to pay at 32.5%.

Suitability

Because of the financial risks, shares should only be purchased by those who can afford to lose the money invested. In return for that risk, shares offer both income and capital gains opportunities but fairly substantial sums need to be invested in a 'portfolio of shares' (ie, several shareholdings in different companies) to produce significant gains.

Shares are often purchased by trustees and may form the bulk of trust investments. Risk: medium/high.

Income: low/medium.

Capital growth: medium/high.

(8) Investment trusts

Investment trusts are quoted companies whose assets consist solely of shares in other companies. The investment trust company may specialise in acquiring shares in companies in one particular sector of the market or it may own shares in a wide variety of companies. The advantage for the investor holding shares in the investment trust is that he can have an indirect interest in a number of companies with the investment management handled by professional managers: the investment trust.

The investment trust pays dividends and the value of investment trust is determined by the stock market.

Tax

Dividends paid on shares in investment trusts are taxed in the same way as dividends on other quoted shares.

When an investor disposes of his shares in an investment trust a liability to CGT can arise.

Suitability

Investment trusts are suitable for anybody, including trustees, who might reasonably consider investing in quoted shares and also smaller investors who lack the expertise to manage their own portfolio or for whom transaction costs on shares are high compared to their amount of investment. The risk of loss as compared with investment in individual companies may be reduced due to the spread of investment by the trust but an investment trust may have to be held for several years to realise much capital growth.

Risk: medium.

Income: medium.

Capital growth: medium/high.

(9) Unit trusts

Unit trusts provide a method of investing on the stock market for anybody who wishes to invest in a range of companies but lacks the time or expertise to manage his own share portfolio.

Unit trusts are offered by a number of banks and other institutions who employ investment managers. The managers charge an annual management fee for their expertise and there is also an initial 'setting-up' charge. The investor hands his investment money to the investment manager in return for a number of units. The value of the units is determined by the value of the shares in the companies in which the managers invest. The investment manager then uses the investor's money to buy shares in other companies. Different unit trusts invest in different types of company, for example, UK Gilt Unit Trust only invests in UK government securities; M&G Far Eastern Unit Trust invests only in companies quoted on stock exchanges of countries in the Far East (eg, Japan and Hong Kong).

An investor can sell his units back to the unit trust managers at any time. If the unit trust has performed well, the sale price should be greater than the price at which the investor purchased his units. Unit trusts have two prices: the bid price which is what an investor will receive if he sells his units, and the offer price which is the price at which the units can be purchased.

Example

Daisy decides to invest £1,100 in the Magic Unit Trust which invests in UK companies. On the day of her investment the bid price is £1 and the offer price £1.10. She receives 1,000 units.

Daisy must wait until the bid price of units in Magic Unit Trust increases to at least £1.10 before she sells in order to get back her full investment. The bid price must increase further for her to make a capital gain on her investment.

Unit trusts also pay dividends to investors.

Tax

From April 1999, dividends paid to unit holders are taxed in the same way as dividends on quoted shares.

Any profit made by an investor on the sale of his units is liable to CGT.

Suitability

Anybody including trustees wishing to invest in UK or overseas companies but without the time or expertise to manage their own portfolio should consider unit trusts. However, the initial costs mean that unit trusts are not suitable for short-term investment.

Risk: medium.

Income: low/medium.

Capital growth: medium/high.

Note: Open-ended investment companies (OEICs) are a more modern version of the unit trust. An OEIC has all the characteristics of a unit trust but uses the structure of a corporation as is commonly done in the rest of Europe and in the USA.

Like a unit trust, an OEIC is a collective investment pooling the resources of many investors. Both are open-ended and have to dispose of assets if here is a run on the fund.

Structurally OEICs are different from unit trusts. They are formed as limited liability companies. People invest in them through the purchase of shares but these are traded in the same way as unit trusts. The shares have a single price for buying and selling. The tax treatment of OEIC funds and their investors' proceeds is identical to that for unit trusts.

(10) Personal equity plans (PEPs)

A personal equity plan (PEP) provided a way of making a tax-free investment in shares. The scheme was introduced by the Government in 1987 as a way of encouraging investment in UK companies. Because they were tax free, a limit was placed on the amount which could be invested in a PEP each year. A maximum of £6,000 per annum per tax payer could be invested in a general PEP plus another £3,000 in a single company PEP (in the shares of a single company) making an overall limit of £9,000 per annum.

New PEPs cannot be started after 5 April 1999 when ISAs (see (21)) became available. Existing PEPs can continue to be held since ISAs were introduced and will have the same tax advantages.

Tax

To obtain any tax benefit from a PEP, the investment must be maintained for a minimum of one year plus one day.

The shares and unit trusts within the PEP will pay dividends in the usual way. Income tax deducted at source by the companies can be reclaimed by the PEP owner, and the dividends are not subject to basic or higher rates of tax. For this reason, high-income shares (instead of capital growth) are often put into a PEP.

Any profits made on sales by the investment managers within the PEP will not be subject to CGT. When an investor withdraws his money from a PEP, any increase in value over the original investment is also free of CGT.

Suitability

PEPs were suitable for anyone considering diversifying their investments by investing in the stock market and, because of the tax advantages, were particularly attractive to higher-rate income tax payers.

PEPs are seen as a medium- to long-term investment which have to be held for more than one year to obtain the tax breaks.

Risk: medium/high.

Income: medium/high.

Capital growth: medium/high.

(11) Insurance bonds

Usually known as 'investment bonds' or 'single premium bonds', insurance bonds are single premium (one off capital payment, not the more usual regular insurance premiums) non-qualifying policies (ie, not satisfying Income and Corporation Taxes Act 1988, s 267 and so attracting tax at maturity). The bonds are normally 'unit linked' with-profit policies so that bonuses are added to the value of the units by the life company.

Income and capital are retained within the bond. Withdrawals up to 5% of the premiums paid can be taken tax free for the first 20 years of the bond.

Tax

No tax is payable by the investor during the life of the bond providing withdrawals do not exceed 5%. Gains arising on maturity of the bond are subject to higher-rate tax (as non-qualifying policies) but not to starting or basic rate tax.

Suitability

These bonds are suitable for higher-rate tax payers with a lump sum to invest as there is no tax to pay during the life of the bond. The 5% tax free withdrawal represents the income entitlement from the investment. Ideally the bond should be planned to mature when the investor's tax rate has fallen below higher rate (so as to avoid income tax), for example, the bond could mature following retirement when income is less.

Risk: medium.

Income: low (max 5%). Capital growth: medium/high.

(12) Guaranteed bonds

These are single premium non-qualifying life policies which last for a fixed period. Guaranteed income bonds guarantee income at fixed rates, and guaranteed growth bonds guarantee a fixed return when the bond ends.

Tax

As non-qualifying life policies, there is no basic rate liability but higher rate tax may be payable.

Suitability

Both bonds may be suitable for basic rate tax payers (as only higher rate tax may be payable) with capital to invest.

Risk: low/medium.

Income: low/medium (none on guaranteed growth bonds). Capital growth: medium (income on guaranteed income bonds).

(13) Enterprise Investment Scheme (EIS relief)

A scheme introduced by the Finance Act 1994 to replace the existing Business Expansion Scheme.

Individuals with capital to invest (maximum £200,000 in any tax year) obtain income tax relief at 20% of the amount invested provided various qualifications are met for the next three years. Capital gains made on disposal are free of CGT.

Qualifying investments are shares in unquoted trading companies carrying on trading activity in the UK. UK resident tax payers may obtain the relief but they are not eligible if they are 'connected with' the company, for example, as an employee or paid director. Further, combined shareholdings of the investor and his 'associates' must not exceed 30% of the share capital.

Example

£50,000 is invested in EIS shares in January 1998 (1997/98).

(a)   The initial investment – attracts 20% relief, so that the effective cost of the shares is £40,000.

(b)   If shares are sold more than three years later – any gain is free of CGT.

Because of the generous nature of the relief, and in an attempt to restrict its abuse, there are many detailed conditions in the Finance Act 1994, Sch 15.

Suitability

Investors with substantial capital to invest in unquoted trading companies with which they are not connected. Although income tax relief at 20% is available on the investment, dividends received will attract income tax. Generally, it should be remembered the company's articles of association and questions of marketability of the shares may make it difficult to find a buyer for the shares. The danger is getting 'locked into' the investment – or perhaps only being able to sell at a reduced price.

Risk: medium/high.

Income: possibly none, depending on whether the company pays dividends.

Capital growth: medium/high (but marketability may make sale difficult).

(14) Offshore funds

These funds are managed by companies registered outside the UK tax and regulatory system under the Financial Services Act 1986 in places such as the Channel Islands and the Isle of Man.

Funds actively marketed in the UK (being approved by the Securities and Investments Board (now the Financial Services Authority)) are either Distributor Funds (ie, a fund which pays dividends equivalent to 85% of its income) or Accumulator Funds (where gross income is retained within the fund to increase its value).

Tax

Dividends from Distributor Funds are paid gross but are taxable on receipt into the UK. Income and capital gains of Accumulator Funds are subject to tax on sale of the investment and rates then prevailing.

Suitability

These funds are similar to UK unit and investment trusts and so are suitable for anyone with capital to invest. Distributor Funds (paid gross) may be particularly suited to non-tax payers. Accumulator Funds are more likely to be attractive to higher-rate tax payers who can afford to retain their investment offshore until after retirement when their tax rates are lower.

Risk: medium/high.

Income: medium/high.

Capital growth: medium/high.

(15) Pensions

Pension schemes are a way of saving for old age, so providing an income after retirement.

The main categories of scheme include State pensions, occupational pensions for employees, and personal pension schemes.

The State scheme

The State scheme is funded by the self-employed, employees and employers paying national insurance (NI) contributions. The scheme has two parts: a compulsory contribution and an additional voluntary state pension. Up to April 2002, the additional state pension was called the State Earnings-Related Pension Scheme (SERPS). SERPS was based on the employee's record of National Insurance contributions and level of earnings as an employee. It was possible for employers and employees to 'contract-out' and was not available to the self-employed.

All employers, employees and the self-employed must contribute to the compulsory part of the scheme. Provided a person has made sufficient contributions during his or her working life, he or she will currently receive the old age pension at 60 (for women) or 65 (for men).

The additional SERPS pension is paid by the State if employer and employee have paid extra NI contributions. Contributions are based on the employee's annual earnings and there is no income tax relief for the employee's contributions. The pension will currently be paid at 60 for a woman, and 65 for a man. It is possible to 'contract out' of SERPS. In this case, a lower level of NI contributions is payable but only the old age pension will be received after retirement. Because of the costs involved in operating SERPS the Government has actively encouraged 'contracting out'.

On 6 April 2002, the Government reformed SERPS and replaced it with the State Second Pension. Any SERPS entitlement already built up is protected. The State Second Pension provides a more generous additional state pension for employees earning up to £24,600 with most help going to those on the lowest earnings (up to around £10,800). It also assists certain carers and people with long-term illness or disability whose working lives have been interrupted or shortened.

Occupational pension schemes

These are often called company pension schemes but apply equally to those employed by partnerships and other non-corporate entities. The scheme must be offered by any employer who wishes to contract out of SERPS and may be contributory or non-contributory.

A non-contributory scheme is one where only the employer pays into the scheme to provide his employees with appropriate pension benefits on retirement. Such payments by the employer are not treated as an emolument of the employee for his income tax purposes and are based on a percentage of the employee's earnings.

In a contributory scheme, both the employer and employee contribute. Again, the employer's contributions are based on a percentage of the employee's annual earnings and do not count as emoluments. The employee's contributions are an agreed minimum percentage of earnings. He may also pay additional voluntary contributions (AVCs) into the scheme or free standing AVCs (FSAVCs) into a separately run scheme. An employee may obtain tax relief only to the extent that his total contributions do not exceed the prescribed limit. The current limit for contributions is 15% of earnings. However, earnings over £105,600 (2005/06) (the earnings limit) are ignored.

All contributions and AVCs are paid into a fund which is invested by the trustees of the pension scheme with the aim of increasing the value of the fund.

There are two main types of scheme:

(a)   Salary related schemes (also known as 'defined benefit' schemes). The pension the employee gets is based on the number of years employed by the scheme provider and the level of earnings (usually at the date of retirement or the date when the employee leaves).

(b)   Money purchase schemes (also known as 'defined contribution' schemes). The employee's contributions (together with any provided by the employer) are invested. The final pension is based on the amount invested and how well the investments have performed. The money is used to purchase an annuity.

Businesses are increasingly closing their salary schemes and turning to money purchase schemes which are cheaper to provide.

On retirement, an employee will receive either an annual pension based on the amount of his final salary or a cash lump sum and a smaller annual pension.

Legislation controls the maximum amount of pension and lump sum which can be received.

Where an employee dies before retirement age, a lump sum based on contributions made to the scheme may be payable to the employee's dependants. Having started to receive a pension, all rights to it ceases on the employee's death. However, an employee can elect to receive a smaller pension than he would normally be entitled to with the guarantee that, on his death, the pension will continue to be paid to his widow for the remainder of her life.

Tax

If the scheme is 'exempt approved' under ICTA 1988, s 612 (which most occupational pension schemes will be – there are other special rules governing unapproved occupational pension schemes), it enjoys a number of valuable tax concessions:

(a)   as stated earlier, the employer's contributions will not be taxed as a benefit in kind as part of the employee's emoluments;

(b)   the employer's annual contributions can be deducted before tax is calculated;

(c)   the employee can obtain tax relief on his contributions up to 15% of remuneration. For the year 2005/06 the 'earnings limit' for this purpose is £105,600.

Example

An employee earning £100,000 per annum can make contributions, ie ordinary contributions, AVCs and FSAVCs of £15,840 (15% × £105,600) and obtain tax relief at his highest rate by deducting this amount from his emoluments for Sch E purposes.

(d)   On retirement the maximum pension is two thirds of the earnings limit of £105,600 (2005/06). If pensionable employment is less than 40 years the amount of the pension will be reduced.

Example

If the employee in the previous example is earning £125,000 per annum at retirement and has put in 40 years' service, his maximum pension will be two thirds of £105,600, ie £70,400 per annum.

(e)   Instead of taking a full pension, the employee can commute part of his entitlement for a tax-free cash sum. Conventional wisdom is that the tax-free cash be taken and invested to produce further income in retirement. Again the earnings limit applies. The maximum which can be taken in this way is 1.5 × final salary subject to the earnings limit.

Example

For the employee in the previous example the maximum tax-free lump sum is 1.5 × £105,600 = £158,400. He would also be entitled to a reduced pension (taxable under Sch E).

(f)   Any payment made to the employee's dependants on his death will not be charged to IHT provided the trustees of the pension scheme have the discretion to choose who should benefit.

(g)   The pension fund builds up free of tax, ie, the trustees do not pay income tax on income received from investment of the contributions; nor do they pay CGT on disposal of investments.

Suitability

An occupational pension scheme is suitable for any employee in paid employment. The ultimate pension benefits are likely to be significantly better than benefits paid by the State. There is, however, no obligation on an employer to set up such a scheme, nor can the employer require an employee to become a member of the scheme, ie, he can 'opt out' in favour of a personal pension should he prefer.

Self-employed pension schemes

These schemes are available to the self-employed and also employees who either do not wish to join their employer's occupational pension scheme or whose employers do not provide an occupational pension scheme.

An individual taking out a scheme for the first time is now limited to a personal pension but until 1988 pension provision was made through retirement annuity contracts. Although it is no longer possible to buy new retirement annuity contracts, it is still possible for contributions to be made to contracts taken out before 1988 and most people who have existing retirement annuity contracts continue to pay into them in preference to acquiring a new personal pension because the various maximum limits are often more favourable.

Personal pensions

Contributions are paid to the pension fund company – usually one of the life assurance companies – which invests them to provide a cash lump sum and/or an annual income and annuity, for the individual when he reaches retirement age. The pension can start at any time between the ages of 50 and 75 years.

Contributions are limited to a percentage of the individual's 'net relevant earnings' (earned income less certain deductions) in the tax year. Once again, the earnings limit of £105,600 (2005/06) applies so that earnings over this amount are ignored. The percentage which can be invested increases with the age of the individual.

Age	Contribution %
Up to 36	17.5
36–45	20.0
46–50	25.0
51–55	30.0
56–60	35.0
61 and over	40.0

Example

An individual aged 50 can pay a maximum contribution attracting tax relief of 25% of £105,600, ie, £26,400.

Individuals, especially when first contributing to a personal pension, may not be able to afford the full permitted contribution each year. In such cases, the contributions shortfall can be carried forward as 'unused contributions' for up to six tax years.

On retirement, the individual can choose to receive an annuity, ie, a pension for life or a reduced annuity plus a tax-free lump sum. This lump sum is calculated as a percentage of the total value of the fund available to the individual.

Tax

Contributions up to the limit attract tax relief at the individual's highest rate. For employed persons, relief at basic rate is obtained by paying the contribution net of basic rate tax. The pension company recovers an equivalent amount from the Revenue. Higher rate relief is obtained through the employee's tax return. The self-employed pay contributions in full and obtain relief by making a claim in their tax return after the income tax year in which the contributions were paid.

The lump sum is tax free. The annuity is taxed as income.

If the individual dies before retirement, the pension company will pay out a lump sum calculated in accordance with the scheme. To avoid this sum forming part of the individual's estate on death, and so chargeable to IHT, death benefits should be settled during the individual's life on, usually, discretionary trusts for the family and dependants.

Suitability

A personal pension is suitable for all self-employed people and those employees who cannot or do not wish to be part of an occupational scheme.

Occupational and personal pensions – summary

Risk: low/medium (trustees hold the funds but investment may be in gilts and/or equities).

Income: low (depending on investment of contributions). Capital growth: medium (due to tax-free nature of the funds).

Stakeholder pensions

In essence these are personal pension schemes which meet the following Government imposed minimum standards:

(a)   annual charges must not exceed 1%;

(b)   there must be no initial charges or exit penalties;

(c)   the scheme must accept contributions of as little as £20 gross;

(d)   the rules must allow for contributions to be stopped, started and changed without penalties;

(e)   scheme managers must be authorised by the FSA or have trustees.

Many providers are offering charges which are substantially lower than 1% (sometimes as little as 0.4%).

For every £1 paid in, the Revenue will pay an extra 28p even if the contributor does not normally pay tax. Anyone can contribute although for persons without earnings, the limit for contributions is £3,600 gross (this means the contributor will pay in £2,808 which with the Revenue's contribution will amount to £3,600). Parents can pay into schemes for their children as can non-earning individuals provided they have sufficient funds.

As from October 2001, most employers will have to offer a stakeholder scheme unless:

(a)   they offer a group pension plan without exit charges, which employees who have been employed for three months can join and into which the employer either pays a contribution of 3%, or will match an employee's contribution of 3%; or

(b)   it offers an occupational scheme which individuals can join within one year of starting employment.

Employees in occupational pension schemes will probably wish to remain. However, the newly employed may find joining a stakeholder scheme more beneficial than an occupational scheme because of its flexibility. Employees can take the pension with them when they change jobs.

(16) Life assurance (insurance)

There are a number of life assurance products only the most common types of which are dealt with below.

Whole life assurance (whole of life assurance)

In return for a regular monthly or annual premium an assurance company will contract to pay out an agreed fixed sum on the death of the life assured.

Most assurance companies refuse to insure the life of anybody over the age of 80 years and the older a person when they enter into a contract, the more expensive the premium. For example, a person aged 30 years might insure his life for a given sum for £50 per annum while a person aged 60 years might pay £100 per annum for the same level of life cover.

Whole life policies can be written on single lives and also on joint lives. In the latter case, two lives are insured and the assurance company will either pay out on the first death or on the death of the survivor of the joint lives depending on the policy purchased. It is also possible for a person to insure a second person's life provided that he has an insurable interest in the second life. The fixed sum is paid out to the proposer on the death of the life assured.

If the policy is non-profit only a specified sum is payable on death. If it is with profit or unit linked there is an investment element. The sum assured will be paid with bonuses (with profit) or accumulated units (unit linked).

Tax

Premiums may be paid out of capital or income. No income tax relief is available for premiums paid.

On the death of the life assured, the assured sum forms part of his estate and will be liable to IHT unless the policy has been written in trust or assigned.

Suitability

Whole life assurance is suitable for anyone who wishes to provide a lump sum for his family or dependants on his death.

This may be to provide another asset, or to provide cash with which to meet debts such as an IHT bill or a mortgage or to provide funds to buy a deceased partner's share or the shares of a deceased shareholder/director whose shares might have to be sold to an outsider if the other members cannot afford to buy them.

It is not suitable for anybody wishing to save to provide a benefit for themselves.

Term assurance

In return for the payment of a regular premium the assurance company will pay out an agreed sum if the life assured dies within a fixed period of time from the purchase of the assurance policy. The term assurance provides protection only. There is no investment element.

If the proposer ceases to pay the premiums during the agreed term or the life assured survives the term, the policy comes to an end. It has no surrender value.

Tax

The tax treatment is the same as for whole life assurance.

Suitability

Term assurance is suitable for anyone, including trustees who needs to provide a lump sum with which to pay IHT which would become chargeable on a lifetime transfer if the transferor died within seven years of the transfer.

It may also be used by an individual to cover a fixed-term commitment such as a mortgage or school fees.

It is not suitable for anyone aiming to provide a benefit for himself.

Endowment assurance

In return for regular premiums, the assurance company contracts to pay the sum assured on the earlier of a given date or the death of the life assured. In these cases, there is clearly the possibility of personal enjoyment of the policy proceeds by the life assured.

The policy may be with profits or unit linked. It can be written on single or joint lives. There is an investment element.

Endowment policies provide protection as well as a sum payable on the maturity date for the policy or the earlier death of the life assured. These policies are frequently used in planning for the repayment of mortgages (where they are linked to the date for repayment of the mortgage) or school fees (where they are planned to mature at a time appropriate to payment of the fees).

Tax

Policies are normally for a minimum period of 10 years so that as 'qualifying policies' under ICTA 1988, s 267 the sum payable on maturity is tax free. If the life assured survives to the given date, he will receive the assured lump sum free of all taxes. If the payment is made on death, the sum forms part of the estate of the assured.

Suitability

Endowment assurance is suitable for any tax payer looking to build up a tax-free lump sum over a long period either for his own benefit or to meet commitments such as the repayment of a mortgage or the payment of school fees.

Keyman assurance

Where a person is a 'key' man or woman within an organisation his premature death will affect the profitability of the company or partnership. The company or partnership may, therefore, insure that person's life so that the company or partnership receives a lump sum on the death of the 'key' man. The life assurance may be a whole life, term or endowment policy.

(17) Permanent health insurance (PHI)

A person who is in employment anticipates receiving a regular wage or salary or share of partnership profits in return for working. If that person becomes disabled and, therefore, unable to continue working, he will lose this source of income. He can, therefore, insure himself by paying an annual premium so that if he is no longer able to work, the insurance policy will provide him with regular sums of money for a stated period or up to a stated age. There is a limit on the annual amount which can be received from PHI.

Payment may not commence immediately after the disability arises as the policyholder can defer claiming benefit, for example, for three months. The longer the agreed period of deferral, the lower the annual premium.

An employer often provides PHI through group arrangements. Contributions paid are generally deductible as trading expenses.

Tax

An individual does not receive tax relief on the premiums paid.

Once benefits are claimed they are taxable as income.

Suitability

Permanent health insurance is suitable for anyone in work who has dependants, but cover may not be available for a person who is already in poor health when he applies to purchase the insurance cover. It is particularly suitable for the self-employed for whom replacement of income when permanently disabled will be essential. The effect on the business through absence of the 'owner' may cause it to fold.

(18) Annuities

In return for the investment of a capital lump sum, a life company will guarantee a regular amount of income (annuity) to the investor – purchased life annuity. The annuity can be paid annually, quarterly or monthly as the investor wishes. A good rate of return can be obtained if the annuity is purchased when interest rates are high. But the cost of the annuity depends partly on the age of the annuitant and may not be worthwhile until he reaches 70 years of age. On the death of the annuitant or expiry of the agreed term, usually no capital is returnable.

Tax

The Revenue regards purchased life annuity payments as being partly income and partly a return of the original capital invested (ICTA 1988, s 656). Only the income element is subject to income tax at the annuitant's income tax rates and is received net of lower rate tax. Some or all of this tax can be recovered by non and lower rate tax payers.

No tax is payable on the capital element.

Suitability

Annuities are suitable for anyone who needs a guaranteed income or income for life and who can afford to spend capital. The main disadvantages are that the real value of the income may be eroded by inflation and that once purchased there is no ability to surrender the annuity or recover the initial capital investment. Annuities may be suitable for elderly clients, or younger clients with children wishing to make provision for school fees.

Risk: low.

Income: medium/high (depending on age at purchase).

Capital growth: nil.

(19) School fee plans

There are a number of commercial plans available or parents can create their own provision. Those listed below are intended to give an indication of how some of these plans work. The deciding factor as to the type of plan is often whether the parent can afford a 'one off' lump sum payment out of capital, or whether the cost of the plan has to be met from income.

Funding from income

Life assurance schemes

Certain qualifying with profits or endowment life assurance policies enable the proceeds to be received completely tax free provided that premiums are payable for at least 10 years. The idea is that a series of such policies are purchased each maturing in consecutive years to provide annual funds for annual school fees.

Deferred annuities

Monthly premiums are paid to purchase an annuity equivalent to the level of fees whose payment is deferred until the fees are needed. The premium payments need not commence until shortly before school fees start to become due and continue until the last term for which fees are required.

The income element of the annuity will be subject to income tax at the parent's highest marginal rate.

Funding from capital

Compounding

Many schools offer their own fee plan. In return for a guaranteed level of fees parents pay a lump sum to the school in advance of the child starting at that school.

This can result in a substantial saving to the parents but care should be taken to check what happens to the lump sum if the child does not subsequently start at that school or leaves before the anticipated year.

There should be no tax consequences.

Educational trusts

There are a number of charitable educational trusts which, in return for an administration fee, invest the parents' lump sum in the purchase of an annuity payable termly to meet the fees. The annuity can start immediately or be deferred. The longer the deferral (eg, the plan is established on the birth of a child, to commence when he is seven years old) the greater the value of the annuity. Any over-provision against the school fees can be paid to the parent.

Any annuity paid to the school is unlikely to be subject to income tax, but any surplus paid to the parent will suffer income tax at his rate(s) on the income element.

Gilt-edged securities

A lump sum can be invested in gilts with a range of redemption dates to mature over the school life of the child. If suitable redemption dates are not available, long-dated gifts can be purchased and holdings sold as and when school fees become due.

There is no CGT to pay on any gains made on the redemption or sale of gilts.

(20) Mortgages

Mortgages cannot be described as investments from the point of view of the borrower. Frequently, but not necessarily, they are linked to insurance policies which are investments. The insurance policy is designed to repay the mortgage debt at the end of the term or on the earlier death of the borrower so that the property on which it is secured can pass free of mortgage to the beneficiary under the borrower's will or intestacy.

There are many types of mortgage. The borrower must be advised to 'shop around' to find the type which best suits his particular circumstances. This is particularly true for the first-time buyer needing a large mortgage (or large as a proportion of the purchase price for the house).

In principle, there are two types of mortgage: the repayment mortgage and the interest only mortgage.

Repayment mortgages

Here, the monthly repayment is partly interest and partly a repayment of the capital sum outstanding. In the early years, the payments are largely of interest but include some capital repayment. As the capital is repaid, the proportion of interest in the monthly repayment reduces and the capital proportion increases.

To cover the possibility of the borrower dying before the capital is repaid at the end of the mortgage term, the lender will require a mortgage protection policy. A decreasing term assurance (with no investment element) is usual. It is decreasing in that the cover provided equates to the reducing capital sum due to the lender.

(Until April 2000, tax relief was available (within limits) on the interest paid to the lender in each year. The amount of this interest was certified to the Inland Revenue by the lender for tax relief purposes.)

Interest only mortgages

In these cases, the lender does not expect monthly repayment of capital but he will require interest on the amount borrowed. The capital remains due at the end of the mortgage term. Arrangements should be made by the borrower to fund this liability (sometimes the lender will only lend if adequate arrangements have been put in place). There are two main types of interest only mortgages.

The 'endowment mortgage'

This is a misleading phrase for a commonly met arrangement. There are two transactions – the mortgage and the endowment policy. The premiums on the policy attract no tax relief and represent a further outlay by the borrower but he is, at least, acquiring a valuable asset.

The policy is assigned to the lender. At the end of the mortgage the policy will mature. After the mortgage debt is discharged, any balance will be paid to the borrower. If the policy was a 'with profits' policy, there will often be a sizeable sum due to the borrower. In this way, the policy may prove to be a good investment.

Some 'with profit' policies assume that when bonuses are added at the end of the term, the sum assured will then be the equivalent of the sum borrowed. In such cases, the premium payable on the policy may be reduced because the sum assured is reduced. This will be attractive to many borrowers but increases the risk that the policy may not be sufficient to pay off the sum borrowed when it matures.

A 'pension mortgage'

This phrase is also misleading. Again there are two transactions – the mortgage and the pension. The assumption is that the repayment of the mortgage at the end of the term is funded from the 'tax free' lump sum payable from a personal pension (see (**15**)).

While superficially very attractive (bearing in mind the favourable tax position of a personal pension), it must be remembered that the real purpose of the pension is to provide an income for retirement (and not a lump sum to repay a mortgage debt).

(21) Individual Savings Accounts (ISAs)

Individual Savings Accounts (ISAs) became available from April 1999 to replace TESSAs (see (**3**) and PEPs (**10**)) from that date. UK resident and ordinarily resident adult savers can subscribe to either a maxi-ISA or up to two mini-ISAs each year.

Maxi-ISA

Until 5 April 2010, £7,000 may be invested annually in a maxi-ISA. Of this, up to £3,000 may be in cash (on deposit) and the rest may be in a mixture of investments (equities and certain life assurance policies). Alternatively, less (or none) may be in cash and the rest (or the whole) in investments.

Many maxi-ISAs contain only investments and are thus seen as a direct replacement for PEPs.

Mini-ISA

Instead of one maxi-ISA, investors may have up to one of each of two mini-ISAs.

Until 5 April 2010, the maximum amounts which can be invested annually are:

(a)   cash: £3,000; or

(b)   investments: £4,000.

If an investor exceeds the annual limit, or invests in a maxi- as well as a mini-ISA, the Revenue has power to close ineligible investments and to require repayment of any tax advantages gained.

Savings are exempt from income tax and CGT. Exceptionally, the 10% tax credit in respect of dividends could be reclaimed until April 2004.

There is no restriction on withdrawals (and no loss of tax relief if withdrawals are made), but once the maximum subscription for a year is made, it is not possible to top up to the maximum again following withdrawals.

A husband and wife can each have their own investments in ISAs. There is no minimum investment, nor is there any overall lifetime limit.

Appendix 3 – Enduring Power of Attorney

SCHEDULE   Regulations 2 and 3

ENDURING POWER OF ATTORNEY

Part A: About using this form

1. You may choose one attorney or more than one. If you choose one attorney then you must delete everything between the square brackets on the first page of the form. If you choose more than one, you must decide whether they are able to act:
- Jointly (that is, they must all act together and cannot act separately) or
- Jointly and severally (that is, they can all act together but they can also act separately if they wish).

On the first page of the form, show what you have decided by crossing out one of the alternatives.

2. If you give your attorney(s) general power in relation to all your property and affairs, it means that they will be able to deal with your money or property and may be able to sell your house.

3. If you don't want your attorney(s) to have such wide powers, you can include any restrictions you like. For example, you can include a restriction that your attorney(s) must not act on your behalf until they have reason to believe that you are becoming mentally incapable; or a restriction as to what your attorney(s) may do. Any restrictions you choose must be written or typed where indicated on the second page of the form.

4. If you are a trustee (and please remember that co-ownership of a home involves trusteeship), you should seek legal advice if you want your attorney(s) to act as a trustee on your behalf.

5. Unless you put in a restriction preventing it your attorney(s) will be able to use any of your money or property to make any provision which you yourself might be expected to make for their own needs or the needs of other people. Your attorney(s) will also be able to use your money to make gifts, but only for reasonable amounts in relation to the value of your money and property.

6. Your attorney(s) can recover the out-of-pocket expenses of acting as your attorney(s). If your attorney(s) are professional people, for example solicitors or accountants, they may be able to charge for their professional services as well. You may wish to provide expressly for remuneration of your attorney(s) (although if they are trustees they may not be allowed to accept it).

7. If your attorney(s) have reason to believe that you have become or are becoming mentally incapable of managing your affairs, your attorney(s) will have to apply to the Court of Protection for registration of this power.

8. Before applying to the Court of Protection for registration of this power, your attorney(s) must give written notice that that is what they are going to do, to you and your nearest relatives as defined in the Enduring Powers of Attorney Act 1985. You or your relatives will be able to object if you or they disagree with registration.

9. This is a simplified explanation of what the Enduring Powers of Attorney Act 1985 and the Rules and Regulations say. If you need more guidance, you or your advisers will need to look at the Act itself and the Rules and Regulations. The Rules are the Court of Protection (Enduring Powers of Attorney) Rules 1986 (Statutory Instrument 1986 No. 127). The Regulations are the Enduring Powers of Attorney (Prescribed Form) Regulations 1990 (Statutory Instrument 1990 No. 1376).

10. Note to Attorney(s)

After the power has been registered you should notify the Court of Protection if the donor dies or recovers.

11. Note to Donor

Some of these explanatory notes may not apply to the form you are using if it has already been adapted to suit your particular requirements.

YOU CAN CANCEL THIS POWER AT ANY TIME BEFORE IT HAS TO BE REGISTERED

Part B: To be completed by the 'donor' (the person appointing the attorney(s))

Don't sign this form unless you understand what it means

Please read the notes in the margin which follow and which are part of the form itself.

Donor's name and address

Donor's date of birth

See note 1 on the front of this form. If you are appointing only one attorney you should cross out everything between the square brackets. If appointing more than two attorneys please give the additional name(s) on an attached sheet.

I _____

of _____

born on _____

appoint _____

of _____

● [and _____

   of _____

Cross out the one which does not apply (see note 1 on the front of this form).

● jointly
● jointly and severally]

to be my attorney(s) for the purpose of the Enduring Powers of Attorney Act 1985

Cross out the one which does not apply (see note 2 on the front of this form). Add any additional powers.

● with general authority to act on my behalf
● with authority to do the following on my behalf:

If you don't want the attorney(s) to have general power, you must give details here of what authority you are giving the attorney(s).

Cross out the one which does not apply.

in relation to
● all my property and affairs:
● the following property and affairs:

Please read the notes in the margin which follow and which are part of the form itself.

If there are restrictions or conditions, insert them here; if not, cross out these words if you wish (see note 3 on the front of this form).

● subject to the following restrictions and conditions

If this form is being signed at your direction:—
● the person signing must not be an attorney or any witness (to Parts B or C).
● you must add a statement that this form has been signed at your direction.
● a second witness is necessary (please see below).

I intend that this power shall continue even if I become mentally incapable.

I have read or have had read to me the notes in Part A which are part of, and explain, this form.

Your signature (or mark).

Signed by me as a deed _____
and delivered

Date.

on _____

Someone must witness your signature
Signature of witness.

in the presence of _____
Full name of witness _____

Your attorney(s) cannot be your witness. It is not advisable for your husband or wife to be your witness.

Address of witness _____
_____
_____

A second witness is only necessary if this form is not being signed by you personally but at your direction (for example, if a physical disability prevents you from signing).

Signature of second witness.

in the presence of _____
Full name of witness _____

Address of witness _____
_____
_____

Part C: To be completed by the attorney(s)

Note: 1   This form may be adapted to provide for execution by a corporation

2.   If there is more than one attorney additional sheets in the form as shown below must be added to this Part C

Please read the notes in the margin which follow and which are part of the form itself.

Don't sign this form before the donor has signed Part B or if, in your opinion, the donor was already mentally incapable at the time of signing Part B.

I understand that I have a duty to apply to the Court for the registration of this form under the Enduring Powers of Attorney Act 1985 when the donor is becoming or has become mentally incapable.

If this form is being signed at your direction:—
● the person signing must not be an attorney or any witness (to Parts B or C).
● you must add a statement that this form has been signed at your direction.
● a second witness is necessary (please see below).

I also understand my limited power to use the donor's property to benefit persons other than the donor.

I am not a minor.

Signature (or mark) of attorney.

Signed by me as a deed and delivered

Date.

on _____

Signature of witness.

The attorney must sign the form and his signature must be witnessed. The donor may not be the witness and one attorney may not witness the signature of the other.

in the presence of _____

Full name of witness _____

Address of witness _____

_____

_____

A second witness is only necessary if this form is not being signed by you personally but at your direction (for example, if a physical disability prevents you from signing).

Signature of second witness.

in the presence of _____

Full name of witness _____

Address of witness _____

_____

_____

Appendix 4 – Discretionary Settlement

Table of contents

SETTLEMENT

DATE: [   ]

PARTIES:

(1)   [   ] (the **'Settlor'**); and

(2)   [   ] (the **'Trustees'**).

RECITALS

(A)   The Settlor wishes to make this Settlement and has transferred or delivered to the Trustees or otherwise placed under their control the property specified in the Schedule. Further money, investments or other property may be paid or transferred to the Trustees by way of addition.

(B)   It is intended that this Settlement shall be irrevocable.

PART 1 – OPERATIVE PROVISIONS

1. Definitions and construction

In this Deed, where the context admits, the following definitions and rules of construction shall apply.

1.1   The **'Trust Fund'** shall mean:

(a)   the property specified in the Schedule;

(b)   all money, investments or other property paid or transferred by

any person to, or so as to be under the control of, and, in either case, accepted by the Trustees as additions;

(c)   all accumulations (if any) of income added to the Trust Fund; and

(d)   the money, investments and property from time to time representing the above.

1.2   The '**Trust Period**' shall mean the period ending on the earlier of:

   (a)   the last day of the period of 80 years from the date of this Deed, which period, and no other, shall be the applicable perpetuity period; and

   (b)   such date as the Trustees shall at any time specify by deed, not being a date earlier than the date of execution of such deed or later than a date previously specified.

1.3   The '**Accumulation Period**' shall mean the period of 21 years from the date of this Deed, or the Trust Period if shorter.

1.4   The '**Beneficiaries**' shall mean:

   (a)   the Settlor's children and remoter issue;

   (b)   the spouses, widows and widowers (whether or not such widows or widowers have remarried) of the Settlor's children and remoter issue;

   (c)   [   ];

   [(d)   Charities;] and

   [(e)]   such other objects or persons as are added under clause 3.

1.5   '**Charity**' shall mean any trust, foundation, company or other organisation whatever established only for purposes regarded as charitable under the law of England and Wales.

1.6   The expression '**the Trustees**' shall, where the context admits, include the trustees for the time being of this Trust.

1.7   References to the children, grandchildren and issue of any person shall include his children, grandchildren and remoter issue, whether legitimate, legitimated[, illegitimate] or adopted [but shall exclude any illegitimate person and his descendants].

1.8   Words denoting the singular shall include the plural and vice versa.

1.9   Words denoting any gender shall include both the other genders.

1.10   References to any statutory provision shall include any statutory modification to or re-enactment of such provision.

1.11   The table of contents and clause headings are included for reference only and shall not affect the interpretation of this Deed.

2. Power to receive additional property

The Trustees may, at any time during the Trust Period, accept additional money, investments or other property, of whatever nature and wherever situate, paid or transferred to them by the Settlor or any other person. Such additional money, investments or other property shall, subject to any contrary direction, be held upon the trusts and with and subject to the powers and provisions of this Deed.

3. Power to add Beneficiaries

3.1   The Settlor, or such person as the Settlor shall have nominated in writing, may, at any time during the Trust Period, add to the Beneficiaries such objects or persons or classes of objects or persons as the Settlor or such other person shall, subject to the application (if any) of the rule against perpetuities, determine.

3.2   Any such addition shall be made by deed:

   (a)   naming or describing the objects or persons or classes of objects or persons to be added; and

   (b)   specifying the date or event, not being earlier than the date of execution of the deed but before the end of the Trust Period, on the happening of which the addition shall take effect.

[3.3   This power shall not be exercised so as to add to the Beneficiaries either the Settlor or any person who shall previously have added property to the Trust Fund or the spouse for the time being of the Settlor or any such person.]

4. Discretionary trust of capital and income

4.1   The Trustees shall hold the capital and income of the Trust Fund upon trust for or for the benefit of such of the Beneficiaries, at such ages or times, in such shares, upon such trusts (which may include discretionary or protective powers or trusts) and in such manner generally as the Trustees shall in their discretion appoint. Any such appointment may include such powers and provisions for the maintenance, education or other benefit of the Beneficiaries or for the accumulation of income and such administrative powers and provisions as the Trustees think fit.

4.2   No exercise of the power conferred by sub-clause 4.1 shall invalidate any prior payment or application of all or any part of the capital or income of the Trust Fund under the trusts of this Deed or made under any other power conferred by this Deed or by law.

4.3   Any trusts and powers created by an appointment under sub-clause 4.1 may be delegated to any extent to any person, whether or not including the Trustees or any of them.

[4.4   Notwithstanding clause [   ], the Trustees may not release or restrict this power during the Settlor's lifetime without his written consent.]

4.5   The exercise of the power of appointment conferred by sub-clause 4.1 shall:

(a)   be subject to the application, if any, of the rule against perpetuities and the law concerning excessive accumulations of income; [and]

(b)   be by deed, revocable during the Trust Period or irrevocable, executed during the Trust Period [; and

(c)   be subject to the written consent of the Settlor during his lifetime].

5. Income trusts in default of appointment

The provisions of this clause shall apply during the Trust Period until, subject to and in default of any appointment under sub-clause 4.1.

5.1   The Trustees shall pay or apply the income of the Trust Fund to or for the benefit of such of the Beneficiaries as shall for the time being be in existence, in such shares and in such manner generally as the Trustees shall in their discretion from time to time think fit.

5.2   Notwithstanding the provisions of sub-clause 5.1, the Trustees may at any time during the Accumulation Period in their discretion accumulate the income by investing it in any investments authorised by this Deed or by law and, subject to sub-clause 5.3, shall hold such accumulations as an accretion to capital.

5.3   The Trustees may apply the whole or any part of the income accumulated under sub-clause 5.2 as if it were income arising in the then current year.

6. Power to apply capital for Beneficiaries

The provisions of this clause shall apply during the Trust Period notwithstanding the provisions of clause 5 but subject to any appointment made under sub-clause 4.1.

6.1   The Trustees may pay or apply the whole or any part of the capital of the Trust Fund to or for the benefit of all or such of the Beneficiaries, in such shares, and in such manner generally as the Trustees shall in their discretion think fit.

6.2   The Trustees may, subject to the application (if any) of the rule against perpetuities, pay or transfer any income or capital of the Trust Fund to the trustees of any other trust, wherever established or existing, under which any Beneficiary is interested (whether or not such Beneficiary is the only object or person interested or capable of benefiting under such other trust) if the Trustees in their discretion consider such payment or transfer to be for the benefit of such Beneficiary.

7. Trusts in default of appointment

From and after the expiration of the Trust Period, and subject to any appointment made under sub-clause 4.1, the Trustees shall hold the capital and income of the Trust Fund upon trust absolutely for such of [ ] as shall then be living and, if more than one, in equal shares per stirpes, provided that no issue shall take whose parent is alive and so capable of taking.

8. Ultimate default trusts

Subject as above and if and so far as not wholly disposed of for any reason whatever by the above provisions, the capital and income of the Trust Fund shall be held upon trust for [ ] absolutely.

9. Administrative powers

The Trustees shall, in addition and without prejudice to all statutory powers, have the powers and immunities set out in Part 2 of this Deed. No power conferred on the Trustees shall be exercised so as to conflict with the beneficial provisions of this Deed.

10. Extended power of maintenance

The statutory provisions for maintenance and education shall apply but so that the power of maintenance shall be exercisable in the discretion of the Trustees and free from the obligation to apply part only of the income for maintenance where other income is available.

11. Extended power of advancement

The statutory provisions for advancement shall apply but so that the power of advancement shall extend to the whole, rather than one half, of the share or interest of the person for whose benefit the advancement is made.

12. Appointment of new trustees

12.1 During the lifetime of the Settlor the power of appointing new trustees shall be vested in the Settlor.

12.2 A person may not be appointed to be a trustee notwithstanding that such person is not resident in the United Kingdom. Remaining out of the United Kingdom for more than 12 months shall not be a ground for the removal of a trustee.

13. Proper law, forum and place of administration

13.1 The proper law of this Trust shall be that of England and Wales. All rights under this Deed and its construction and effect shall be subject to the jurisdiction of, and construed according to, the laws of England and Wales.

13.2 The courts of England and Wales shall be the forum for the administration of these trusts.

13.3 Notwithstanding the provisions of sub-clauses 13.1 and 13.2:

(a)   The Trustees shall have power, subject to the application (if any) of the rule against perpetuities, to carry on the general administration of these trusts in any jurisdiction in the world. This power shall be exercisable whether or not the law of such jurisdiction is for the time being the proper law of this Trust or the courts of such jurisdiction are for the time being the forum for the administration of these trusts, and whether or not the Trustees or any of them are for the time being resident or domiciled in, or otherwise connected with, such jurisdiction.

(b)   The Trustees may at any time declare in writing that, from the date of such declaration, the proper law of this Trust shall be that of any specified jurisdiction. No exercise of this power shall be effective unless the law of the jurisdiction specified is one under which this Trust remains irrevocable and all, or substantially all, of the trusts, powers and provisions contained in this Deed remain enforceable and capable of being exercised and so taking effect.

(c)   Following any exercise of the power contained in sub-clause 13.3(b), the Trustees shall, by deed, make such consequential alterations or additions to this Deed as they consider necessary or desirable to ensure that, so far as may be possible, the trusts, powers and provisions of this Deed shall be as valid and effective as they were immediately prior to such change.

(d)   The Trustees may, at any time, declare in writing that, from the date of such declaration, the forum for the administration of these trusts shall be the courts of any specified jurisdiction.]

14. Exclusion of Settlor and spouse

14.1   No discretion or power conferred on the Trustees or any other person by this Deed or by law shall be exercised, and no provision of this Deed shall operate directly or indirectly, so as to cause or permit any part of the capital or income of the Trust Fund to become in any way payable to or applicable for the benefit of the Settlor or any person who shall previously have added property to the Trust Fund or the spouse for the time being of the Settlor or any such person.

14.2   The provisions of sub-clause 14.1 shall not preclude the Settlor or any such person from exercising any statutory right to claim reimbursement from the Trustees for any income tax or capital gains tax paid by him in respect of income arising to the Trustees or capital gains realised or deemed or treated as realised by them.

14.3   Subject to sub-clause 14.2, the prohibition in this clause shall apply notwithstanding anything else contained or implied in this Deed.

15. Exclusion of Trusts of Land and Appointment of Trustees Act 1996, s 11(1)

Section 11 (trustees' duty to consult beneficiaries) of the Trusts of Land and Appointment of Trustees Act 1996 shall not apply to the trusts contained in this Deed.

PART 2 – ADMINISTRATIVE PROVISIONS

SCHEDULE
[The initial Trust Fund]

Signed as a deed and delivered   )

by [   ]   )

in the presence of:)

Appendix 5 – Accumulation and Maintenance Settlement

Table of contents

SETTLEMENT

DATE: [   ]

PARTIES:

(1) [   ] (the **'Settlor'**); and

(2) [   ] (the **'Trustees'**).

RECITALS

(A) The Settlor wishes to make this Settlement and has transferred or delivered to the Trustees or otherwise placed under their control the property specified in the Schedule. Further money, investments or other property may be paid or transferred to the Trustees by way of addition.

(B) It is intended that this Settlement shall be irrevocable.

PART 1 – OPERATIVE PROVISIONS

1. Definitions and construction

In this Deed, where the context admits, the following definitions and rules of construction shall apply.

1.1 The **'Trust Fund'** shall mean:

(a) the property specified in the Schedule;

(b) all money, investments or other property paid or transferred by any person to, or so as to be under the control of, and in either case, accepted by the Trustees as additions;

(c) all accumulations (if any) of income added to the Trust Fund; and

(d) the money, investments and property from time to time representing the above.

1.2   The **'Trust Period'** shall mean the period ending on the earlier of:

(a)   the last day of the period of 80 years from the date of this Deed, which period, and no other, shall be the applicable perpetuity period; and

(b)   such date as the Trustees shall at any time specify by deed, not being a date earlier than the date of execution of such deed or later than a date previously specified.

1.3   **'Primary Beneficiary'** shall mean:

(a)   the existing grandchildren of the Settlor, namely

[   ] who was born on [   ];

[   ] who was born on [   ];

[   ] who was born on [   ]; and

[   ] who was born on [   ]; and

(b)   every other grandchild of the 'Settlor' born after the date of this Deed and before the Closing Date.

1.4   **'Beneficiary'** shall mean any person actually or prospectively entitled to any share or interest in the capital or income of the Trust Fund.

1.5   The **'Closing Date'** shall mean whichever shall be the earlier of:

(a)   the date on which the first Primary Beneficiary to do so attains the age of 25; and

(b)   the date on which the Trust Period shall determine.

1.6   The **'Accumulation Period'** shall mean the period of 21 years from the date of this Deed, or the Trust Period if shorter.

1.7   **'Interest in possession'** shall have the meaning it has for the purposes of s 71 of the Inheritance Tax Act 1984 or any statutory modification or re-enactment of such section.

1.8   The expression **'the Trustees'** shall, where the context admits, include the trustees for the time being of this Trust.

1.9   References to the children, grandchildren and issue of any person shall include his children, grandchildren and remoter issue, whether legitimate, legitimated[, illegitimate] or adopted [, but shall exclude any illegitimate person and his descendants].

1.10 Words denoting the singular shall include the plural and vice versa.

1.11 Words denoting any gender shall include both the other genders.

1.12 References to any statutory provision shall include any statutory modification to or re-enactment of such provision.

1.13 The table of contents and clause headings are included for reference only and shall not affect the interpretation of this Deed.

2. Power to receive additional property

The Trustees may, at any time during the Trust Period, accept additional money, investments or other property, of whatever nature and wherever situate, paid or transferred to them by the Settlor or any other person. Such additional money, investment or other property shall, subject to any contrary direction, be held upon the trusts and with and subject to the powers and provisions of this Deed.

3. Principal trusts

3.1   The Trust Fund shall be held upon trust for such of the Primary Beneficiaries as:

(a)   attain the age of 25 before the end of the Trust Period; or

(b)   are living and under that age at the end of the Trust Period

and, if more than one, in equal shares absolutely.

3.2   The provisions of sub-clauses 3.3 and clause 4 shall apply to the share of the Trust Fund to which any of the Primary Beneficiaries is or may become entitled under sub-clause 3.1. In those provisions, such share is called the '**Share**' and that one of the Primary Beneficiaries who is primarily interested in the Share is called the '**Primary Beneficiary**'.

3.3   If any Primary Beneficiary shall die during the Trust Period, under the age of 25 and leaving children who survive him, the Share of such Primary Beneficiary shall be held upon trust for such of the children of the Primary Beneficiary as attain the age of 25 before the end of the Trust Period, or are living and under that age at the end of the Trust Period, and, if more than one, in equal shares absolutely.

3.4   No Primary Beneficiary shall be entitled to any share of the Trust Fund without bringing any assets or interest advanced to him or paid or applied for his benefit (in exercise of any of the powers conferred by sub-clause 4.2 or clause 9) into account in such manner as the Trustees shall in their discretion determine with a view to achieving an equitable division of the unadvanced part of the Trust Fund.

4. Trusts for Primary Beneficiaries under 25

This clause shall apply, during the Trust Period, in respect of the Share of any Primary Beneficiary who is living and under the age of 25.

4.1   During the Accumulation Period the Trustees may pay or apply any income of the Share to or for the maintenance or education or otherwise for the benefit of the Primary Beneficiary, or any other Primary Beneficiaries who are for the time being living and under the age of 25.

4.2   The Trustees may also pay or apply any capital of the Share to or for the maintenance, education, advancement or otherwise for the benefit of the Primary Beneficiary. No capital may be so applied in a way which would or might prevent the Primary Beneficiary from becoming entitled to it, or to an interest in possession in it, on or before attaining the age of 25, nor in such a way that the income of it might meanwhile be dealt with except by being applied for the maintenance, education or otherwise for the benefit of one or more of the Primary Beneficiaries for the time being living and under the age of 25 or by being accumulated.

4.3   Subject as above, the income of the Share shall, during the Accumulation Period, be accumulated as an accretion to the capital of the Share. Any such accumulations may, at any time, be paid or applied in the manner set out in sub-clause 4.1 as if they were income of the Share arising in the then current year.

4.4   Subject as above, s 31 of the Trustee Act 1925 (as modified below) shall apply to the income of the Share.

4.5   Notwithstanding the above, the Trustees may, at any time during the Trust Period, by deed direct that the Primary Beneficiary shall become entitled to the income of all or any part of the Share from such a date as they shall specify. Such date shall not be earlier than the date of the deed, nor later than the date on which the Primary Beneficiary shall attain the age of 25. Such income shall be paid to the Primary Beneficiary from the date specified, or, if and so long as he is under the age of 18, applied or retained for his sole and absolute benefit and the trusts declared by sub-clauses 4.1 to 4.4 shall determine.

5. Trust to accumulate

Subject as above, during the Accumulation Period, so long as no Primary Beneficiary has attained the age of 25 and further Primary Beneficiaries may come into existence, the income of the Trust Fund shall be accumulated.

6. Ultimate default trusts

In the event of the failure or determination of the above trusts, the capital and income of the Trust Fund shall be held upon trust for [such of the Primary Beneficiaries as are living at the date of this Deed, and if more than one, in equal shares] absolutely.

7. Administrative powers

The Trustees shall, in addition and without prejudice to all statutory powers, have the powers and impunities set out in Part 2 of this Deed. No power conferred on the Trustees shall be exercised so as to conflict with the beneficial provisions of this Deed.

8. Extended power of maintenance

The statutory provisions for maintenance and education shall apply, but so that the power of maintenance shall be exercisable in the discretion of the Trustees and free from the obligation to apply part only of the income for maintenance where other income is available.

9. Extended power of advancement

The statutory provisions for advancement shall apply, but so that the power of advancement shall extend to the whole, rather than one half, of the share or interest of the person for whose benefit that advancement is made.

10. Restrictions on certain powers

10.1 In this clause, 'qualifying property' means any part of the Trust Fund which is for the time being property to which s 71 of the Inheritance Tax Act 1984 (or any statutory modification or re-enactment of such section) applies.

10.2 Where the Trust Fund or any part of it would (in the absence of the restrictions imposed by this sub-clause) fail to be qualifying property by reason only of powers conferred on the Trustees by this Deed or by law, those powers shall be capable of being exercised only in a manner which does not prevent the Trust Fund or that part of it from being qualifying property.

11. Appointment of new trustees

11.1 During the lifetime of the Settlor, the power of appointing new trustees shall be vested in the Settlor.

11.2 A person may be appointed to be a trustee notwithstanding that such person is not resident in the United Kingdom. Remaining out of the United Kingdom for more than 12 months shall not be a ground for the removal of a trustee.

12. Proper law, forum and place of administration

12.1 The proper law of this Trust shall be that of England and Wales. All rights under this Deed and its construction and effect shall be subject to the jurisdiction of the courts, and construed according to the laws, of England and Wales.

12.2 The courts of England and Wales shall be the forum for the administration of these trusts.

12.3 Notwithstanding the provisions of sub-clause 12.1 and 12.2,

[(a)] The Trustees shall have power, subject to the application (if any) of the rule against perpetuities, to carry on the general administration of these trusts in any jurisdiction in the world. This power shall be exercisable whether or not such jurisdiction is for the time being the proper law of this Trust or the courts or such jurisdiction are for the time being the forum for the administration of these trusts, and whether or not the Trustees or any of them are for the time being resident or domiciled in, or otherwise connected with, such jurisdiction.

[(b)] The Trustees may at any time declare in writing that, from the date of such declaration, the proper law of this Trust shall be that of any specified jurisdiction. No exercise of this power shall be effective unless the law of the jurisdiction specified is one under which this Trust remains irrevocable and all, or substantially all, of the trusts, powers and provisions contained in this Deed remain enforceable and capable of being exercised and so taking effect.

(c) Following any exercise of the power contained in sub-clause 12.3(b), the Trustees shall by deed make such consequential alterations or additions to this Deed as they consider necessary or desirable to ensure that, so far as may be possible, the trusts, powers and provisions of this Deed shall be as valid and effective as they were immediately prior to such change.

(d) The Trustees may, at any time, declare in writing that, from the date of such declaration, the forum for the administration of these trusts shall be the courts of any specified jurisdiction.]

13. Exclusion of Settlor and spouse

13.1 No discretion or power conferred on the Trustees or any other person by this Deed or by law shall be exercised, and no provision of this Deed shall operate directly or indirectly, so as to cause or permit any part of the capital or income of the Trust Fund to become in any way payable to or applicable for the benefit of the Settlor or any person who shall previously have added property to the Trust Fund or the spouse for the time being of the Settlor or any such person.

13.2 The provisions of sub-clause 13.1 shall not preclude the Settlor or any such person from exercising any statutory right to claim reimbursement from the Trustees for any income tax or capital gains tax paid by him in respect of income arising to the Trustees or capital gains realised or deemed or treated as realised by them.

13.3 Subject to sub-clause 13.2, the prohibition in this clause shall apply notwithstanding anything else contained or implied in this Deed.

14. Exclusion of Trusts of Land and Appointment of Trustees Act 1996, s 11(1)

Section 11 (trustees' duty to consult beneficiaries) of the Trusts of Land and Appointment of Trustees Act 1996 shall not apply to the trusts contained in this Deed.

PART 2 – ADMINISTRATIVE PROVISIONS

SCHEDULE
[The initial Trust Fund]

Signed as a deed and delivered   )

by [   ]   )

in the presence of:)

Appendix 6 – Will – Outline Structure

Opening	Name, address, occupation and date (unless at end of will)
Revocation	Previous wills and codicils
Executors and trustees	Individuals (lay, professional); trust corporation
Specific bequests/devises	Particular items owned
Pecuniary legacies	Money
Residuary gift	Absolute or contingent gifts to individuals or class of individuals
	Substitution provision in case prior gift fails
Powers of executors and/or trustees	Implied by statute Express provision
Attestation	Signed by the testator in the presence of two independent witnesses
	Witnesses sign in the presence of the testator

Appendix 7 – Trust Distribution Account

John Bale Trust

(a) Tom Bale set up an accumulation and maintenance trust for his nephew John under which John became entitled to the trust capital on his 18th birthday on 10 February 200–.

(b) The trustees being satisfied that no capital tax liability arises (no IHT since the trust is an accumulation and maintenance trust; no CGT because their annual exemption covers the gain on their deemed disposal caused by John's absolute entitlement) have transferred the investment in ABC plc to John.

(c) The dividend shown in the income account was received on 25 March 200– and it, together with the remaining cash has been transferred to John.

Capital account

	£
Assets held on 10 February 200–	
ABC plc ordinary shares	10,000.00
Cash	50.00
	10,050.00
Less: Lowe, Snow & Co's costs, disbursements and VAT on distribution of the funds	30.00
Balance held for John Bale	10,020.00

Income account

Income tax year 200–/200–	
Dividend	
ABC plc ordinary shares	10.00
Balance held for John Bale	10.00

Beneficiary's account

Capital, per capital account	10,020.00
Income, per income account	10.00
Total due	10,030.00
Represented by	
ABC plc ordinary shares	10,000.00
Balance of cash, now due	30.00
	10,030.00

Index